5/08

Carolina Home Gardener

Carolina Home Gardener

by Chris Florance

with drawings by Kaye Florance
and others

The University of North Carolina Press
Chapel Hill

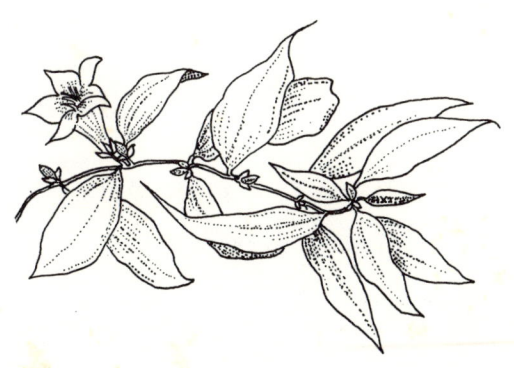

*The author wishes to acknowledge the kind assistance of
the Library of the Department of Botany, The University of
North Carolina at Chapel Hill.*

*Copyright © 1976 by
The University of North Carolina Press
All rights reserved
Manufactured in the United States of America
Library of Congress Catalog Card Number 75-23480
ISBN 0-8078-1258-7*

Library of Congress Cataloging in Publication Data

Florance, Chris, 1910–
    Carolina home gardener.

    Bibliography: p.
    Includes index.
    1. Gardening—North Carolina. 2. Gardening
—South Carolina. 3. Landscape gardening.
I. Title.
SB453.2.N8F55   635.9′09756   75-23480
ISBN 0-8078-1258-7

*Dedicated to
Kaye, Bill,
and the spirit of
Fannie B.*

Contents

Foreword / ix

Part One
Basic Gardening Techniques

First There Must Be Tools / 2
Preparing Soil for Outdoor Planting / 3
How to Make Compost / 5
Mulching / 6
Planting Seeds—Outdoors and Indoors / 7
Plant Propagation by Cuttings / 10
Planting Techniques
 for Trees and Shrubs / 12
Feeding the Garden / 14
Pruning: A Year-Around Chore / 17
The Espalier: A Special Kind of Pruning / 22
Pesticides / 23
Keeping Garden Records / 25
Garden Calendar / 26

Part Two
An Introduction to Garden Design

Base Plantings / 34
Locating the Garden / 35
Framing the Garden / 36
Shrubs and Trees Come First / 37
The Green-Garden Concept / 38
The Large Family of Hollies / 39
Deciduous Shrubs of Importance / 41
Guide to Selecting
 Evergreen and Deciduous Shrubs / 41
Shrub Flowering Sequence / 44
How to Select Healthy Shrubs / 46
Trees in Landscape Design / 46
The Addition of Bedding Plants / 48
Wild Flowers Are Also for Gardens / 52
Herbs Are for Both Kitchen and Garden / 56
Putting the Garden Together / 58
Color in the Garden / 59
Landscaping the Farm Home / 60
Design and Garden Maintenance / 61

Part Three
A Year in My Garden

My Approach to Gardening / 64
January / 65
February / 70
March / 75
April / 79
May / 86
June / 89
July / 93
August / 98
September / 102
October / 106
November / 109
December / 111

Part Four
Sources of Gardening Information

County, State, and
 Federal Governmental Agencies / 118
State and National
 Garden Club Organizations / 118
Gardening Centers / 118
Local and Regional Flower Shows / 118
Garden Classes / 119
Correspondence Courses / 119
Public Gardens and Arboreta / 119
Plant Societies / 120
All-America Selections / 121
Where to Buy Seeds,
 Plants, and Garden Supplies / 121
Gardening Books and Periodicals / 122

Glossaries and Index

Glossary of Scientific Plant Names / 128
Glossary of Common Plant Names / 132
Index / 136

Foreword

Throughout the writing of this book the problems of the inexperienced gardeners who have always lived in the Carolinas, as well as those of the many newcomers, have been uppermost in mind. Because of a wide diversity of plants, soils, temperatures, and topography existing in a relatively small space, gardening in the Carolinas is unique. Special cognizance of these conditions has been taken throughout the book. Fully aware that there are usually a number of ways to get gardening jobs done, I have selected the ways I have found most easily understood and feasible for the skills and means of the average gardener. My suggestions are based on experience with generations of gardeners whom I have known and advised for more than a quarter of a century as a garden consultant in the Carolinas.

Part one, "Basic Gardening Techniques," deals with such fundamental gardening activities as the preparation and maintenance of good growing soil, how to increase the supply of plants, planting techniques for trees and shrubs, and the management of such garden functions as feeding, pruning, spraying, and mulching. Part two, "An Introduction to Garden Design" points the way to combining bedding plants, trees, and shrubs into a harmonious and easily maintained garden. The importance of enclosures, the green-garden concept, formal and informal design, and suggestions for the use of color have been included. Part three, "A Year in My Garden," is an application of the ideas set forth in the first two sections of the book. It is a monthly record of what was done to plant and maintain my own small garden where flowers predominate, but where fruits and vegetables are also cultivated. Since I believe that my garden is the prototype of future Carolina gardens, I have emphasized in this section the ways and means of successfully integrating a relatively large variety of both flower and food plants within a small garden area.

It is hoped that this book will serve as a useful reference for the beginner as well as a source of regional information for the more experienced gardener. Familiar plant names are employed throughout the text. At the end of the book a botanical glossary of these familiar names has been provided to point the way to further study. A topical index has been organized for the reader's convenience in finding quickly how to make a geranium cutting or when to feed a boxwood, plant a tomato, or prune a crape myrtle. A calendar of basic garden chores (see page 26) as well as a monthly summary of my own garden activities are featured in this book to serve as guideposts for beginners and reminders for experienced gardeners. To facilitate the continuing learning process necessary to becoming a good gardener, I have listed additional sources of garden information in part four, which includes books on special garden subjects, other sources of information, regional gardens to visit, sources of seeds and plants, and other information of interest to gardeners.

Part One
Basic Gardening Techniques

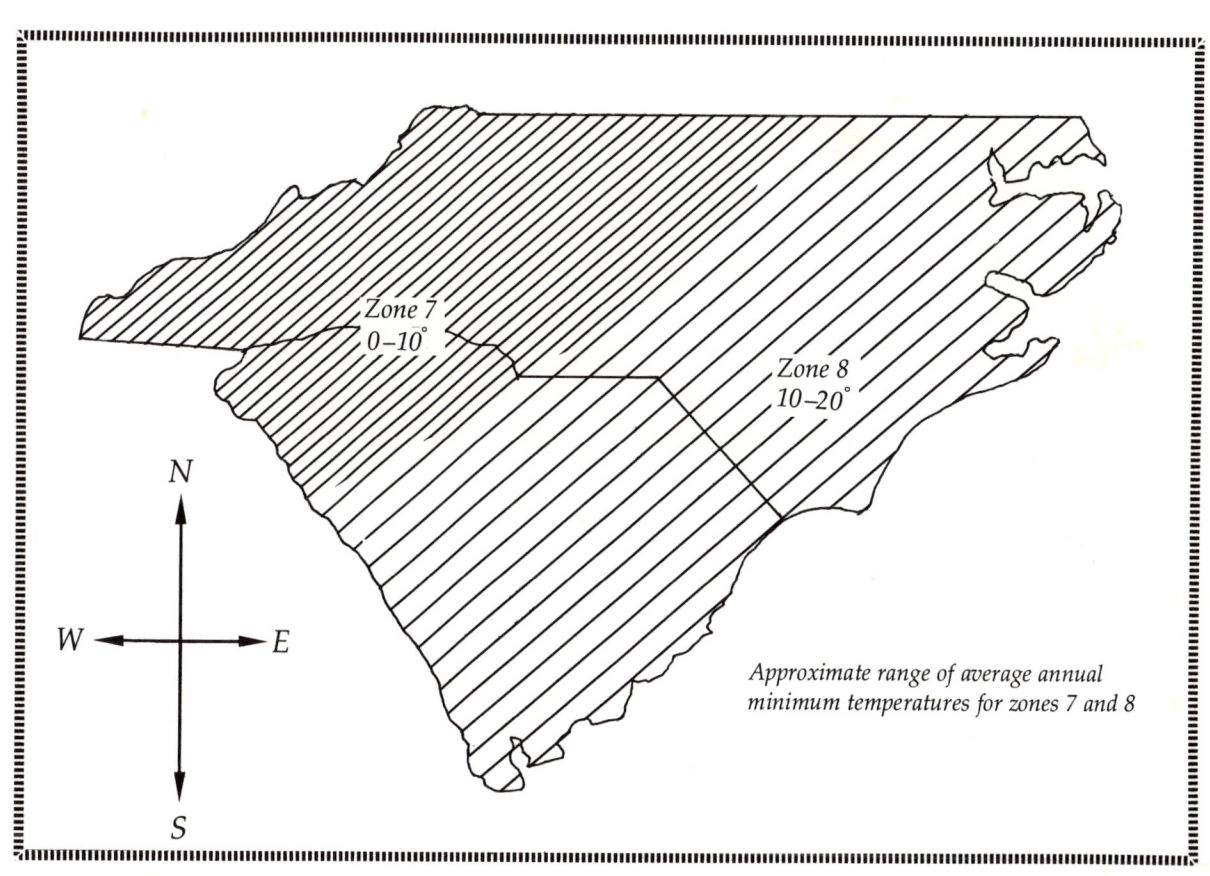

Approximate range of average annual minimum temperatures for zones 7 and 8

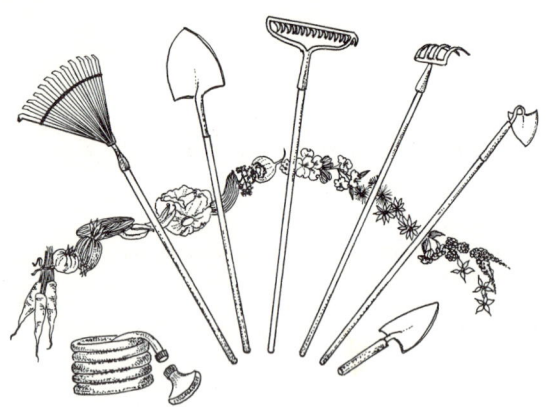

First There Must Be Tools

It is no accident that the canny makers of the seed and plant catalogs adorn their opening pages with pictures of dew-kissed roses or plump juicy tomatoes—and relegate to the back pages the less glamorous tools, sprays, and fertilizers that made them possible. In the beginning of this writing effort, I had planned, subconsciously perhaps, to emulate the seed-catalog psychology by putting the tools and techniques of gardening in the last section of the book.

But that was before I met Abdul and Ayesha. Abdul and Ayesha moved into the house behind me by way of New York and Cairo when the New York firm by whom Abdul was employed moved their offices from New York to North Carolina. The first sign I observed of an awakening gardening interest was when I saw Abdul sitting flat on the ground one warm spring day digging a hole with a sharp rock. With my usual crusading zeal (my husband has a different name for it!), I hung my head over the fence with advice and the loan of a tool or two. Abdul, in spite of his college degrees and Continental charm, did not know how to hold a shovel. Like any other Carolinian of my vintage who still has one foot in the country regardless of where we live, I could not believe what I was seeing.

Now, in recognition of the changing times and peoples in the Carolinas, and with apologies to my peers to whom shovels and rakes are as familiar as the knife and fork, I shall begin at the beginning.

First, there must be tools. If I were allowed only seven hand tools for gardening, I would choose a shovel, two rakes, a hoe, a trowel, a leaf broom, and a garden hose.

Shovel: My favorite shovel has a long handle and a diamond-pointed cutting blade and is absolutely indispensable to my gardening even though we own a rotary tiller. As a digging implement the shovel has no equal; by placing the foot on the top edge of the blade and using the body weight to push downward, large clean bites of soil may be lifted easily by using the leverage supplied by the long handle. It is far superior to the shorter-handled, square-bladed shovel or spade and should be the first tool purchased by the beginner.

Rake: Two types of rakes are needed by the gardener. One variety, called the bow rake, has several teeth about two and a half inches long attached to the wooden handle with a bowed member. Buy one of good quality because it will be needed for such sturdy tasks as leveling and removing coarse trash, roots, and debris from garden beds. The second rake, known in the Carolinas as the "potato digger," has only four tines just under five inches long. The potato digger is an excellent cultivating tool that I use for mixing compost and fertilizer with soil to the proper depths and consistency.

Hoe: There are several kinds of hoes, and it takes experience to determine which type is best adapted to your needs. I prefer the Warren hoe, a heart-shaped tool with sharp upper points, which can be used in reverse to push out weeds and grass from beds. The narrow, sharp blade of the tool allows for delicate maneuvering without damage to the flower and food crops and is also useful for laying open shallow furrows such as those I use for planting onions.

Trowel: Like hoes, trowels come in several sizes and styles. My favorite style has a strong wooden handle and a no-nonsense wide blade for doing fairly heavy garden chores such as planting bulbs and bedding plants.

Garden Hose: The hose equipped with a nozzle that breaks the water spray into droplets (similar to that used on shower baths) is the best all-purpose hose. (Misting devices are helpful for watering seed flats and small plants but are not indispensable.)

Leaf Broom: This is almost as useful in the cultivated garden areas as it is for clean-up duties about the yard. No other tool is better for the final cultivation of seed-bed surfaces.

Additional Tool Supplies

The seven tools listed above are starter tools; as soon as you can, add to this group a pitchfork, bucket, wheelbarrow or cart, hose-gun-sprayer, fertilizer spreader, lawn-edger, sprinkling pot, and the basic pruning tools. The four basic pruning tools are a pruning saw, hand pruner, long-handled lopper, and tree paint.

Motorized Rolling Stock

I suppose the lawn mower is the most important item in this group of garden tools, and a motorized one is now considered a must, though I can remember when the pushing kind was thought of as a sign of affluence.

Of much greater importance to the garden proper is a rotary cultivator or tiller, which is almost a necessity for any extensive flower or vegetable gardening. This rather expensive piece of power equipment and others such as the leaf shredder are the kinds of tools that might be jointly owned by two or three garden-minded neighbors, provided the ground rules for communal use are worked out and agreed upon beforehand. Rental agencies usually stock these items in larger urban areas.

Incidentally, the power mower can also be used to shred leaves. Pile the leaves in a heap and make several passes through them with the mower. The resulting fragments are coarser than those put through the leaf-shredder, but they are quite acceptable as composting and mulching materials.

Regardless of the number and type of tools you may acquire in the pursuance of gardening, never waste money on cheap ones. Good-quality tools, kept clean, oiled, and stored in the dry, will usually last a lifetime of good service. Poor-quality ones must be constantly replaced.

To build up a stock of tools, visit some of the yard-and-garage sales that are prevalent nowadays. Many old tools are made of better materials than some of the new ones, and quite frequently they are practically unused.

Preparing Soil for Outdoor Planting

The measure of the importance of soil preparation to successful gardening should not be judged by the amount of space I am allotting to it. Rather, it can be judged as a measure of my knowledge. Although I have worked in the soil and planted many gardens for myself and others, I consider the substance beneath my feet both mysterious and complex. It pleases me that my gardening efforts have been reasonably successful in spite of my lack of knowledge.

It gave my professional ego quite a lift to have such a shining horticultural light as R. Milton Carlton, a gardener and writer of long experience, state in one of his most recent books, *Vegetables for Today's Garden*, that he, too, considers the soil a very complicated matter.

"A basic fact to note in your garden scrapbook," Carlton wrote, "is that no one really knows much about soils. I do not exclude from this statement experts who have spent a lifetime studying the subject." Carlton continues, "I must confess that the stuff baffles more often than not." It is reassuring to know that soil can produce a bounty of both food and flowers without the gardener knowing exactly how it is able to do so.

It further develops, in the reading of Carlton's books and others on the subject, that most successful gardeners prepare soil in basically the same way. Most garden soils, whether sandy or heavy clay, can be mixed with various forms of organic matter (compost, manures, sawdust, peat moss, or sphagnum) to grow everything the average gardener wants.

Making a New Bed

When a new planting bed is to be prepared, first remove all grass, weeds, etc. from the surface. (If you have Johnson grass [*Sorghum halepense*], Bermuda grass or wire grass [*Cynodon dactylon*], or other stolonate grass or weeds, deeper and harder digging will be in order.) The entire surface is then dug with a spade or shovel to a depth of eight to ten inches. The digging must be deeper for planting shrubs and trees. Distribute evenly over the surface a layer of three to four inches of organic matter. Top-dress the organic matter with a balanced fertilizer such as 8-8-8.

At this stage a rotary cultivator is worth its weight in charley horses. (In some areas this tool is available on a rental basis.) Make two or three slow runs with this tool through the spaded bed to mix thoroughly the soil, organic material, and fertilizer. The results will look like potting soil. If a tiller is unavailable, a hand tool such as a potato digger used diligently can do a satisfactory mixing job.

Two Discouraging Notes

I wish that I could say that when such a bed is made it is done for once and all, but I cannot. The organic material, or a good part of it, is consumed with each crop it produces. With each successive new crop planted, another two or three inches of organic matter should be added.

The second discouraging note is the high price of peat moss, sphagnum, and other commerical forms of organic material. I have discovered only one way to reduce the cost of this vital organic matter. I use leaves.

Perhaps you have no trees on your lot. Neither do we, at least not enough to supply our needs, but in the fall we are diligent in assisting the city sanitation department with the removal of the leaves other people sweep to their curbs for destroying at the city dump. These new leaves require at least a year or more of composting to bring them to the stage of decay best suited for use in the soil. For a short cut, run the lawn mower through the pile several times. The resulting smaller bits can be used immediately in the soil preparation. In some urban areas, where regular fall collection of leaves is a public service, it is possible to get loads of these chopped leaves (the trucks grind them coarsely as they are collected to save space) delivered to your garden when the trucks are making their regular pick-ups in your vicinity.

In my vegetable-growing areas, bushels of these chopped leaves are spaded into the soil in October and November. By the following March they have decayed enough to make a fine planting bed with only a couple of passes with the tiller. Some of the leaves are stockpiled for similar use in flower beds when they are planted anew each season. These chopped leaves are also excellent surface mulches, and now that pine needles are scarcer and costlier, I am using leaves almost exclusively for mulching. A three-inch to four-inch layer applied in the fall eliminates most of the winter and summer weeding and watering, and it slowly improves the soil as well.

A Special Kind of Soil Problem

A special problem faces the gardener whose house is built on a lot where the topsoil was hauled off or covered for grading purposes with several feet of subsoil.

In my own yard the existing thin layer of topsoil was covered in some spots to a depth of three feet. It is without question the hardest, poorest, and most nearly hopeless soil I have ever worked in my whole garden life. It is futile to dig it out, haul it off, and refill the holes with topsoil. We tried that, but the holes filled with surface water that drained so slowly that the plants eventually drowned. We solved this problem by laying gravel-filled paths where the water flowed naturally, and putting the beds and planting sites on top of the hardpan rather than in it. This approach necessitated the expense of extra topsoil, but after only three years I can see a definite improvement in the top inches of the hardpan. In time I am sure that even this impervious soil will be good enough to grow the plants of my choice.

We could all take a lesson from the wisdom of the farmer who yearly turns to the surface a few inches of the subsoil before the cold weather arrives. All winter it rains and snows. At night the hard clods freeze; the next day they thaw. By winter's end the hard dirt has crumbled and, with a few turns of the harrow, has become a part of the friable topsoil. With a spade, a rake, and a good mind to garden, you can do the same.

How to Make Compost

Those who expect to garden successfully must have some form of organic matter to mix with their existing soil. A general definition of organic matter would be what remains of certain living organisms, and the forms familiar to the gardener are leaf mold, peat moss, animal manures, sawdust, wood chips, sphagnum moss, tobacco stems, various types of hulls, ground corncobs, and grass clippings.

Organic matter is equally important for hard clay soils or sandy porous soils. Its addition improves the drainage in heavy clay by helping to separate the finely packed soil particles; in sandy soil where water drains too quickly, organic matter lengthens moisture retention. All root systems grow better in soils containing organic matter, and if the roots are vigorous, the plants they support will be more productive.

Leaves comprise our greatest potential source of organic matter, and the process of turning the autumn leaves into leaf mold is one of the easiest of garden chores. Nature makes compost in the forests the year around; in fact it is the only food supply of countless thousands of trees that sprout, grow, and die in a never-ending cycle of woodland ecology.

It is puzzling that gardeners do more than half the work needed to make compost simply by sweeping the leaves into piles and setting them on the street rather than depositing them in a compost bin. Some people even take the trouble to bag the leaves before placing them on the curb. Wouldn't it be just as easy to put them in the compost pile? Perhaps it is not understood that such a leaf pile will self-compost in due time, without further aid, into a mellow, friable layer of excellent compost that could be used in place of costly commercial substitutes.

How to Make Leaf Compost

The nature-does-it method of leaf composting requires eighteen to twenty-four months. During the years when I lived on a larger lot, it was my custom to keep two such piles going simultaneously, and after the first two years, I had a plentiful supply of seasoned leaf mold ready at all times.

For a faster method, and one better suited to a smaller lot, it can be done in this manner: Choose an out-of-the-way spot where ground space six to ten feet square (rectangular or circular) can be cleared to receive the leaves. For the sake of neatness a wire enclosure not more than four feet high is helpful but not mandatory. The leaf pile is made in a layer-cake arrangement with alternating layers of leaves rolled or trampled to a six-inch depth and a nitrogenous fertilizer (8-8-8, 10-6-4, or other) applied at the rate of a pint of fertilizer for each square yard of leaf surface. The fertilizer nourishes the bacteria and fungi that do the work of breaking the leaves up into compost. Water after depositing each layer.

A slight saucer-like indentation should be made in the center of each layer of leaves and fertilizer to hold rainfall or water applied during dry periods. When the pen is full of layers of leaves and fertilizer, water it thoroughly. A six-inch layer of topsoil can be used, if desired, to top off the pile to act as an anchor for the leaves and to help retain moisture.

In early spring, late spring, and mid-summer, turn the pile to mix the outside leaves with the inside ones for more equal decaying action. Water during drought periods. By fall of the year following the compost-bed beginning, your pile will be about one-fourth its original size and the humus therein will be dark, moist, partially rotted, and ready for incorporation into the garden.

Using Grass Clippings and Other Matter in Composting

Some gardeners use everything vegetative left over around their premises in their compost pile: grass clippings, spent annuals, twigs, manures, and table scraps. All these are indeed vegetable matter in one form or another and potentially compostable. Bear in mind, though, that grass clippings and manures may contain noxious weeds, that twigs and grapefruit rinds are slow to break down, and that flower remains might harbor and pass on various insects and diseases. If leaves are plentiful, either from your own or your neighbor's discards, they are relatively clean and decay at a more constant rate. Chopping with the lawn mower or grinding in a power leaf-shredder can hasten the process.

The Chemical Nature of Leaf Compost

Leaf mold made of oak leaves and pine needles is definitely acid in reaction, an advantageous fact to know for those who garden with such acid-requiring plants as camellias, azaleas, rhododendrons, gardenias, pieris, and dogwoods.

A majority of our deciduous trees make a leaf mold that is either mildly acid or neutral in reaction. It is doubtful that leaf mold of any trees would create a problem, but in case of doubt, a soil analysis would indicate the extent and nature of the problem and suggest remedial measures.

Mulching

Mulch is compost, peat moss, ground bark, pine needles, or other types of organic matter applied to the surface of the ground. It is useful around shrubs, foundation planting, vegetables, bedding plants (except for iris and peonies), and trees. Organic matter used as mulches is valuable for several reasons:

1. It is an aid to temperature controls, keeping the ground cooler in summer and warmer in winter.

2. It helps to retain ground moisture, thus reducing the amount of watering required during conditions of drought.

3. Mulch is a neat and attractive ground cover that helps control grass and weeds.

4. It gradually enriches the soil, though this requires maintaining a constant supply of mulch for several years.

Mulches should be replenished twice yearly, in the spring for summer and in the fall for winter. Spot replenishing may be done at any time as needed. The depth of mulch depends on the size of the plant. Shrubs, trees, and roses need four inches, while smaller bedding plants do best with half that amount.

Pros and Cons of Mulching Materials

Leaf Compost: Partially decayed leaves, composted as described earlier, are excellent when used as a mulch. Fresh leaves, whole or chopped, may be applied to tree and shrub plantings as mulches. In fact, where such plantings exist, the deciduous autumn leaves can be shaken or picked from the shrubs and left where they fall. It is, however, necessary to anchor these loose leaves with pine needles, bits of soil, or poultry wire until they have absorbed enough water to hold them down.

Hay and Straw: Both materials are porous and useful unless too many weeds were harvested along with the grain. Quite frequently some grain will also sprout, but it can be easily pulled out and left on the surface for decomposing.

Sawdust and Wood Chips: Both are weed-free and attractive in appearance. Both materials (as well as corncobs, hay, and straw) deplete the nitrogen content of the soil to some degree. This is easily corrected by the addition of extra nitrogenous fertilizers.

Grass Clippings: These should be allowed to cure for a time before use as mulch. Freshly cut grass generates considerable heat for a week or ten days after cutting and should be allowed to cool down before use around plants. Grass clippings also tend to form a hard crust that sheds water. Break it up occasionally to maintain porosity.

Peat Moss: Peat-moss mulches are very good looking, but they also crust and shed water in addition to being quite expensive.

Hulls: Peanuts, buckwheat, barley, and pecan hulls may be used as mulch if available. Except for the pecans, however, they blow about considerably.

Ground Corncobs: These are long-lasting and attractive but field mice come to find the bits of corn.

Tobacco Stems: Experts recommend using tobacco stems only as a fertilizer since they contain about 6 percent potash. Shallow-rooted plants might be damaged by such a mulch. The nicotine in the stems is said to have some value as an insect repellent.

Pine Needles: No mulching material is better looking or longer lasting. Acid-forming in nature, it is perfect for use around azalea-camellia-rhododendron plantings. Like hay or straw, however, pine needles are inflammable.

Paper Products: Old newspapers, magazines, cardboard, and the like are useful as mulching materials, but they are relatively short-lived and require some anchoring from winds as well as camouflage for aesthetic reasons.

Polyethylene Film: Black plastic of agricultural grade is sold in rolls of a thousand feet by many garden stores. Like the newsprint, it requires anchoring and camouflaging. However it lasts a full season and saves watering as well as weeding.

Planting Seeds— Outdoors and Indoors

For outdoor planting of seeds, start with large seeds such as those of zinnia (*Zinnia elegans*), castor bean (*Ricinus communis*), string bean, corn, etc. When the weather is warm enough for germination (see tables for dates), cover the seeds just enough to hide them from view; deep burial is unnecessary and unwise. Very small, delicate seeds, such as those of the petunia (*Petunia hybrida*), begonia (*Begonia* spp.), or snapdragon (*Antirrhinum majus*), will disappear from view on contact with the soil or other growing media, and no additional covering is required. A gentle watering is all that is needed to settle the seeds to the proper depth for growing.

Watering is also required for larger seeds, and the soil should be kept consistently moist, but not sodden, at all times until germination. There is no way to establish a schedule for watering since winds, temperature, humidity, and sunshine determine the rate of evaporation. Learn to check moisture needs by feel. Water only when the soil surface is dry to the touch.

A light covering of pine straw or wheat straw will reduce the amount of watering needed; or temporary shade can be provided with tree branches, burlap scraps, etc.

It is wise to plant more seeds than you will require and thin later to a proper stand. A "proper stand" varies with each plant since the space must be what the mature plant will require. Observation, questions to experienced gardeners, and a perusal of garden literature* will provide this information.

Don't take too literally the length of germination time printed on the seed packets. The time required varies widely in response to an equally wide variation in growing conditions. If you fail on your first trials, try again. Surely if so many seeds can grow without any aid at all from man, some will grow eventually as a result of your patience and efforts.

Planting Seeds Indoors

There are several varieties of vegetables and flowers in both the cool- and warm-weather groups (see lists) which may be started indoors earlier than it is safe to plant them outdoors. You must decide for yourself whether indoor planting is worth the extra trouble.

Some varieties that lend themselves most advantageously to the indoor-starting procedures are as follows:

Cool-Weather Vegetables:
Broccoli, cabbage, endive, lettuce

Cool-Weather Flowers:
Calendula (*Calendula officinalis*), sweet alyssum (*Lobularia maritima*), Drummond phlox (*Phlox Drummondii*), cornflower (*Centaurea cyanus*)

---

*Some seed catalogs include handy guides for seed planters which include germination tables, uses, and cultural information.

Warm-Weather Vegetables:
Cucumber, eggplant, pepper, squash, pumpkin, melon, tomato

Warm-Weather Flowers:
Aster (*Callistephus chinensis*), Browallia (*Browallia americana*), Christmas cherry (*Solanum pseudocapsicum*), marigold (*Tagetes* spp.), zinnia, petunia, begonia, snapdragon, vinca or the annual periwinkle (*Vinca rosea*)

If you have a greenhouse or growing lights, you could start these plants as early in the winter as you please and probably have fruits or flowers showing by safe outdoor-planting dates. Without these special growing aids, there is little to be gained by planting any of the varieties listed more than two or three weeks earlier than the proper time to put them outside.

Every year thousands of seeds and seedlings perish on window sills put there by hopeful gardeners trying to beat the calendar. Modern houses do not provide the proper heat, light, or humidity that growing plants require. In spite of these disadvantages, some indoor-bred seedlings do survive, and with more knowledge aforehand their numbers should increase.

A Growing Medium for Indoor Seeds

There are several commercial products used for starting seeds indoors. Horticultural vermiculite, which comes in several sizes, is an excellent growing medium for certain seeds that are susceptible to some of the harmful bacteria usually present in less sterile media.

Potting soils sold under several brand names are also popular with many gardeners. My own favorite recipe for sowing seeds is a combination of commercial potting soil (labeled as containing sand, vermiculite, soil, and peat), builder's sand, and peat moss—one-third each by volume. The texture and consistency of this mixture suits me perfectly. I use it for everything—starting seeds, making cuttings, and potting plants both large and small. Small amounts of 8-8-8 chemical fertilizer may be added to the mixture as desired.

Containers for Indoor Seed Growing

To eliminate the labor and the shock to the seedling of transplanting, I recommend starting the seeds in containers suitable for planting in outside beds, containers and all. The peat-fiber pot, made of a mixture of wood pulp and finely ground peat moss, is available in 2½ inch and 3 inch sizes (and larger). These may be filled with the potting mixture described above, and each small pot planted with two or three seeds of as many varieties as your windows will accommodate.

When the seedlings have developed four to six leaves and all danger of frost is over, they can be planted outside pot and all. In planting outside, never allow the rims of the peat pot to project above the ground level. The exposed edges act as a wick to draw water away from the seedling. This lack of water stunts growth and prevents the plant from developing new roots outside the pot. To avoid this situation, simply peel away the upper half of the pot at planting time.

In purchasing peat pots, check to see if they will crumble under gentle pressure or if there is so much wood fiber in the composition that plant roots will have difficulty getting through. The softer one requires more careful handling, but it will permit a faster breakthrough of the roots. There is also a choice of round or square peat pots. The square shape packages more economically where space is a problem.

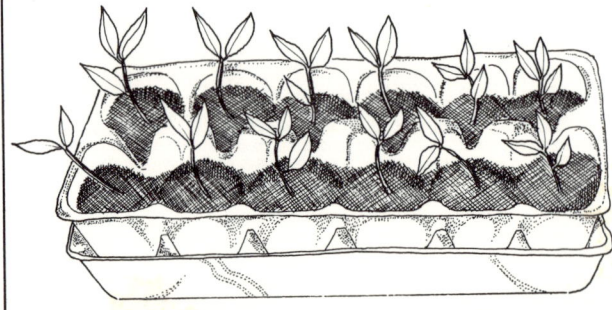

[8] Carolina Home Gardener

Food, Water, and Light Requirements

Just as the experienced cook knows what constitutes "a pinch" of this and that, so does the gardener learn to judge the proper amounts of food, water, and light the seedlings require.

For a starting point to acquiring this knowledge, withhold all fertilizer for the first week after germination. The seed itself has enough stored food inside its own coat to get it through the first few days of its life. After this first week or ten days, use only a water-soluble fertilizer that is recommended for potted plants and use it strictly according to the frequency and quantity suggested by the manufacturer for seedlings.

Water only when the surface of the soil feels dry to the touch. Frequency will be greatly affected by the prevailing weather conditions. In cool, cloudy weather, very little if any watering will be needed. On clear, warm days, look at your seedlings two or three times daily to check on their moisture content. A six- to eight-hour lapse in watering on a warm sunny day can kill seedlings you have nursed for weeks. It is better, as a general rule, to run seedlings a little too dry than a little too wet. The white, fuzzy molds that sometimes occur at the roots of your seedlings usually indicate too much water, shade, or warmth. These soil molds can be avoided when you understand their cause. Regardless of your knowledge and skill, you must always keep a constant vigil on seedlings during the early stages of their growth. I put mine where I can see them on my routine comings and goings. Remember that old saw: out of sight, out of mind.

How water is applied is important. Never subject seeds or seedlings to hard overhead pressures. Peat pots can be placed in shallow pans and watered from the bottom. A perforated sprinkling head, such as those used to dampen laundry when steam irons were not so common, will work fine if overhead watering is necessary. Whatever the method, keep it gentle.

The light requirements of seedlings must also be learned from experience since the amount needed varies with the seeds and the seasons. In early spring when sunlight is gentle and benign, seedlings can benefit by all the light you have available. (In fact, the lack of sufficient light in the house is one of the main reasons that growing plants indoors is so difficult.) On warmer days, watch out for the effects of the midday sun shining through the glass. It can get a lot hotter than you think, causing wilting and damage to seedlings. On such days, shift the seedlings to a shadier spot for an hour or so until the heat is less intense. Tall, spindly plants, the results of insufficient light, might as well be discarded, for seldom if ever do they overcome this inauspicious start.

From Indoors to Outdoors

Slow and easy are the keywords for the critical period when seedlings grown indoors are introduced to the outside world. Whether the plant is a small seedling, a rooted cutting, or an old plant that wintered indoors, the changes are drastic and the plant is unprepared.

Adjust your plants for this change by taking them outside for ever-increasing lengths of time during the warmest part of the day. A sheltered sunny spot protected from drafts, beating rains, and frolicking dogs is an ideal place. A week to ten days of this interim care should guarantee your plants' survival in the open garden.

Using Last Year's Seeds

This seems as good a place as any to mention the feasibility of using leftover seeds from the previous season. Most vegetable (and flower) seeds are viable for a year or longer, and a substantial economy may be realized from the use of leftover seeds. Those over a year old should be tested before planting to determine their viability. A simple way of doing this is to place ten seeds on a double layer of moistened paper towel fitted into a plate or flat dish. Cover the seeds with another moistened double layer of paper towel and cover with another dish the same size as the bottom one. After six or seven days of storage in a warm place, count the number of seeds which have sprouted. If half have growing signs, plant twice as many seeds. If less than five germinate, buy some fresh seeds.

Plant Propagation by Cuttings

In addition to planting seeds as an easy and inexpensive way of increasing the plant supply, the gardener can also root cuttings or "slips" of favorite plants. A cutting is a small portion or piece taken from certain specified parts of a larger plant at a certain stage of growth, placed in a rooting medium, and shaded, watered, and cared for until new roots are formed.

Propagation by cuttings has two advantages over the seed-grown plant. It starts out larger and it will be an exact duplicate of its parent, rather than a cross between two parents, as is the case of the seedling. New plants grown from cuttings can be propagated from a large group of plants including evergreen and deciduous shrubs, house plants and many bedding plants, herbs and wild flowers.

For the beginner the three types of cuttings most easily made are the softwood cuttings, hardened green cuttings, and the hardwood cuttings.

Softwood Cuttings

The cuttings made from plants with relatively soft tissues are called softwood cuttings. Several such cuttings have been mentioned elsewhere and include those of all species of begonia, geranium (*Pelargoniums*), coleus (*Coleus Blumei*), impatiens (*Impatiens balsamina*), *Dianthus* spp., rose, chrysanthemum, wandering Jew (*Zebrina pendula*), and others.

Generally, cuttings from this group may be rooted the year around, but the months from May through August are the best. Many—especially begonias, geraniums, coleus, impatiens, and wandering Jew—may be rooted in water in a kitchen window, while all can be rooted in sharp sand, potting soil mixture, and vermiculite.

In addition to the foregoing plants, these plants can also be readily rooted using the same methods: Arabis (*Arabis albida*), cactus (*Opuntia* spp.), dahlia (*Dahlia pinnata*), fuchsia (*Fuchsia procumbens*), gerbera (*Gerbera Jamesonii*), hibiscus or the rose mallow (*Hibiscus coccineus*), lantana (*Lantana camara*), Boston daisy, a *Chrysanthemum* spp., penstemon (*Penstemon*), scabiosa (*Scabiosa japonica*), petunia, phlox in variety, sedum, verbena, and viola.

There is hardly a simpler way to grow a new plant than to break or cut a stem or small end section of a healthy plant and put it where moisture and partial shade are present as needed for the rooting process. It is one of my private pleasures to insert such pieces into pots of established flowers that receive fairly regular watering and protection. A few weeks—or a season later, after I have forgotten it—I "discover" a new plant ready for its own pot or place in the garden.

Begonia Cutting

Hardened Green Cuttings

Semiripe cuttings of all varieties of azalea, camellia, and boxwood that are at the right stage for rooting in July and August are called hardened green cuttings. Other shrubs that may be rooted easily at this season are abelia (*Abelia grandiflora*), *Bougainvillea* or bougainville, scotch broom (*Cytisus scoparius*), daphne (*Daphne cneorum*) and other daphnes, hoya or wax-vine (*Hoya carnosa*), *Escallonia*, all the hollies (*Ilex*), the mahonias, including *Mahonia Bealei* and *M. repens*, oleander (*Nerium oleander*), Confederate- or star-jasmine, (*Trachelospermum jasminoides*), *Aucuba japonica*, and others.

Hardened green cuttings can be rooted in plastic-covered, sand-filled clay pots or other containers and stored in shaded places. Like other cuttings, they will need some winter protection for the first year or two of their lives.

Hardwood Cuttings

Still a third group, hardwood cuttings, may be made in November or in the early spring. November-made hardwood cuttings and spring ones are made alike but are handled differently.

Cuttings are made from the current season's growth, either from long canes that grow from the base of the plant or from the terminal branches of this new growth. The lengths of the cuttings vary depending on the character of individual growth. If the nodes or growth buds occur close together, the cutting can be about six inches long; if they are widely spaced, such as they are on grapes and butterfly bushes (*Buddleia Davidii*), the length must be greater. (The minimum number of buds required is two, but three or four are better.) The cuttings are severed either straight across the stem or at a slight slant, and there should be an inch of stem left below the bottom node and above the top node. The ideal size for such cuttings is the diameter and length of a lead pencil.

The November-made hardwood cuttings should be buried in containers of moist sand, sawdust, peat moss, wood shavings, or vermiculite and stored at forty to forty-five degrees temperature to prevent drying out until calluses, which look like scar tissue, form on the cut ends of the wood. Burial position can be either vertical or horizontal.

By the first of March remove the cuttings and plant upright in an outside bed with a bud or two above ground to complete rooting. Water and mulch until top growth is well underway. Transplant in the fall to permanent sites.

A second method bypasses the interim callus-forming stage by making the cuttings in February or early March and planting them directly outdoors in partly shaded exposures to form their new roots during the warming weather of spring.

Among garden plants that may be propagated in this manner are such favorites as deutzia (*Deutzia gracilis*), forsythia (*Forsythia intermedia*), honeysuckle (*Lonicera fragrantissima*), kerria (*Kerria japonica*), mock orange (*Philadelphus coronarius*), pearlbush (*Exochorda racemosa*), lilac (*Syringa vulgaris*), snowberry (*Symphoricarpos albus*), spirea (*Spiraea Vanhouttei*), vitex or chaste-tree (*Vitex agnus-castus*), beauty bush (*Kolkwitzia amabilis*), weigela (*Weigela florida*), willow (*Salix* spp.), flowering quince or Japanese quince (*Chaenomeles japonica*), snowball (*Viburnum tomentosum*), flowering almond (*Prunus glandulosa*), crape myrtle (*Lagerstroemia indica*), winterberry (*Ilex verticillata*), and others.

Two More Ways to Increase Plant Supplies

In addition to the three general classes of stem cuttings described above, there are two additional easy ways for the home gardener to increase the supply of plants. They are called layerage and division or separation.

Layerage frequently occurs in the garden with no help at all from the gardener. Low-hanging branches of such plants as boxwood (*Buxus sempervirens*), forsythia, winter jasmine (*Jasminum nudiflorum*), azalea, aucuba, and euonymus form roots at spots where their limbs touch the soil or are covered by a layer of mulch. Follow this example by fastening low branches to the soil of these and other plants you may have use for in the garden. After a year's growth in the anchored position, leave the new plant in place but sever the stem between the new roots and the parent plant, and allow it to grow for another season to develop a stronger root system. After two seasons, or longer if the layered plant seems to need additional growth, transplant the new shrub to a permanent site in the garden and treat the same way you would any other freshly moved garden material.

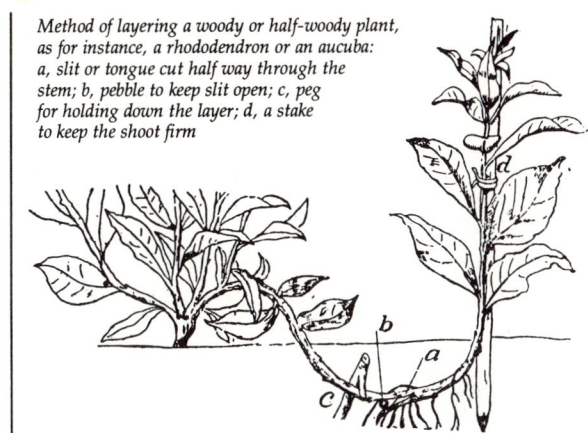

Method of layering a woody or half-woody plant, as for instance, a rhododendron or an aucuba: a, slit or tongue cut half way through the stem; b, pebble to keep slit open; c, peg for holding down the layer; d, a stake to keep the shoot firm

Additional plants that may be layered successfully are candytuft (*Iberis sempervirens*), all varieties of dianthus, aubrietia (*Aubrietia deltoidea*), pachysandra (*Pachysandra terminalis*), ivies (*Hedera helix*), perennial periwinkles (*Vinca major* and *V. minor*), hoya or wax-vine, Carolina jessamine (*Gelsemium sempervirens*), daphne, cotoneaster (*Cotoneaster horizontalis*), magnolia (*Magnolia grandiflora*), oleander, mock orange, pyracantha (*Pyracantha coccinea*), and goldenchain tree (*Laburnum alpinum*).

Almost everyone who has gardened at all has divided a plant. It is done by digging up the entire plant, or taking it from a container, and breaking or cutting it with a spade or knife into small pieces.

Basic Gardening Techniques [11]

Fleshy-rooted plants such as the bearded iris (*Iris germanica*), siberian iris (*Iris sibirica*), peony (*Paeonia lactiflora*), day lily (*Hemerocallis* spp.), canna (*Canna generalis*), liriope (*Liriope muscari*), dahlia, rhubarb, and Irish potato must have buds or growth points on each division in addition to a part of the root.

Fibrous-rooted plants, of which the ajuga (*Ajuga reptans*), primrose (*Primula vulgaris*), and the coral-bell (*Heuchera sanguinea*) are examples, can be easily divided without tools into small sections suitable for planting; on the other hand, plants with a single taproot system, such as the balloon flower (*Platycodon grandiflorum*) or the columbine (*Aquilegia canadensis*) and other columbines, do not lend themselves to this form of propagation.

Planting Techniques for Trees and Shrubs

Hundreds of chapters have been written on how to transplant trees and shrubs, and I want to add a thought or two of my own. By no means would I leave the impression that I take the matter of planting costly trees and shrubs lightly, but I must confess that it never ceases to astound me how many of the badly planted ones survive. The point I do wish to stress is that timidity and inexperience should not deter you from planting. As it is in the case of unskilled pruning, a majority of the plants will survive in spite of inexperience.

One style of planting trees and shrubs which I would like to see abolished is the residential subdivision method of planting. Each new house, in order to meet mortgage loan requirements, gets a quota of eight to ten shrubs and a tree or two, depending on the cost of the house. All too frequently the shrubs selected turn out to be whatever was cheapest at the time and the trees are almost invariably silver maples—the least expensive and least valuable of all the maple family. Small holes, exactly the size of the root ball, are shoveled out of the tangle of clay subsoil, concrete fragments, brickbats, beer cans, etc., and the hapless plants are stuffed in. A little loose dirt is kicked around them, and the whole sorry mess is covered with enough pine needles to hide the poor workmanship.

I once observed one of the new houses being "landscaped" in my neighborhood. It took three men exactly twenty minutes to finish the job, load their tools and be gone. The shrubs died within three months and the replacements appear to be headed for a similar fate.

A Better Way to Plant

Dig holes for trees and shrubs twice the diameter of the root ball but only two or three inches deeper than the ball's depth.

If the excavated soil is of such poor quality that it cannot be mixed with peat moss or other forms of organic matter, get some topsoil that can. Make a mixture of two-thirds soil, one-third peat moss,

and a handful of 8-8-8 fertilizer. Mix thoroughly. Line the bottom of the hole with two inches of the improved soil. Place the plant in the hole in a vertical position and with its best side facing garden-viewers. Fill in the remaining cavity with good soil and press in gently with the foot to fill all the spaces.

It is unnecessary to remove burlap or other decayable fabric wrappings. Tin or plastic containers should be removed, of course. Where drainage is normal, make a rim of earth around the dirt-ball perimeter to conserve water and to prevent rapid runoff.

Surface-rooted plants (boxwood, camellia, azalea, rhododendron, pieris, etc.) should be set three or four inches above the surrounding ground levels. Other plants should be set an inch or two higher. In a few months, they will settle to the right level.

[12] *Carolina Home Gardener*

Watering

Regardless of the moisture in the soil, or the raindrops falling on your head, water each plant as soon as it is planted. The water will drive out the air pockets and settle the loose new soil around each small root and rootlet.

Thereafter, water weekly for a full year unless there is substantial rainfall during that time. Dogwood trees often need extra watering for two years or more after planting. A three- to four-inch layer of pine needles or other form of mulch aids in moisture retention in addition to serving as a deterrent for weeds.

Staking

Trees that are larger than an inch in diameter should be staked to hold them in an upright position until they are firmly anchored by their own roots. This may be as long as twelve to eighteen months. Most of the staking I see in local gardens isn't worth the time it took to gather the materials. Ropes and twines rapidly become slack; stakes and cables are a nuisance to the lawn mowers and a menace to children at play. Most of the trees bought for residential gardens are small enough to be staked with the double-stake method. So far I have found no better way. (See illustration.)

When To Plant Trees and Shrubs

Less than 10 percent of the families in our three-year-old subdivision are native-born North Carolinians. It is a varied and interesting neighborhood with people from many parts of the United States and several foreign countries.

With all their diversity, there does seem to be one gardening idea in common: the planting of trees and shrubs must be done in March or April. All the other months are too hot or too cold.

Some of my neighbors have been surprised (and informed, I hope) to see that I plant off and on throughout the entire year. Although our climate is subject to wide fluctuations, it is seldom that cold weather periods last long enough to freeze more than an inch or two of the top soil of our gardens, and such thin crusts are short-lived. Many a time I have officiated at tree-and-shrub plantings in thirty-five-degree weather. It was a bit uncomfortable, but I always dressed in the best polar-bear style, and I can't recall a cold of any consequence in the past twenty-five years. Small frozen clods left around such plantings thawed out into friable soil the first few hours of more temperate weather. (Small bedding plants, of course, must be planted on warmer days in loose, friable soil. Otherwise there would be no loose soil to cover and protect the delicate shallow roots.)

Planting Container-Grown Plants

A plentiful supply of container-grown trees and shrubs has made planting a truly year-around business, since such plants can be safely planted at any time. The gardener should be alerted to the possibility that some of these plants may have been in the containers too long, leaving them root-bound. Such plants may require several seasons to recover from this handicap, and the worst cases may never recover. Avoid buying large plants in small containers, and if possible, examine the root structure. If the roots have formed a solid overlapping network with the overflow growing through the drainage holes of the container, the plant is not apt to be a wise investment.

Specimen Trees and Shrubs

Specimen-sized trees and shrubs that must be dug with earth balls around their roots and wrapped in burlap are more likely to grow and prosper if dug and replanted in the cool weather of late fall, winter, and early spring. Deciduous trees and shrubs should be planted when they are not in leaf, approximately during the same seasons mentioned above.

Top Pruning

Broad-leaved evergreens are more likely to survive transplanting at any time of the year if a portion of their leaves is pruned to balance the root loss caused by digging. For example, when I transplanted a large magnolia to my new garden three years ago, I removed every leaf. No die-back followed. However, I have never been able to persuade others to practice defoliation, and I have seen many large-specimen magnolias die after transplanting. This failure to prune was certainly part of the reason for such losses.

Root Pruning

Dogwoods and other native trees that abound in rural areas or city lands marked for clearing can often be transplanted successfully. Survival chances are substantially increased by root pruning. This is a simple process of cutting a circle around the tree with a long spade just as though digging a root ball for transplanting. The tree is left in place, after cutting a circle, for a period of six months for new roots to grow inside the root ball. For all deciduous trees—which, of course, includes dogwoods—the ideal timing would be to root prune in early autumn and transplant to the new site in late February or early March before the new leaves appear.

Inexpensive Planting Insurance

Many garden stores stock, under various trade names, a pressurized antitranspirant plastic spray product that improves the survival chances for transplanted evergreens or deciduous plants in full foliage. A thin coating of this quickly applied substance eases the shock of transplanting by reducing the loss of moisture through the pores of the leaves. A few hosings or rainshowers will clear away all traces of the spray.

A coating of this substance is also excellent as a protection against winter weather damage for such established plants as boxwood, camellia, rhododendron, and other broad-leaved evergreens.

To summarize:

1. Container-grown plants may be safely planted at any time of the year.

2. Large evergreens and deciduous plants are more safely transplanted from December to March.

3. The use of pressurized weather-protection sprays is an added safeguard for broad-leaved evergreens transplanted at any time and for deciduous plants transplanted when in leaf.

Feeding the Garden

The first and most important step in developing a program of plant nutrition is to have samples of your soil tested. These tests can be made at any time of the year, but early spring and late fall testings are the most reliable. This testing service is provided by state agricultural experiment stations, and in North Carolina there is no charge for this assistance. Contact your local farm agent for instructions on the collection and mailing of soil samples. You will receive a prompt analysis with specific recommendations. If you need any further help, the local representatives of our state department of agriculture will give it. With all this expert advice you can proceed with confidence.

The Nature of Fertilizer

Plant nutrition is even more complex than human nutrition, and there are still many things about it that remain unknown. Plant scientists have determined that plants need for their growth ten major elements and twenty minor or trace elements. The major ten include nitrogen, phosphorus, potash, calcium, magnesium, sodium, sulphur, chlorine, aluminum, and silicon. Among the twenty trace elements are such chemicals as iron, manganese, zinc, boron, copper, barium, and iodine.

How happy I am to leave the combining of these elements entirely in the hands of the plant scientists and commercial manufacturers. Until you have gained much knowledge and experience, I advise you do the same. So far, I am perfectly satisfied with the premixed, balanced chemical fertilizers sold at my favorite garden store. On these bags of fertilizer are three hyphenated numbers. They come in many combinations such as 8-8-8, 5-10-10, 0-14-14, and several more. The first number in the series of three denotes the percentage of nitrogen; the second digit is the percentage of phosphorus, and the third number is the percentage of potash.

In addition to nitrogen, phosphorus, and potash, the bag contains some additional major elements as well as some small amounts of the trace elements. The remainder of the bulk is inert matter that acts as a "carrier" for the chemicals.

As an example, I have just checked the contents of a bag of 8-8-8 fertilizer in my storeroom. The label shows this analysis: nitrogen 8 percent, phosphorus 8 percent, potash 8 percent, calcium 10 percent, sulphur 8 percent, and magnesium 1.2 percent. The remainder is made up of the trace elements and the necessary inert carriers (sand or lime).

The Importance of Nitrogen, Phosphorus, and Potash

Nitrogen is necessary to stimulate the top growth of a plant—the stems and leaves. Phosphorus aids in proper root development and potash improves all the functions of the plant. For the inexperienced gardener and unless a soil test indicates otherwise, I would suggest a simple program that calls for feeding a multipurpose 8-8-8 fertilizer or similar formula from February through June. In the fall when top growth has slowed down, change to an 0-12-12 or similar formula with a low nitrogen content. In fact, if the growth and color are satisfactory, the fall feeding of shrubbery might be omitted altogether.

Suggested Calendar for Fertilizing

Crop	Fertilizer	Date
Azalea, camellia, rhododendron, pieris, boxwood*	Half-and-half combination 8-8-8 fertilizer & cottonseed meal	15 Feb.–1 Mar.
Azalea, camellia, rhododendron, pieris	8-8-8 fertilizer	15 Apr.–1 May
Azalea, camellia, rhododendron, pieris, boxwood	8-8-8 fertilizer	15–30 June
Other evergreens	8-8-8 fertilizer	15 Feb.–1 Mar.
Other evergreens	8-8-8 fertilizer	15–30 June
Trees and deciduous shrubs	8-8-8 fertilizer	15 Feb.–1 Mar.
Vegetables and bedding plants	8-8-8 fertilizer	At monthly intervals during growing period
Rose	8-8-8 fertilizer	At 5-6 week intervals from 1 Mar.–Sept.
Bulbs	8-8-8 fertilizer	Jan. and Oct.†

*This group includes the following:

AZALEAS: Kurume, macrantha, Glen Dale hybrids, Gable hybrids, Gumpo and Satsuki hybrids, and various deciduous azaleas.

CAMELLIAS: *Camellia japonica, Camellia sasanqua*, and other camellia species.

RHODODENDRONS: Hybrids and native varieties.

BOXWOODS: American boxwood (*Buxus sempervirens arborescens*), English or dwarf boxwood (*Buxus sempervirens suffruticosa*), and other boxwood species.

†Bulbs planted among shrubs and other bedding plants receive a share of the fertilizer applied to these larger plants and do not require separate feedings.

Basic Gardening Techniques

How Much to Feed

Only experience can determine exactly what timing and quantities are best. If growth lags and color is poor, try a little more fertilizer or a different formula of fertilizer. Keep in mind that soil conditions, drainage, and watering practices are also important factors in plant growth, and all failures cannot be attributed to the kind or quantity of the fertilizer.

Amount Based on Height or Spread of Shrub

1 ounce for one foot of height or spread
2 ounces for two feet of height or spread
½ pound for three feet of height or spread
3 pounds for six feet of height or spread
5 pounds for eight feet of height or spread

For feeding azaleas, boxwoods, camellias, rhododendrons, pieris, and other highly valued evergreens, I add to the first spring feeding one-half the fertilizer measurement of cottonseed meal, mixing the two together. Cottonseed meal is high in nitrogen, nonburning, and slow-acting. For a long period of time after the faster-acting chemical fertilizer has been exhausted or leached away by heavy rainfall, the cottonseed meal is there to keep the plants green and growing.

Roses: Apply three ounces to each bush beginning in early March and repeat at six-week intervals through 1 September. Newly planted roses should be fed sparingly during the first season.

Trees: Small trees can be top-dressed (scattering fertilizer on the surface) if the fertilizer is applied in the late winter or early spring when the soil is thoroughly wet. Large trees should be fed every three years by putting the fertilizer in holes punched to a depth of at least twelve inches (deeper is even better). A power auger is a handy tool for this operation, but it can be done with a crowbar. Start a few feet from the base of the tree and punch holes two to three feet apart in concentric circles to a distance of ten feet beyond the spread of the outer branches.

The amount of fertilizer used is based on the size of the tree. For example, a tree with a six-inch diameter, measured four feet above the ground, should be fed two to three pounds per inch of diameter, or a total of twelve to eighteen pounds. Distribute the fertilizer in approximately equal amounts into the holes and refill with potting-soil mixture or a good grade of topsoil.

Some General Suggestions on Fertilizing

Foundation Planting: No amount of fertilizer can counterbalance the soil conditions that exist around some house foundations. Builders deposit all the scraps of mortar, bricks, boards, tar-paper siding, and what-have-you in the open spaces dug for the foundation. The landscape contractor covers it up with a thin layer of sorry dirt and plants in it. Remove at least enough of this debris to make a hole full of good soil and replant. It is worth the extra effort.

Wood Ashes: Wood ashes contain valuable amounts of potash. Save them for use around roses, lilacs, and peonies.

Specialty Fertilizers: Special formulae are manufactured for feeding roses, acid-requiring plants (azalea, camellia, and rhododendron), and lawns. These are excellent fertilizers but cost considerably more than standard, all-purpose plant foods. If soil contains humus and proper care is given to watering, spraying, and other special needs, the less expensive fertilizers will produce satisfactory results.

Feeding Large Shrubs: Specimen shrubs of boxwood, holly, cherry laurel, ligustrum, and the like should be punch-fed in the manner described above for large trees.

Fertilizer Storage: Chemical fertilizers must be stored in a dry place, and they should be used within six months after the bag is opened.

Dehydrated Manures and Bone Meal: I do not consider either product to be of much value. Processing methods now in use destroy too much of their food value to be worth their cost. Fresh manures are not in this day generally available to gardeners.

Lime: Lime serves several important functions. Not only is it useful in several ways as a soil conditioner, it is also essential in the control of soil acidity. Southern soil usually tends to be acid in nature; your soil-test analysis will indicate how much lime and the type to use in your garden.

Applying Fertilizer: Spread fertilizer evenly around the plant in a circle as wide as the spread of its outer branches. Never dump it by the handful into the center of a plant or allow any fertilizer to come in contact with any part of the plant. When feeding small bedding plants or ground cover areas, follow the feeding with a thorough shower bath to remove any particles of fertilizer that may have lodged among the leaves.

Yellowing Foliage: The leaves of roses, azaleas, and many other plants sometimes begin to turn yellow in the spring and summer. This lack of green color, or chlorosis (lack of chlorophyll), may be due to a lack of nitrogen, one of the three main elements required for healthy plant growth, or lack of one of the three trace elements, iron, manganese, or sulphur. How to determine exactly what is lacking is a difficult problem for both amateur and professional gardener.

If the regular application of a balanced chemical fertilizer such as the 8-8-8 formula, which I have found satisfactory, fails to correct the problem, try a couple of applications of an iron chelate according to the directions on the container. (Caution: apply iron chelate at the root level of roses and bedding plants to avoid foliage burn.) If the discoloration persists, consult your county extension agent.

Fertilizer and Water: It is important to keep in mind that plant roots can absorb and utilize fertilizers only when they are in soluble form. Apply fertilizer just before a rain or water with the hose immediately after application. On the other hand, heavy rainfalls may leach or wash away most of the benefits of your fertilizer. When this happens, extra amounts may be needed. (Even this problem has a positive application: in case you have inadvertently applied too much fertilizer, a heavy watering can minimize the burning caused by too much fertilizer.)

Feeding Lawns: Lawns are fed seasonally according to the type of grass. Cool-weather grasses (fescue and bluegrass) are fed in the fall and spring and the warm-weather grasses (Bermuda, zoysia, and centipede) from April to August. For help with the types of fertilizer and quantities to use, consult Extension Circular 292 available at your county agricultural extension office.

In dealing with the problems of plant growth such as feeding, watering, and the like, I think it has never been better expressed by anyone than in these words of Laurence Manning (*The How and Why of Better Gardening*, p. 60):

"The best rule to follow is that of moderation in all things. Feed a starved soil a little at a time, rather than its entire estimated deficiency all at once. Water only when you need to and in reasonable quantity, neither flooding or surface-sprinkling. Drain, dig, and cultivate only for a specific reason; unless there is one, leave your soil alone."

Pruning: A Year-Around Chore

In matters of pruning, many gardeners have no self-confidence whatever. They take timid hold on the pruning tool and approach the subject as if it harbored mice or black widow spiders. There is nothing to fear. Just think of all the thousands of shrubs that are butchered, maimed, and carved into balls each year by some of the so-called pruning "experts" and yet survive it all.

Plants have no feelings in spite of the twaddle we hear about prating to one's posies. Shrubs in tolerably good health will put on a burst of growth after pruning, and if you have unwittingly cut a few twigs you think you shouldn't have, there will be two or more to replace each one by the end of the growing season. If the health of a shrub is so uncertain that it cannot survive such pruning, the garden will look better without it.

The one big asset that the gardener has over the hired hand is in caring how the shrub looks and whether it survives. For this reason I believe the gardener will do a better job of pruning than anyone else. The basic reasons for pruning are quite simple and a knowledge of them, however superficial, improves the confidence and the skill of the gardener.

Why Pruning Is Necessary

To Control Size: If heavy, repeated prunings are necessary to control the size of a shrub it is likely that the site is wrong. Large, vigorous shrubs such

as the Burford holly and ligustrum are totally out of place in the base planting of the one-floor house. They are better suited, and need less pruning, around large buildings, in hedges, screens, or as specimens in the shrub garden.

To Produce Compact, Bushy Growth: Pruning to achieve compactness is necessary and should be initiated when the shrub or tree is quite small. For example, I have seen container-grown camellias two feet tall, or taller, without any lateral branches. To promote this lateral growth, pinch out the terminal bud of the camellia whip. As the side branches develop harmonious proportions, pinch off their bud tips as well. In a few seasons of such care your reward will be a well-formed, sturdy plant with ample wood to produce the flowers you want.

To Produce More Fruit or Berries: The pruning of fruit trees, grapevines, and the small fruits (raspberries, blueberries, etc.) is done solely for the purpose of making more fruit. Strangely enough, such practical pruning is very aesthetic as well. If you have seen a peach orchard pruned and in flower, you have seen beauty that is unsurpassed by any art form or expression.

To Maintain Good Health: When the free access of air and light are shut out from the interior of a tree or shrub by dense, twiggy inner growth, disease and decay have found the perfect home. Such a plant should be thinned all over from bottom to top, and a few of the largest and oldest canes or branches should be cut as near the base of the plant as possible.

Where surface shearing, such as is done in hedge trimming, has been the only type of pruning done for several seasons, a thin, twiggy shell of outer leaves encloses the plant. These must also be thinned. Long sleeves and sturdy gloves, as well as a lot of patience, are required for this job. Individual branches varying in length from six inches to two feet, depending on the type of shrub, must be cut from the entire perimeter of the shrub. Don't be afraid you will cut too many. Just keep in mind that you must let the sunshine enter the heart of the plant, and if half the total surface is removed it will not be too much.

Pruning To Achieve Special Effects: The formal and the informal espaliering of trees and shrubs is the very old and still popular technique of pruning certain types of plants to a flat form attached to a wall, frame, or other vertical surface. More will be said later on this subject.

Plants can also be pruned into other shapes such as hedges, archways, and topiary. For the uninitiated, topiary pieces are plants pruned to look like ducks, peacocks, cones, spirals, and the like. Such pruning may be well beyond the skill, patience, and tastes of the average gardener. I do like a few plants here and there in a garden clipped to a neat, compact form. It is a refreshing change of pace from the blowsy informality of most gardens.

To Counteract the Loss of Roots at Transplanting Time: Regardless of the size and firmness of the earth balls dug in transplanting, some of the root system is inevitably destroyed. Pruning away a compensating portion of the top produces a more healthful balance between the functions of the root and the foliage. (Exception: boxwoods have very dense fibrous roots and, unless they are quite large specimens, will not require top pruning when transplanted.)

The amount to be top-pruned varies with the size and type of the plant. If my experience with gardeners is any indication, there is little likelihood that too much top pruning will be done. Most would prefer to lose a finger than remove an inch from a new plant.

Some Guidelines for Pruning

Would that I could write a set of rules for pruning that would cover all the problems and questions about the subject. Since I cannot, I offer the following guidelines that I believe can be applied to pruning generally:

1. Remove all diseased, dying, and dead wood.

2. Remove crossed, rubbing limbs that damage the bark and invite infections and insects. Select the less important of the crossing pair for removal.

3. Avoid leaving stubs when pruning by cutting limbs as close as possible to the next larger stem. Rotting stubs left by improper pruning will eventually spread infection to the healthy wood. Undercut larger limbs whose weight might tear the surrounding bark if only a single uppercut is made.

4. Use a commercial pruning paint to cover each cut the size of the thumb and larger. Paste tree paint does a better and cleaner job than the spray paint. Both types are sold at garden stores.

5. Preserve the natural shape of the plant unless some other special form is desired. Cutting terminal branches to different lengths will help to maintain a natural appearance.

6. Avoid stubs by cutting just above a node or joint.

7. Begin pruning when the plant is small and prune lightly and regularly to achieve compact growth. Broad-leaved evergreens that grow throughout the summer often require several light prunings throughout that growing season.

Pruning Notes of Special Interest

The following alphabetical list of pruning suggestions for individual plants answers some of the questions I have been asked the most frequently by other gardeners over the years.

Azalea: Light and moderate pruning can be beneficial to most types of azaleas, especially those varieties that develop long, straggly branches. Why not cut these tall pieces when they are in bloom for use in the house? If this is done each spring, no other pruning will be needed except for removal of dead branches or those broken in ice and snow storms.

Boxwood: Slow-growing English boxwood normally requires only surface thinning to allow light to reach the interior. Breaking out the short sections used in making Christmas decorations is pruning enough to serve this purpose. Faster-growing American and Korean boxwoods can be pruned much more severely, if needed, to improve the form and quality. I have restored unsightly old specimens from this group by cutting 50 percent of the total volume. Such drastic cutting requires from three to five years for full restoration, but there are times when it seems the only solution. Boxwood growth begins by the middle of February or earlier. January pruning is recommended.

Burford holly (Ilex cornuta var. *Burfordi):* The natural grace of the Burford holly is one of its two superlative assets. The second is its shining red berries. To preserve both assets, leave some of last year's growth each time pruning is done. Although Burford holly, as well as ligustrum (*Ligustrum* spp.), pyracantha, aucuba, elaeagnus (*Elaeagnus pungens*), and many other large evergreens will tolerate drastic pruning, they should be used where such heavy-handed pruning is not necessary. If the occasion arises for heavy cutting, do it in January or February before the new growth begins.

Camellia (both *Camellia japonica* and *Camellia sasanqua*): Many gardeners don't dare to prune a camellia. Don't be afraid. Compact hedges or elegant espaliers formed from camellias are the products of heavy pruning. I remember an ice storm that broke a large camellia in my garden leaving a naked stub about a foot high. I cleaned up the break, painted it, and waited. In time it restored itself completely. Normally, light pruning through the cutting of blooms for arrangements will be enough, but if heavier cutting is required, don't hesitate to do it.

Clematis (Clematis Jackmanii and others): There are few plant varieties that have such involved pruning requirements as the hybrid clematis. Since most of those used in southern gardens belong either to the Jackman or Lanuginosa groups that bloom in spring and early summer, I recommend that they be pruned annually before the end of January. Better flowering will surely result from the new growth that such cutting engenders. I prune my own vines to a height of eighteen to twenty-four inches. Old, unpruned plants will bloom some without pruning, but in a couple of seasons there is apt to be too much dead and unfruitful wood. And, if you have ever tried to remove these old stems in midseason, you know that it is impossible to do so without breaking and damaging the new wood. Clematis is a very brittle plant. Varieties grown in my garden and pruned yearly in January are Jackman, Romona, Henry, Prince Phillip, Crimson Star, and Nelly Moser.

Crab apple (Malus spp.) (and ornamental cherry, plum, peach, and pear): If the blooms of these trees are more important than their graceful shape, prune immediately after they flower. I prefer to prune these trees in the winter when there are no leaves or flowers to confuse the pruning eye. Superfluous and crossing limbs, as well as the sucker growth made each season along the main trunk and large limbs, can be removed. There will be plenty of wood left to flower on a much handsomer tree. Cherry trees (weeping types) and some of the crabapples and pears are grafted on various types of understock. Branches that sprout below the graft joint should be removed. Terminal branches of all varieties can be shortened as needed to preserve the natural symmetry of the tree.

Crape Myrtle: When it comes to "bone" structure, no other ornamental, with the possible exception of the dogwood, can surpass the crape myrtle—that is, when it is properly pruned. Treat it not as a fat-headed shrub, but as a queen-sized Ming tree with glorious silver bark topped by great trusses of summer color.

Start when the plant is young. Choose three to five of the largest base stems to save; cut all others to the ground and never let them grow again. As the tops grow, thin and prune to enhance the picturesque angular lines of the branches and, as far as height is concerned, give it its full head. Eventually you will have a small, spreading tree of surpassing beauty and distinction. Reward it with a specimen spot in your garden.

Dogwood (Cornus florida): This tree somehow seems to get left out of the regular pruning program. Like the fruit trees and the crape myrtle, it should be pruned regularly to enhance its natural form. Annual sucker stems should be pruned and crossing wood removed from the main body of the tree. The dogwood has remarkable recuperative powers and it is a common sight to see a fine young tree growing from the stump of an old one.

Junipers and Pines (Juniperus spp. and Pinus spp.):[*] Needle-leaved plants do not have the recuperative growth characteristic of broad-leaved plants. Therefore, approach them with caution. Restrict your cutting to finger-sized branches and try to leave some green needles below each cut. Removal of half the "candles" of new growth that occurs in the spring on the pines is the safest kind of pruning. If the terminal branch of a pine is broken accidentally, the nearest lateral branch can be trained upwards to take its place.

Mahonia and Nandina (Nandina domestica): These two shrubs have a similar growth habit with a few tall stalks reaching quite high above the main portion of the plant. Each spring remove these tallest canes to ground level. The prunings make dramatic interior decoration and should be so used.

Quince, Flowering: In its old age the thorny quince is literally a pain to prune, and I have seen specimens with a girth of fifteen feet. At this age and stage, most of the shrub would have to be pruned in order to reach the core of the plant. Avoid this stage by annually removing a few of the oldest canes both from the center and around the perimeter of the numerous stalks that make up this plant. Restrict height by cutting stems of terminal branches to varying lengths, just the sort one uses in arranging.

---

[*]See Curtis May, *Pruning Shade Trees and Repairing Their Injuries*, U.S. Department of Agriculture Home and Garden Bulletin no. 83 (Washington, D.C.: Government Printing Office, 1965) for help with pines and other yard trees. The price for this bulletin is ten cents.

Rhododendron: This shrub is frequently allowed to grow to a rangy, unattractive stage that requires drastic pruning for restoration. Well-established plants react favorably to such treatment. For example, the native varieties in our mountain areas are cut to the stump a couple of years before digging to insure the compact quality required for commercial uses.

Hybrid varieties usually are pruned from the beginning by nurserymen and arrive in your garden as compact, well-formed shrubs. Removal of faded flowers immediately after blossoming is usually enough pruning to maintain their good shape. If not, don't hesitate to take off some of the heavier growth.

Roses, Climbers (Rosa spp.*):* Depending on their vigor, climbers should have from one to four of the oldest canes cut to ground level as soon as their main flowering season is over. Remaining young canes can be shortened enough to keep them under control.

Hybrid Teas: Around Thanksgiving cut vigorous hybrid teas to one half their size; weaker bushes by one third. The purpose of this November pruning is to minimize winter wind damage to the brittle-wooded rose. In late March they are pruned again, this time to produce new flowering wood for summer. Many gardeners prune the first of March, but I have had roses badly damaged several times by the late freezes that sometimes occur in early March, and I have learned to prune a little later and wait a little longer for the first blooms.

Pruning Timetable

These shrubs should be pruned immediately after flowering:

Azalea (*Rhododendron* spp.)
Brooms (Scotch broom)
Camellia
Deutzia
Flowering almond
Flowering quince
Forsythia
Fringe tree (*Chionanthus virginica*)
Hydrangea, florists' types forced for Easter (*Hydrangea hortensia*)
Lilac
Sweet-Breath-of-Spring, also winter honeysuckle
Mock orange
Pearlbush
Pieris (*Pieris japonica*)
Redbud (*Cercis canadensis*)
Rhododendron (*Rhododendron* spp.)
Rose (climbers)
Spirea (early spring-flowering varieties)
Viburnum (*Viburnum tomentosum, Viburnum Carlesii* and other viburnums)

Shrubs that should be pruned between January and March:

Abelia
Althea
Beautyberry (*Callicarpa americana*)
Barberry (*Berberis vulgaris*)
Butterfly bush
Crape myrtle
Hydrangea (oak-leaf and peegee varieties)
Hypericum (*Hypericum calycinum*)
Kerria
Spirea (summer-flowering varieties)
Vitex

Pruning for berry-bearing shrubs should be done lightly in early spring and at end of fruiting season:

Aucuba
Cotoneaster
Holly (red-fruited varieties)*
Mahonia
Nandina
Pyracantha
Snowberry
Viburnum

*Hollies and other fruiting plants require second-year growth for fruits. Prune lightly to retain some of the fruiting-age wood.

The following shrubs will produce some secondary blooms if pruned immediately after flowering:

Althea (*Hibiscus syriacus*), butterfly bush, crape myrtle, oak-leaf hydrangea (*Hydrangea quercifolia*), peegee hydrangea (*Hydrangea paniculata* var. *grandiflora*), smoke tree (*Cotinus*), summer spirea (*Spiraea bumalda*), vitex, weigela

Basic Gardening Techniques [21]

The Espalier: A Special Kind of Pruning*

It takes thinking and planning to achieve good garden design in a limited space. Where the small garden is enclosed by fences or walls, you may enjoy an extra dimension provided by a specialized type of pruned plant called the espalier, and at the same time you can save precious bedding space at the base of the espaliered plant.

The term espalier means a framework of stakes, wires, or supports upon which trees and shrubs are attached and trained to a flat plane that can be formal or informal in pattern. Espaliering is an ancient gardening technique that owes its origin to the same dearth of growing space that has brought about its current return to popularity. The main difference between espaliering of the past and that of the present is that in the old days when food was grown within the protected walls of castle and village, espaliering was entirely utilitarian. Fruit trees were carefully trained to produce maximum crops of highly prized fruits. Remaining arable space was planted with pot and medicinal herbs. Modern application of this historic garden form is mainly ornamental, although there are indications that shrinking lot sizes and the high costs of fruits may bring a revival of interest in the culinary aspects of espaliering.

*Henry J. Smith, *Space Sculpture with Trees and Shrubs*, Agricultural Extension Service Publication no. 291 (Raleigh, N.C.: Agricultural Extension Service, 1971).

Formal and Informal Espaliers

The formal espalier may be trained to a single shoot with the terminal branches spread out and attached fanlike to the espaliering frame. A second method of formal espaliering is the training of two, four, or six pairs of opposite limbs branching at regular intervals from a main stem. This method is called the cordon. The informal espalier more nearly resembles a vine, with flowing and irregular lines capable of being exceedingly artistic when executed by creative hands.

Espaliering, whether of formal or informal patterns, should begin when the plant is quite small. It is well to select a plant that already has a strong single stem (for the fan espalier) or one with two strong opposite lateral branches (for the cordon). Plant the shrub or tree as close as possible to its supporting frame. Cut off all the surplus branches, both front and back, as near the stem as you can. From the outset prune away any branches that are contrary to the pattern you have in mind. Fasten the growing branches at regular and short growth intervals in order to allow the branches to adapt safely to the established pattern.

In bending the branches of all patterns, bend only a little at the time to avoid breakage. It may take several tyings to finally have a branch in the desired position. Have no fear of removing surplus branches of ornamentals, but for fruit-tree espaliering, care must be exercised to leave fruiting spurs long enough to produce the blooms and their subsequent fruit.

Plants Suitable for Espaliering

Evergreen: Almost any plant can be trained to the flat vertical plane of the espalier. In Carolina gardens, the pyracantha and camellia sasanqua are very popular. The pyracantha is thorny and mean by nature for the extra handling an espalier requires. However, there are few sights as magnificent as a well-trained espaliered pyracantha loaded with glistening red or orange fruits.

The camellia japonica is also an excellent espalier subject as well as the loquat (*Eriobotrya japonica*), evergreen magnolia, cotoneasters, and the Burford holly.

Deciduous: Dwarf forms of fruiting pear, apple, plum, and cherry are suitable for espaliering and with skilled pruning will produce fruits. The fig bush lends itself well to the fan-shaped espalier on a protected house or garden wall. Several deciduous shrubs are fine espaliering subjects and should replace some of the heavy evergreen espaliers that tend to overpower the surrounding beds by their weight and mass. I enjoy two forsythias that I have attached to my garden fence as one would a climbing rose. In winter the twigs are loaded with the tiny buds of the flower clusters and the bark is a clean light brown. In bloom in the early spring it is a breath-taking sight. The dogwood tree is excellent espaliering material as well as flowering quince, jasmine, viburnum, weigela, and the deciduous azalea.

Regardless of the choice of pattern or plants, espaliered materials are subject to the same cultural requirements of proper exposures, feeding, spraying, and watering as their nonespaliered counterparts. Only their pruning is different.

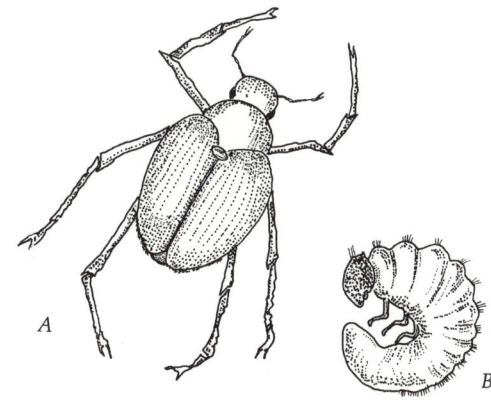

The Japanese Beetle
A. Summer form
B. Winter underground stage

Pesticides

Both my use of pesticides and my attitude towards this controversial subject could be described as moderate. It seems certain that their excessive and indiscriminate use is harmful to the environment, yet how could sufficient food for the world's population be produced without some controls?

As for me, the ballooning costs of insecticides, plus the work and messiness of applying them, are strong safeguards against their excessive use. My spraying program is minimal—delayed as long as possible, and once begun, sparingly practiced. It is true, of course, that I do not produce blue-ribbon roses or the biggest tomatoes in the neighborhood, but competitive gardening is the least of my concerns.

Beginners in gardening often experience well-founded confusion in the selection of spray materials, and no wonder. There are hundreds on the market and more new ones are added each year. For a starting point one needs to know that plants have two groups of enemies: insects and bacteria-fungi. Of course, all insects and all bacteria-fungi are not harmful, but entirely too many are. Insects of many shapes and sizes eat or suck the life-bearing juices from plants, and the bacteria-fungi group causes a host of plant diseases such as mildews, rots, rusts, and blights.

I manage my own garden problems with a very limited number of sprays, and my own spraying program is offered solely as a point of departure. A little experience will soon equip the earnest gardener to formulate a program for his or her own purposes. And, in acquiring this experience, he or she will also discover that healthy, well-tended plants, like their human counterparts, will have a good deal of natural immunity.

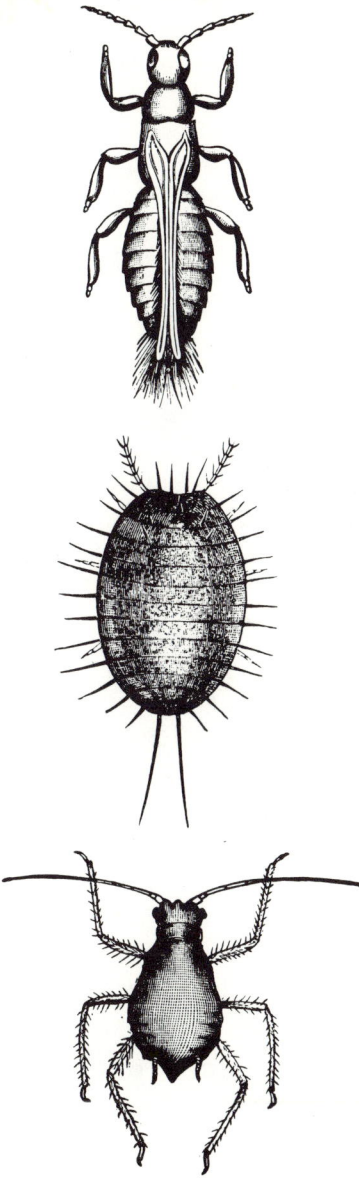

Basic Gardening Techniques

My Bug-and-Bacteria Arsenal

(Trade names are used solely for the sake of convenience and in no way imply superiority over other brands.)

Spray	Enemy	Crops	Dates
Volck oil spray	Scales, whitefly, mealybug, aphid, etc.	Evergreens, roses, trees, shrubs	15 Feb.–15 Apr.
Sevin	Many insects, including Japanese beetles	Vegetables, flowers	As needed
Metaldehyde baits*	Slugs, snails	Vegetables, flowers	As needed
Systemics	Leaf miners, borers	Boxwood, holly, columbine, iris	15 Feb.–1 Apr.
Benlate, Phaltan (fungicides)	Mildews, blights, rots, rusts, smuts, and many more	Roses, lilacs, phlox, mums, and others	As needed
Isotox, Malathion (insecticides)	Wide range of insects	Roses and many ornamentals	As needed
House-and-garden pressurized sprays	Insects	Potted plants	As needed

*Beer in shallow pans will attract slugs and snails to a joyous drowning. It also attracts neighborhood pets.

[24] *Carolina Home Gardener*

Spraying Roses

Roses require more spraying than anything I grow, needing attention on a weekly basis. However, in actual practice, every ten to fourteen days is more likely what they really get. They perform quite well for me with this laxer regimen.

The fungicide (Benlate or Phaltan) can be combined with an insecticide (Isotox or Malathion) to make an all-purpose rose spray. Mix the Phaltan or Benlate with a small amount of water to form a paste as in making a gravy or sauce. Fill the jar with water, add the Isotox or Malathion and mix thoroughly. A six-gallon capacity hose-gun application will spray approximately twenty bushes, and both top and lower surface of all leaves should be spray-coated.

During the hottest part of the summer I reduce the amount of spray ingredients by one-third to one-half. This saves money and reduces the possibility of burning the leaves. For this reason it is also advisable to spray in early morning to permit drying before the warmest part of the day.

A Word on Natural Repellants

Some gardeners plant marigolds, onions, flowering tobacco, garlic, and other plants that are said to discourage various and sundry plant pests. Since I have not tried any of these methods, I have no opinion as to their efficacy. It surely would do no harm to try them, however.

One garden writer suggested the following intriguing folk recipe for an organic, all-purpose spray: chop three ounces of garlic bulbs and soak twenty-four hours in two teaspoons of mineral oil. Add one pint of water, mix, strain, and apply. If the mixer can survive the mixing, it ought to repel something. I cannot state it for an absolute fact, but I do think that mothballs scattered among my pansies have been some help in holding the rabbits at bay in midwinter when greenery is not so plentiful.

(While on the subject of old-time gardening ideas, I might add that I do not plant by the signs either. I also hasten to say that I have no objections whatever to others doing so. It has never been quite clear to me how one could tell if a crop failure occurs because of planting in the wrong sign or for other reasons such as unfavorable weather, barren soil, or poor cultural practices.)

For the Best Help with Garden Pest Problems

Before closing the subject of pesticides, I would like to call your attention to two helpful publications on the subject which are available without charge from your county agent or from the North Carolina Agricultural Extension Service, Raleigh, N.C. James R. Baker, *Insect Control on Ornamental Plants in and around the House*, Agricultural Extension Service Publication no. 561 (Raleigh, N.C.: Agricultural Extension Service, 1974) includes drawings of more than thirty of our most common ornamental plant pests and recommendations for control measures. H. E. Scott, Charles H. Brett, and K. A. Sorenson, *Insect Control for Vegetable Gardens*, Agricultural Extension Service Publication no. 177 (Raleigh, N.C.: Agricultural Extension Service, 1973) deals specifically with twenty-five pests that are most likely to give the home gardener trouble.

Keeping Garden Records

Keeping records of your growing activities is not mandatory, but it can be very helpful both to the record keeper and to others as well.

Very few gardeners would take the time and effort to keep and share the kind of records Elizabeth Lawrence and her mother maintained for many years. North Carolina author and landscape architect, Elizabeth Lawrence, in a book called *A Southern Garden*, writes about a garden notebook she and her mother made during several years of gardening at Raleigh, N.C. Together they noted and recorded the early and late flowering dates in that area of hundreds of annuals, biennials, perennials, bulbs, shrubs, and vines. The first edition of *A Southern Garden* (1942) and a subsequent revision (1967) have been useful to me many times throughout my gardening years. In planting private gardens for special events, scheduling flower shows, and designing gardens for seasonal flowering sequence, Elizabeth Lawrence's notebook has been an invaluable tool.

What is needed in the Carolinas is many more garden notebooks. Perhaps the records you keep will not be as extensive as my own, which have been the basis for this book, nor that of the Lawrences, but even the simplest of records are excellent aids and reminders, especially during the formative years of mastering the fundamentals. A simple, easily kept record might be in the form of a monthly calendar with divisions to cover the four basic gardening activities of pruning, spraying, planting, and feeding.

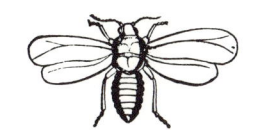

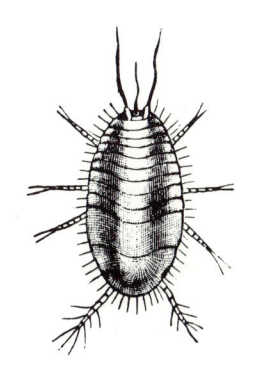

Basic Gardening Techniques

Such a record might look like this:

FEBRUARY

Activity	Trees	Shrubs	Bulbs	Plants, Bedding	Vegetables	Other	Materials
Pruning	Apple	Althea				Grapes	
Spraying	Trees	Evergreens, deciduous plants					Volck oil
Planting	Trees	Shrubs		Day lily	Salad greens, lettuce, peas	Poppies	
Feeding	Trees	Shrubs	Spring bulbs				8-8-8 fertilizer

A second approach to keeping garden records might be an alphabetical listing of the plants you grow or plan to grow. A sample entry might look like this:

AZALEA: *var. Coral-bells*

Comments	Fed	Pruned	Sprayed	Other
Size: 3'–5'	15 Feb. 15 June	Lightly after flowering	Iron chelate 15 July 1 Aug.	Mulched, watered in dry spells

Color: Salmon pink

Growth habit: Spreading

Evergreen or Deciduous: Evergreen

Flowering date: 10 Apr.

Garden Calendar

On Using a Garden Calendar

There is nothing arbitrary in the suggested monthly garden regimen that follows. It is offered merely as a guide for beginners and as a reminder for more experienced gardeners. Obviously many of the tasks listed for January could be as efficaciously done in late December or early February. However, human nature being what it is, I would advise that most of the garden chores mentioned be done within five to six weeks of the times recommended.

I would also urgently recommend that my calendar be adjusted by the individual to the average frost dates of the locality. For mountain and foothill gardeners it is especially important to take full advantage of their shorter growing season; for coastal and southern gardeners, additional crops may be possible through more exact knowledge of regional frost dates. The most reliable information on these dates can be had from county agricultural agents, who are located at county seats, and from experienced gardeners in the neighborhood.

Year-Around Garden Chores

Throughout most sections of the Carolinas there are a number of gardening activities that can and should be done as needed without too much attention to the date. These include weeding, watering when it is dry, cleaning up, composting, mulching, making cuttings, light feeding (especially following heavy rainfalls), moderate pruning, and the removal of faded flowers. In the Carolinas gardening is truly a year-around hobby.

January

1. Plant trees and shrubs, both evergreens and deciduous, including fruit trees, berries, and grapes.

2. In coastal and southern areas, apply a dormant spray (Volck) to fruits and ornamentals, both evergreen and deciduous, on any day when the temperature is not below freezing for twenty-four hours. Follow directions explicitly.

3. Prune grapes and fruit trees.

4. Prune evergreens as needed. January (and February) are good months to do heavy amounts of pruning, since new growth beginning in March will rapidly cover the cutting signs.

5. Provide extra care for house plants. Wash foliage of smooth-leaved varieties, remove weak and dead portions, pinch back long runners of begonias, geraniums, coleus, and wandering Jew. Maintain pebble-filled saucers with water to hold pots for greater humidity.

6. Root the pruned stems from begonias, geraniums, and wandering Jew in glasses of water on a bright, but not necessarily sunny, window ledge. The kitchen is a good place for such cuttings because of the extra humidity existing there.

7. In case of snow, shake fresh drifts from boxwoods, hollies, and azaleas to minimize breakage.

8. Feed beds of daffodils an application of 8-8-8 fertilizer as soon as their tops appear above ground, usually in January.

9. In case of scant rainfall, keep evergreens watered and mulches intact. For overly exposed boxwoods and camellias, apply a coating of plastic spray such as Wiltpruf to reduce foliage sun scald. Apply when temperatures are around 45 degrees.

10. In case you haven't done so earlier (see calendar for November and December), sow seeds of hardy annuals (annual poppy, cornflower, larkspur, and Drummond phlox) on surface of the beds where they are wanted.

11. Check new catalogs that arrive in early January and prepare seed order for spring.

12. If you are not a believer in feeding the birds in winter, do at least provide water for them when the natural supplies are frozen. Many gardeners provide both feed and water during the winter months.

February

1. On sunny days when the ground is workable, divide and replant perennials before their tops begin to grow. These would include hosta, day lily, iris, liriope, spring phlox, loosestrife, evening primrose, cowslip, shasta daisy, coral-bell, and other fibrous-rooted perennials.

2. Cut back the tops of Christmas ferns and liriope before new spring growth begins.

3. From mid-February on, plant such cool-season vegetables as English peas, broccoli, lettuce, endive, cabbage, salad greens, radishes, onions, and Chinese cabbage.

4. Biennials such as pansy, hollyhock, canterbury bell, forget-me-not, wallflower, English daisy, and foxglove may be planted for spring bloom, provided you buy well-established plants.

5. Feed trees and shrubbery with an equal mixture of cottonseed meal and 8-8-8 chemical fertilizer. Use special azalea-camellia fertilizer for these plants if you prefer.

6. Cut a few tall stalks of nandina and mahonia to the ground to induce compactness; prune summer-flowering shrubs such as crape myrtle, althea, vitex, oleander, butterfly bush, and the peegee and oak-leaf hydrangeas.

Basic Gardening Techniques [27]

7. In piedmont and mountain areas, apply dormant spray (see January).

8. Have soil samples from garden tested. Call your county farm agent for instructions. Follow the recommendations based on the test results.

9. Prune boxwood (*Buxus sempervirens*) in early February before new growth begins; prune at an earlier date in warmer areas.

10. Check small bedding plants put out in the fall for signs of frost heaving. Press displaced plants back in the soil and cover the exposed roots with fresh soil. Replenish mulches to minimize frost action.

11. Weed for removal of winter chickweed, dock, dandelions, and henbit.

12. Gather branches of pussy willow, forsythia, flowering quince, and Sweet-Breath-of-Spring for forcing in the house.

March

1. Continue plantings of cool-weather vegetables (see list on page 70).

2. Feed, prune, and spray old roses; plant new ones. These rose gardening activities may begin two weeks earlier in coastal and southern areas.

3. Feed cool-season grasses (fescue and bluegrass). If crabgrass is a problem, add a preemergence chemical to the fertilizer, but do not use it (chemical) under trees. Reseed bare spots.

4. Continue pruning begun in January and February. Cut back old stands of ivy to three-inch heights.

5. Refrain from removal of mulch around bedding plants. There is still frost ahead and plenty of it.

6. Remove faded daffodil blossoms but leave the foliage to ripen. It takes three to four months to complete the ripening.

7. Put a cupful of lime around each clematis.

8. Continue weeding.

9. Cut back leggy house plants and feed.

10. Apply wood ashes to peonies, roses, and hostas.

11. Do *not* cultivate around surface-rooted shrubs (azalea, boxwood, camellia, rhododendron, dogwood, and pieris).

12. Apply systemic insecticides to boxwoods and holly trees.

13. Start the seeds of tomatoes, cucumbers, squash, eggplant, and peppers indoors. NOTE: Late March for window growth.

14. In case you didn't get it done in February, feed everything in the garden in March.

15. Prune red raspberries, removing oldest canes to ground; shorten remaining canes to about twelve inches.

April

1. Feed warm-season grasses (Bermuda grass, St. Augustine, zoysia, and centipede). Seed new lawns or reseed old ones.

2. Continue planting new roses; feed established ones again in late April. Continue weekly spraying.

3. Transplant seedlings of tomato, pepper, squash, cucumber, eggplant, and bell pepper as soon as they reach the four-leaf stage. Continue to grow them under protected conditions until danger of frost is past.

4. Remove covering mulch from low bedding plants at the end of April.

5. In late April take house plants outside to a sheltered location for hardening before final placement in the garden and terrace areas.

6. Spray and stake growing peonies. This is the time to prevent the botrytis blight that blackens the buds while they are forming. Use Ferbam or other fungicides.

7. Prune the early flowering deciduous shrubs: forsythia, flowering almond, flowering quince, and spirea. Prune lightly any azaleas that have completed their flowering.

8. Dig and pull apart old chrysanthemums and reset all portions except the old stalk.

9. Plant Christmas poinsettias, with tops cut back to four to six inches, outside in the garden. Ditto with your Easter lily.

10. Watch out for a late frost.

May

1. Continue removal of faded flowers.

2. Feed cool-season lawns. Cut grass to a height of two inches as weather heats up.

3. Plant all tender vegetables and annuals outside. *Vegetables:* tomato, corn, field pea, lima bean, snap bean, cucumber, squash, okra, pepper, melon, Swiss chard, etc. *Flowers:* petunia, zinnia, marigold, scarlet sage, nasturtium, cleome, periwinkle, Browallia, celosia, strawflower, etc.

4. Herbs and wild flowers may also be planted in May.

5. Cut stalks of faded blossoms on columbine, sweet rocket, foxglove, sweet william, wallflower, and dianthus in late May (or early June) to allow for secondary blooms.

6. Sprig or seed new and old lawns of warm-weather grasses (Bermuda grass, zoysia, centipede, and St. Augustine).

7. Continue spraying roses.

8. Apply iron chelate to yellowed azaleas and other shrubs as a foliar spray. For bedding plants, pour iron solution around the roots only. Follow amounts specified on container.

9. Plant tender summer bulbs: caladium, tuberous begonia, canna, dahlia, tuberose, etc.

10. Place potted plants outside for the summer in spots where proper growing conditions exist.

11. Prepare and install hanging baskets and outdoor containers.

12. Pinch tips of chrysanthemums as soon as they are six inches tall. Dwarf varieties may not require pinching, but a moderate amount may be helpful for compactness.

13. Make cuttings of rose, geranium, begonia, dianthus, candytuft, impatiens, wandering Jew, coleus, and Boston daisy for use later in the summer.

14. Continue removing the tips from fast-growing evergreens at growth intervals of six to eight inches.

15. Stake tomato, eggplant, and pepper plants.

16. Plant second crop of beets, squash, cucumbers, tomatoes, and lettuce for continuous harvesting.

Basic Gardening Techniques [29]

June

1. Prepare Japanese beetle sprays for ready use. June is beetle month—and July—and August! Sevin is the best insecticide I have found for beetle control.

2. Continue planting chrysanthemums, gladioli, and all other summer bedding plants.

3. Provide plenty of water for rapidly growing flowers and vegetables. Light applications of 8-8-8 fertilizer applied at three- to four-week intervals through the summer season will increase the flower and vegetable yields.

4. Apply iron chelate again to azaleas and shrubbery.

5. Keep up with the weeding.

6. Remove blossom stalks of peony, iris, and day lily as soon as flowers have faded.

7. Apply a second and final feeding to shrubs and trees.

8. To save labor and water during the remainder of the summer, mulch as many vegetables, shrubs, and flowers as possible with several layers of newspapers or strips of black polyethylene. Camouflage and anchor these materials with two to four inches of pine needles or chopped leaves. (NOTE: If plastic is used, perforate large pieces with the pitchfork to permit water to reach root areas.)

9. Water thoroughly at weekly intervals during periods of sparse rainfall.

10. Tops of hyacinths, tulips, and most of the daffodils have completed their ripening by June. These bulbs may be lifted, cleaned, and stored for fall planting or may be replanted immediately. Bulbs still blooming satisfactorily may be left undisturbed.

11. Sow a second crop of fast-growing summer annuals: marigolds, zinnias, etc.

12. Prune climbing roses as soon as their main crop of blooms has faded.

13. Prune lilacs by removal of oldest canes and two-thirds of the suckers around the main plant.

14. Prune wisteria drastically if it has been blooming sparsely.

15. Shear perennial candytuft to promote new growth for next season.

16. Pinch pine "candles" of new growth as a light pruning.

17. Feed roses.

July

1. Make cuttings of ivy, pachysandra, and periwinkle and put in a shady place to root. Use standard potting mixture as rooting medium or sharp sand mixed with peat moss or sand alone. Keep watered.

2. Prune hybrid tea roses moderately, according to individual vigor, to promote vegetative growth for fall flowering. (If roses are still blooming well in July, this pruning can be done in August.)

3. Continue weeding, removal of faded blooms, and watering of garden in July.

4. Make cuttings of azalea, camellia, holly, boxwood, and other evergreens.

5. Transplant to larger containers or garden beds rooted cuttings made in May.

6. Scatter ripened seeds of honesty wherever such plants are desired for flowering next spring.

7. Continue staking tall flowers and vegetables as needed (mums, dahlias, gladioli, and others).

8. Clear from the premises spent vegetable plants of squash, cucumber, and anything else that is no longer productive.

9. Dig and divide iris and Oriental poppies.

10. Sow in cool shaded locations seeds of such perennials as columbine, gaillardia (*Gaillardia aristata*), painted daisy (*Pyrethrum*), shasta daisy, veronicas (*Veronica incana*), stokesia (*Stokesia laevis*), lupines, and sages (*Salvia*).

11. Remove last vestiges of ripened daffodil foliage.

August

1. Remove faded crape myrtle and oleander blooms to get a second flowering.

2. Feed warm-season grasses.

3. Continue tip-pruning of evergreens that continue to grow throughout the summer.

4. Water according to need.

5. Order seeds for fall garden.

6. Have soil samples tested in case this was not done in February.

7. Prepare batches of potting soil for fall use.

8. Continue making cuttings of broad-leaved evergreens, roses, and bedding plants.

9. Sow seeds or set plants of broccoli, cabbage, Chinese cabbage, and collards.

10. Give roses final feeding, continue regular spraying.

September

1. Feed and reseed old lawns or make new lawns of cool-season grasses. Cut grass two- to two-and-a-half-inch heights.

2. Sow Italian ryegrass (*Lolium multiflorum*) over Bermuda grass, zoysia, or other warm-season lawns.

3. Sow seeds of radish, lettuce, endive, and salad greens and plant onion sets.

4. Purchase any spring bulbs (tulip, daffodil, hyacinth, scilla, crocus, etc.) that you want for your spring garden. Store in a cool dry place until late October and November planting.

5. Sow seeds of pansy, English daisy, forget-me-not, wallflower, and sweet william.

6. Continue to fight insects, especially on the late cool-season vegetable crops.

7. Continue spraying roses.

8. Plant lily bulbs.

9. Begin fall cleanup of spent vegetation of summer annuals and vegetables.

10. Prepare a compost bed to receive fall leaves.

11. Transplant and prepare house plants for wintering inside.

Basic Gardening Techniques [31]

October

1. Before heavy frost arrives, harvest the remaining tender flowers and vegetables for indoor enjoyment.

2. Replenish organic matter, add fertilizer, and thoroughly cultivate beds where summer annuals grew so that they will be ready to replant with bedding plants for spring bloom. Such beds can be planted immediately if desired.

3. Divide and transplant established perennials and add new ones.

4. Take up and store tender bulbs.

5. Sow seeds of hardy annuals (larkspur, poppy, Drummond phlox, cornflower, etc.) where they are to bloom.

6. October is often a dry month. Don't forget to water regardless of temperatures.

7. Wait for natural defoliation of deciduous trees and shrubs before planting new ones or transplanting old ones.

8. Wait until spring to plant new roses.

9. October is a perfect month to get construction done. Build walks, terraces, arbors, and fencing during the fine Indian summer weather.

10. Spray azaleas and pyracantha with Isotox or Malathion for lace bugs that are rampant October feeders.

November

1. Plant evergreen trees and shrubbery throughout November and December.

2. Plant deciduous trees, shrubbery, fruits, and berries in late November and December.

3. Complete planting of spring bulbs, biennials, and perennials.

4. Replenish mulches throughout garden.

5. Continue composting leaves.

6. Apply lime to lilacs.

7. Prune roses to avoid wind and ice damage through winter.

8. Store outdoor furniture.

9. Complete garden cleanup.

10. Make hardwood cuttings.

11. Weed and water as needed.

12. Apply final feeding to cool-season lawns.

13. Plow or spade vegetable-growing areas to take advantage of the freezing-thawing action of winter weather. Mix chopped leaves with soil for composting.

14. Sow in November or December seeds of hardy annuals where they are to grow.

December

1. Complete outdoor plantings of all kinds.

2. Prune evergreens as needed for holiday decoration.

3. Apply spray of plastic (Wiltpruf or other) to provide protection for choice broad-leaved evergreens from prolonged periods of subfreezing temperatures.

4. Save wood ashes for spring application to peonies, roses, and hostas.

5. Soak roots of living Christmas tree in water for several hours before bringing indoors. Plant outside as soon as possible after the holidays.

6. Enjoy the holidays.

Part Two
An Introduction to Garden Design

Base Plantings

Plantings that are situated from three to eight feet from the exterior house walls are called base or foundation plantings. Although their planting should be a carefully integrated part of the overall garden design, they may be the only materials ever planted other than the lawn grass and (I hope) a few trees.

Base-planting styles still in use today had their inception in Victorian times when houses were built on raised foundations and heavy plantings of shrubbery were used to fill the voids between house and ground. The houses of today are built on flat slabs of concrete, and their outside walls extend to the ground. In spite of these architectural improvements, we are still planting in the Victorian tradition with a heavy-handed manner that overpowers both house and gardener within a very short time after the planting.

Giving specific directions for planting any particular example of a house foundation makes the same amount of sense as saying that I have a fine new dress pattern and plan to make a dress by it for every lady in my neighborhood. Each base planting, as well as the garden that surrounds it, is unique as to neighborhood, site, house-style, growing conditions, and, last but not least, the interests and means of the owner.

Recalling, however, the uncounted times I have heard my clients say, "First, let's do something with this base planting," I have given extra thought to the following general suggestions that ought to receive consideration in designing a base planting.*

1. In choosing plants, select those varieties suited to the exposures, using sun and heat-resistant varieties on southern and western exposures unless there is enough existing shade to mitigate the heat. Keep in mind that heat is intensified and reflected by walls, especially those made of brick or stone. Save plants of doubtful hardiness for northern exposures.

2. A majority of the plants used in the base planting should be evergreen because of their year-around appearance. Use herbaceous plants with caution, bearing in mind the long winter months when their places will be vacant.

3. Restrict your base plants to three or four varieties for the sake of harmony and continuity of design. Save the varietal display for the garden proper.

4. Use dwarf, slower-growing plants for one-floor houses; taller types for two-floor structures. In general, the tallest shrubs should not be permitted to grow taller than approximately half the height from the ground to the eaves.

*The North Carolina Agricultural Extension Service has available from your county agent or their offices at State College Station, Raleigh, N.C., a booklet by John H. Harris, *Landscaping Your Home*, Agricultural Extension Service Publication no. 476 (Raleigh, N.C.: Agricultural Extension Service, 1968). In addition to helpful suggestions on site selection, planning, and planting, there is an extensive list of plants adapted to Carolina gardens.

5. Shrubs or shrub groups should be placed where they will serve as accents for the strong structural lines of the house. These strong structural lines are the outside and inside corners, chimneys, and doorways—and occasionally a large blank wall space.

6. In order to avoid the monotony of straight unbroken lines of shrubs marching shoulder to shoulder around the house, leave the ground space under the windows vacant or use only low shrubs or evergreen ground covers if the sight of any unplanted foundation space is uncomfortable for you.

7. If the tallest shrubs are used at the outside corners, intermediate heights at inside corners, and the lowest shrubs at the entrance, the resulting silhouette of descending heights not only adds beauty and interest to the planting as a whole but also creates a distinctive focal point at the entrance.

8. Base plantings for houses that are architecturally balanced with the entry in the center and the same window treatment along the front facade are the easiest to design because the plant arrangement can be identical on both sides, particularly if the terrain is more or less even.

9. On the other hand, the asymmetrical house with the entrance off center may prove a bit more of a problem for the amateur. In this case it is helpful to find the actual center of the house and plan groups of plants to balance each other in weight on both sides of the actual center. Where this method is used the entrance planting becomes

merely a part of the total planting rather than a focal area. Such plantings may indeed take a little more effort, but they are quite frequently more distinctive and interesting than those with the formally balanced treatment described in paragraph 8.

10. Houses erected on uneven terrain require heavier and taller plants on the low side to compensate for the opposing higher land elevation. A tree or two on the lower side can be very effective in helping to counteract the weight.

11. Most houses have four sides. Do extend the base planting to all four. Whereas it may be more prudent to treat the public sides with the conventional evergreen plantings, the base planting in the private areas of the property furnish golden opportunities for the creation of flowering borders and small gardens that may be added to the basic foundation evergreens.

12. The distance to plant shrubs from the house walls varies according to the mature size of the plant, the width of the overhangs, and whether or not the plant is designed for espaliering. The largest shrubs to be used should have enough growing space from the house to permit them to attain the maximum height and spread you deem most suitable. A rule of thumb might allow three to three and a half feet for the dwarf shrubs and up to eight feet for the larger varieties to be used. Many contemporary houses have quite wide eaves that sometimes adversely affect the progress of plants by reducing the amount of light and water they receive. Arrange plants to allow at least the minimum light and rainfall required for their growth. (In extreme cases it might be wiser to gravel such areas or mulch with pine bark and plant outside the zone ordinarily accepted as the base-planting area.) Espaliered plants should be sited as close to the wall as possible, unless a trellis is to be used for securing or supporting the espaliered plant.

13. Base plantings are more attractive when the groups of shrubs are connected with plantings of ground covers such as the ivy, pachysandra, periwinkle, ajuga, or low-spreading shrubs such as azalea, dwarf holly, trailing junipers (*Juniperus horizontalis*), etc. Attention in particular must be called to the fact that ivies are poor companions for dense, low-growing boxwoods, azaleas, and dwarf hollies because of their propensity for climbing and smothering these slower-growing shrubs.

14. Dwarf azaleas and low-growing hollies are also popular as companions for the slow-growing boxwoods in many base plantings in the Carolinas. The faster-growing azaleas and hollies should be regularly pruned for the removal of any contact between them and the choicer boxwoods. Speaking of boxwoods, Southern gardeners are justly devoted to these dark green and lustrous shrubs that are so firmly entrenched in generations of garden lore. If boxwoods are selected with the proper height variations, no additional shrubs are needed for a base planting. Ground coverings of pachysandra, where there is enough shade for it to thrive, are especially beautiful when used to tie together a base planting of the fine-textured boxwood. (With boxwood, as with other shrub selections, the tallest ones should go to the outside corners and the smaller specimens to the entrance.)

15. Avoid strongly pointed plants of all varieties in base plantings. Plants that spread horizontally are far more effective in uniting the house with the earth, which is the main reason for a base planting in the first place.

16. Keep always in mind that a tree or two is worth a hundred shrubs in the garden. A tree is superbly proportioned to frame a doorway or the end of the house. It casts shadows and lights in uncounted patterns on walks, doors, windows, and walls and imparts a subtle feeling of permanence that makes a house unmistakably a home.

Locating the Garden

Flowers, whether in beds or borders, are located traditionally in the private areas of the property. The public areas, or front yards, receive a more conventional, parklike treatment using grass, trees, and shrub groupings of evergreens and deciduous plants around the foundation of the dwelling and along the property lines. This is generally the best division of the ground areas of a residential property. However, there can be exceptions. If you prefer to use the entire backyard as a playground, I think that you should do so, both for the safety of the children and the tranquility of the neighborhood.

In addition to providing a safe playground space, there may be other reasons why flowers could and should be grown in the public or front-yard areas. If the house is plain or unattractive, the facade can be improved by the addition of flowers in window boxes, planters, neat beds, or on trellises. In case, of course, the house itself is architecturally elegant or outstanding, the extra embellishment of flowers is entirely superfluous.

Cases also occur in which heavy shade, stubborn soils, or other site problems in the private area preclude the growing of a favorite flower such as the rose or the iris. Grow these, if you like, in the front yard. On the other hand, if the only trees on the lot are in the front yard, that is the place for an azalea bed. In all instances where flowering material is to be grown in the public areas, special effort must be devoted to the harmonious integration of these plantings into the design of the yard as a whole. It must be remembered that the year-around appearance of all plantings in the public areas becomes a matter of constant concern. Mulches, pruning, and regular grooming can do much to keep these beds presentable at all times.

Perhaps there will come a sensible day, as some progressive land planners have suggested, when city ordinances will permit residential housing to be placed nearer to the street than is allowed by present standards. Soundproofing and screening would of course be needed, but imagine the size of the private area one could have if the house could occupy the foreground of the lot rather than splitting it in the middle.

Regardless of how the house is situated, the backyard is likely to continue to be the most popular location for the garden and family activities. When in the process of making the final decisions as to where the service areas and the ornamental portions are to be developed, don't overlook the importance of garden-viewing from indoors. People are so busy all the time that every indoor glimpse of outdoor beauty is a thing to cherish.

From the standpoint of the cook—a post of doubtful privilege that I occupy at my house—I find that my aversion to kitchenery is somewhat mitigated by the many gardenward glances to where the flowers toil not, and the birds frolic in a shade-sequestered bath. No wonder my husband has taken up cooking!

Framing the Garden

A well-designed garden is a picture, regardless of its size and location, and like any other picture, it is never complete without a suitable frame.

There are several ways to frame a garden. There are walls, fences, hedges, panels, and sides of buildings. Walls and fences can be made of wood, stone, brick, reeding, plastics, or metal. These materials can be used in a variety of design combinations to suit and enhance any style of house and garden. Whatever your choice, don't fail to ascertain the placement and size restrictions for enclosures in your city. It might save the cost of making changes later on.

If cost is not too great a factor, walls and fences of brick and stone are long-lasting, maintenance-free, and elegant. Needless to say, if the house is a fine one, the wall or fence should be equally distinctive. As a matter of fact, wooden walls and fences can also be elaborate and expensive. Painted wooden fences require as much maintenance as a painted house, but if unpainted woods are appropriate for the house, the cost of maintenance can be greatly reduced.

Decay-resistant woods such as cedar, cypress, and redwood require no painting to be attractive; fences of unpainted soft woods such as pine and poplar should be treated with wood preservatives before erection. All wooden posts, regardless of the type of lumber, should be set in a foundation of concrete for sturdiness and protection from ground moisture.

Reed screening is attractive and lasts several years if it is snugly and firmly framed on rot-resistant timbers. It is airy and blends well with a woodsy setting. However, this style of enclosure is highly susceptible to mechanical damage from falling tree limbs and stray baseballs.

Chain-link fencing is strong, durable, carefree, and uncompromisingly ugly unless something is added to warm its cold and institutional mien. Evergreen ivies may be hand-trained to completely hide the metal framework beneath. Since ivy rootlets cannot cling to the nonporous metal, it is necessary to tie and fasten branches wherever they are needed. The year-around cover of ivy, however, is worth the trouble. Other varieties of vines such as clematis, climbing rose, Carolina jessamine, trumpet creeper (*Campsis radicans*), bittersweet (*Celastrus scandens*), and a host of annual vines may be used and have the advantage of doing their own attaching. Shrubs (pyracantha, camellia, holly, and euonymus) may be fastened in flat, vinelike, semiespaliered forms to chain link or other types of wire fencing. Deciduous shrubs of willowy growth habits (forsythia, cotoneaster, beautybush, weigela, spirea, althea, and the winged euonymus [*Euonymus alatus*]) can also be used in the same manner as the evergreens to soften and adorn unattractive fencing. Still another method of imparting some warmth to a chain-link fence is to interweave filler strips of redwood, cypress, cedar, or enamel-baked aluminum. The last mentioned strip is available in white, light green, or dark green, but such an ostentatious background detracts somewhat from the garden, whereas the natural wood filler strips of redwood, cypress, and cedar blend and harmonize with natural plant colors.

Hedges* are not always satisfactory for framing the garden, and shrub plantings in tree-shaded areas seldom fulfill their desired role, mainly because they fail to grow. In the perpetual competition that takes place between the shrubs and existing trees for food, light, and water, the trees always win. If space, light, and water are available in ample quantity, backgrounds of trees or shrubs are quite satisfactory. They do, however, require regular attention by way of pruning, feeding, spraying, and mulching—so

---

*Privet (*Ligustrum vulgare*), a frequently used plant for hedges, is a high-maintenance risk because of its rapid growth habits.

much so, in fact, that it is debatable as to whether, in the long haul, a structural enclosure might not be less costly. There is a third factor, in addition to cultivation problems and cost, that must be considered in choosing between plants or fences as enclosures. The shrub or tree planting in the small garden requires a goodly amount of space that might be more effectively used for less bulky types of plants. In this area it is not uncommon to see a small garden almost filled by a hedge of white pines or the vigorous ligustrum. It is difficult to create garden designs of proper scale and proportion in such cases.

If a plant hedge is used to frame the garden, select evergreens that can be kept within bounds with a reasonable amount of pruning. Shrubs well suited for hedges are the Japanese holly (*Ilex crenata*), Chinese holly (*Ilex cornuta*), photinia (both *Photinia serrulata* and *P. glabra*), osmanthus (*Osmanthus aquifolium* and *O. fortunei*), camellia, especially the fall-flowering sasanqua camellia, and certain of the ligustrums, notably the *Ligustrum lucidum* varieties.

Perhaps this is the time to mention the changing attitudes concerning all styles of enclosures. There was a time, and traces of this feeling linger on, when a fence or hedge was taken as a personal insult. (It was never my good fortune to be so "insulted"!) With today's burgeoning populations and shrinking lots, more and more people are installing fences, many of them jointly owned. If a neighbor seems receptive to the idea of joint ownership of hedging or fencing, it might help to dispel future hard feelings to discuss the advantages of such an arrangement. If garden framing and privacy strike a sour note, try such ideas as using enclosures as windbreaks, dog pens, line markers, or as a barrier to save your neighbor from sweeping your leaves.

Shrubs and Trees Come First

For those busy with families, earning a living, or those who prefer golf or bridge in their leisure time, a permanent garden of evergreens, seasoned with a sprinkling of deciduous plants, is the best answer for ease of maintenance and year-around good looks. In the Carolinas and surrounding states, we are generously endowed with a variety of beautiful evergreens and deciduous plants unsurpassed by any section of the country. Because of these plant resources, it is well within the scope of the gardener to develop distinctive garden and home settings composed entirely of shrubbery and trees. In order to achieve satisfactory design and composition in such a garden, selections should be based on the following:

1. Year-around beauty of foliage with special emphasis on leaf size, texture, and form.

2. Color as related to flowers and fruits, if any, and the seasonal changes of foliage color in spring and fall.

3. The structural form and character of bark and stems of deciduous plants in winter.

The Green-Garden Concept

Evergreen shrubbery is the backbone of the southern garden, providing a basic permanent framework. In winter, when blooms are scarce, evergreens are alive and full of promise, holding the fort, so to speak, while the bulbs and herbaceous perennials are sleeping. In the growing seasons of spring, summer, and early fall, the evergreens continue to aid and abet the garden with blooms, fruits, and fragrances of their own.

Southern gardeners are fortunate, not only for the great variety of evergreens that thrive in our gardens, but also for their ability to grow satisfactorily in a wide range of garden environments, particularly pertaining to light requirements. It has been a matter of long and happy observation on my part to note that plants needing partial shade for their optimum success can often thrive in far sunnier sites than I had thought possible. Conversely, sun-loving plants can be quite happy, though perhaps less floriferous and fruitful, in deeper shade than one might imagine.

In instances in which plant varieties are grown in less than ideal conditions, their success seems to depend on the extra care in soil preparation and on the faithful provision for their food, water, and mulching needs. In the case of shade plants, extra attention to providing artificial shade in winter is also important.

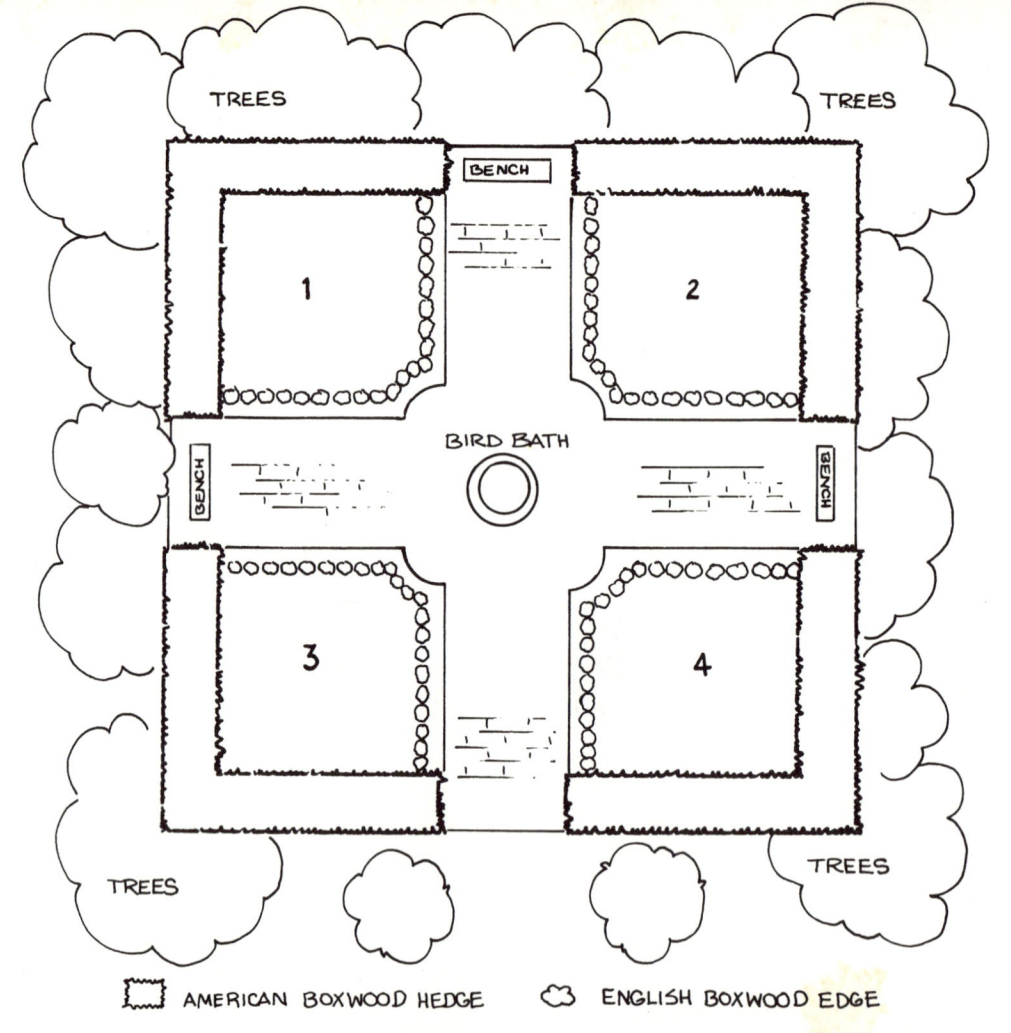

☐ AMERICAN BOXWOOD HEDGE   ⌇ ENGLISH BOXWOOD EDGE

BEDS 1, 2, 3 AND 4 PLANTED OVERALL WITH PACHYSANDRA COMBINED WITH DAFFODIL 'FEBRUARY GOLD'

FORMAL GARDEN LAYOUT FOR SHADE

FOR FORMAL GARDEN IN THE SUN, SUBSTITUTE AS FOLLOWS:
FOR HEDGE: JAPANESE HOLLY (ILEX CRENATA CONVEXA)
FOR EDGE: CANDYTUFT (IBERIS SEMPERVIRENS)
FOR BEDS: ST. JOHN'S-WORT (HYPERICUM REPENS) INTERPLANTED WITH DAFFODIL 'GOLDEN HARVEST'

Evergreens for Partial Shade

Perhaps at this point I should point out that there are several qualities of shade. In the deepest shade, very few plants will grow at all, and the group of evergreens listed on pages 42–43 should have filtered sunlight for at least four hours each day. This is what is meant by partial shade.

The most popular evergreens for partial shade in southern gardens are the azalea, camellia, rhododendron, pieris, mahonia, and aucuba. Azaleas, camellias, and aucubas are grown in relatively large quantities in my garden. They are situated in more direct sunlight than I would wish for them. Yet, with the extra care mentioned above they are thriving.

It is, in fact, the winter sun, and not the summer sun, that harms them most. On days when the ground is frozen, as it is on occasions, the roots cannot supply the necessary moisture for the leaves. As they become drier, the sun burns the foliage and the plant is weakened. Such severe and prolonged exposure can be fatal in a few seasons. Where such drying conditions exist, artificial shade should be devised for the duration of the freeze. Burlap or reed-covered frames, limbs of pines, discarded Christmas trees and the like, blend fairly well with the winter landscape and can be tolerated for the few days their use is indicated.

Fortunate indeed are those coastal gardeners where the fabled Spanish moss festoons the native trees for miles and miles. Strands of this lightweight, natural-looking material crisscrossed on a tender plant furnish effective and attractive protection. Covers of poreless polyethylene are not recommended, since light and air should have free access at all times.

It might be of interest to point out that, in cases of borderline hardiness of certain plants, the very best place for their growth is the north wall of the house or another building. There is total protection from winter sunshine, and the cooler ground temperatures delay the start of new growth in the spring until the danger of hard freezing is past.

Evergreens for Sun

In garden sites exposed to full sun, the most suitable evergreens are holly (*Ilex* spp.), ligustrum, pyracantha, osmanthus, abelia, laurel (*Prunus laurocerasus* spp.), nandina, and juniper.

The Large Family of Hollies

The holly is the most numerous and versatile group of sun-loving southern evergreens. So varied are they, in fact, that new gardeners are often bewildered with their classification and garden uses. Among the most popular hollies for southern gardens are those from the American, Chinese, and Japanese groups. Within these three groups or types of holly are many well-known varieties having a diversity of leaf shape and size, and the plant forms range from very dwarf and spreading to dense, rounded, and upright. Their fruits vary in color from red to yellow and purplish-blue to black.

For the beginner I suggest visits to private and public gardens where hollies are a specialty. Inspection trips to nurseries and garden centers will also yield helpful information as to varieties, their uses, and their faults and merits.

Although my garden is small, I have several varieties from each of the three large groups listed above. They thrive in the hottest, most exposed areas of the garden.

American Holly

Hollies in My Garden

Botanical Name	Common Name	Characteristics
Ilex opaca (American holly)	American holly tree varieties: Foster and Croonenburg hollies	Small evergreen tree with prickly "Christmas Card" leaves and red berries; for fruits, a staminate (male) tree is necessary within at least half a mile.
Ilex cornuta (Chinese holly)	Burford holly	Most popular of prickly-leaved hollies, dark and waxy green; prolific bearer of red fruits.
Ilex crenata (Japanese holly)	Japanese holly varieties: Heller, Hetz, convexa, and round-leaved holly	Small leaves with smooth edges; usually dense growth in sizes from dwarf to intermediate; fruits black or dark purple.

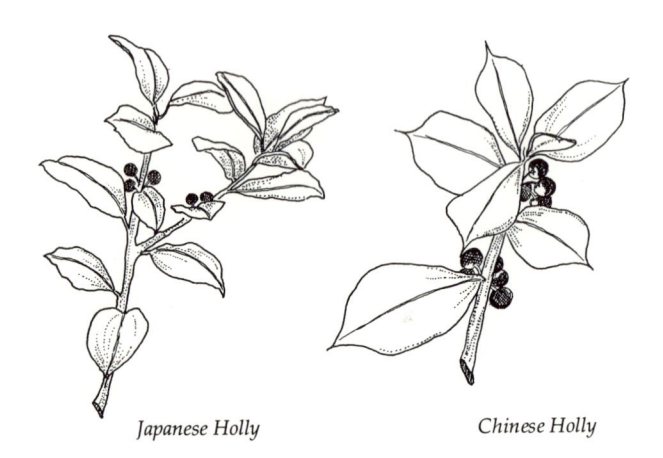

Japanese Holly

Chinese Holly

Evergreen and Deciduous Native Hollies

From the miscellaneous group of hollies worthy of note for Carolina gardens are the native evergreen yaupon (*Ilex vomitoria*), and the Cassine or Dahoon holly, both native to coastal, swampy areas in North and South Carolina. Commercial growers have developed a dwarf form of the large-growing native yaupon (*Ilex vomitoria compacta*), which is becoming quite popular for landscaping uses.

Although most native hollies are evergreen, some recognition is in order for the deciduous members of this large family. There are approximately a dozen species of deciduous native hollies growing in this country, and most of the twelve are found in the Appalachian states. Of the three or four deciduous varieties considered garden-worthy in the Carolinas, one variety is outstanding. I have glimpsed this holly, commonly known as winterberry,* along woodland edges where the stems were completely covered with masses of glistening red berries. When snow is on the ground, they are spectacular, and there should be a winterberry in every woodland garden.

---

*The possum-haw holly (*Ilex decidua*) is also one of our good deciduous hollies but is not as well known to the trade as the winterberry.

Deciduous Shrubs of Importance

Evergreen shrubs of various leaf sizes and textures, especially selected for suitability to their intended sites, should account for approximately three-fourths of the shrub garden constituents. To this base of evergreens some deciduous trees and shrubs should be added. The evergreens, in spite of their importance for mass and year-around foliage, cannot supply the special qualities of form and grace, distinctiveness of stem and bark, and the brilliance of seasonal color characteristic of the deciduous group of plants.

My own garden includes the following from the deciduous plant group: star magnolia, the crape myrtle called "Near East," dogwood, redbud, river birch (*Betula nigra*), a green-stemmed kerria, a red-stemmed dogwood (*Cornus stolonifera*), viburnum, Russian olive (*Elaeagnus umbellata*), and a dwarf Japanese maple (*Acer palmatum*). If I had the space I should also like to have such deciduous plants of distinction as a Japanese quince—particularly a white-flowered one—a dwarf winged euonymus, a corkscrew willow (*Salix matsudana* var. *tortuosa*), and some of the exquisite hybrid deciduous azaleas. (Some of the deciduous azaleas available in Carolina nurseries are the Exbury, Mollis, Vaseyi, and Calendulaceum varieties.)

Guide to Selecting Evergreen and Deciduous Shrubs

In order to make effective use of evergreen and deciduous shrubs, it is helpful to know as much about them beforehand as possible. Height, exposure, use, leaf size (for textural composition), and a particularly special feature are important factors in making final choices. This information is supplied in the following chart for more than seventy-five of the most widely used garden shrubs of the Carolinas.

It should always be kept in mind that shrub sizes are relative. The height classifications I have chosen are small shrubs (1 to 4 feet), medium shrubs (4 to 6 feet), and large shrubs (6 to 12 feet). This does not signify that there can be no further growth beyond these upper size limits. Given enough time and proper growing conditions, a small shrub may grow into the medium-size class and the medium-size shrub may reach an ultimate height of ten feet. The size categories that I have formulated are based on the average heights that may be expected in a growth period of five to eight years under average growing conditions and with average pruning.

Planting Distances

The distance between shrubs is still another variable. For immediate garden effects, shrubs must be planted close together. If long-range growth needs are to be served, greater space must be allowed. In practice I have found the following compromise spacing allowance to be satisfactory.

For shrubs 1 to 4 feet tall, plant 3 to 4 feet apart.
For shrubs 4 to 6 feet tall, plant 5 to 6 feet apart.
For shrubs 6 to 12 feet tall, plant 8 to 10 feet apart.

An Introduction to Garden Design [41]

Evergreens and Deciduous Shrubs for Carolina Gardens
(Key to Leaf Sizes: S—Small, M—Medium, L—Large)

Familiar Name	Catalog Name	Best Exposure	Uses and Leaf Size	Special Features
Low-Growing Evergreens (1'–4')				
Azalea	Azalea	Part shade	Mass planting (S)	Prolific flowering
Boxwood	Buxus	Part shade	Base planting, edging, hedge (S)	Dense, dark green leaves
Chinese holly	Ilex cornuta rotunda	Sun to light shade	Base planting, edging, or mass planting (M)	Dense, relatively slow growth
Cotoneaster	Cotoneaster horizontalis	Sun	Rockery, espalier (S)	Interesting form
Creeping mahonia	Mahonia repens	Part shade	Ground cover (M)	Foliage color, blooms
Curly-leaf ligustrum	Ligustrum coriaceum	Part shade or sun	Planter, specimen (M)	Unique curling leaves
Dwarf pieris	Pieris japonica compacta	Light shade	Garden, or mass planting (M)	Early white flowers
Dwarf yaupon	Ilex vomitoria compacta	Light shade or sun	Base planting, edging, or mass planting (S)	Dense, relatively slow growth
Heller holly	Ilex crenata Helleri	Light shade or sun	Base planting, edging, or mass planting (S)	Dense, relatively slow growth
India hawthorne	Raphiolepsis indica	Sun to light shade	Planter, garden, specimen (M)	Foliage texture and color
Juniper Blue Rug	Juniperus Wiltoni	Sun	Sunny ground cover (S)	Finely textured, gray green foliage
Leucothoe	Leucothoe Catesbaei	Shade to part shade	Woodland garden, mass planting (M)	Graceful form
Mountain andromeda	Pieris floribunda	Shade to part shade	Woodland garden, mass planting (M)	Early white flowers
Mugo pine	Pinus mugo compacta	Sun	Planter, garden specimen (S)	Dramatic form
Repanden holly	Ilex crenata repandens	Sun to light shade	Base planting, edging, or mass planting (S)	Dense, relatively slow growth
Sargent's juniper	Juniperus Sargenti	Sun	Ground cover for hot, dry areas (S)	Fine foliage texture
Shore juniper	Juniperus conferta	Sun	Ground cover for hot, dry areas (S)	Fine foliage texture, gray green foliage
Skimmia	Skimmia Reevesiana	Shade to light shade	Woodland garden, ground cover (M)	Dwarf form
Stokes holly	Ilex crenata Stokes	Sun to light shade	Base planting, edging, or mass planting (S)	Dense, relatively slow growth
Yucca	Yucca	Sun to light shade	Accent for problem area (L)	Bold, gray green leaves

Familiar Name	Catalog Name	Best Exposure	Uses and Leaf Size	Special Features
Low-Growing Deciduous Shrubs (1'–4')				
Deutzia	Deutzia gracilis	Sun to light shade	For small gardens (S)	Graceful form, white flowers
Flowering quince	Chaenomeles	Sun to light shade	Specimen for shrub garden (S)	Unusual form, early flowers
St.-John's-wort	Hypericum	Sun to light shade	Ground cover for poor soil (M)	Healthy foliage, yellow flowers
Winter jasmine	Jasminum nudiflorum	Sun to light shade	Ground cover (S)	Attractive foliage and stems, yellow flowers
Intermediate Evergreens (4'–6')				
Abelia	Abelia	Sun to light shade	Hedge, or base plantings	Foliage color (reddish)
American boxwood	Buxus	Shade to part shade	Hedge, or base planting (S)	Dense dark green foliage
Aucuba	Aucuba	Shade to part shade	Hedge, or base planting (L)	Bold large leaves
Cleyera	Cleyera japonica	Sun to light shade	Planter, garden, or base planting (M)	Shrub and leaf form, foliage color, fruits
Convexa holly	Ilex crenata convexa	Sun to light shade	Hedge, base planting, or mass planting (S)	Dense growth, resembles boxwood
Hetz holly	Ilex crenata Hetzi	Sun to light shade	Hedge, base planting, or mass planting (S)	Dense growth, resembles boxwood
Hybrid rhododendron	Rhododendron	Shade to light shade	Woodland garden, shady planter (L)	Distinctive large leaves, large flowers
Japanese yew	Taxus cuspidata nana	Shade to light shade	Base planting, planter, specimen (S)	Lustrous dark green foliage, red fruits
Mahonia	Mahonia Bealei	Shade to light shade	Base planting, planter, specimen (L)	Bold leaves, late winter blooms, turquoise fruits
Nandina	Nandina domestica	Sun to light shade	Mass planting, or base planting (S)	Red berries, brilliant red winter foliage
Pieris	Pieris japonica	Shade to light shade	Shrub garden, planter (M)	Early white flowers, rosette leaf form
Roundleaf holly	Ilex crenata rotundifolia	Sun to light shade	Hedge, base planting, or mass planting (S)	Dense growth
Intermediate Deciduous Shrubs (4'–6')				
Beautyberry	Callicarpa	Sun to light shade	Mass planting, woodland garden (M)	Purple fall berries
Flowering quince	Chaenomeles	Sun to light shade	Garden specimen, shrub garden (S)	Early blooms, interesting shrub form
Mollis azalea	Azalea molle	Shade to light shade	Woodland garden, planter, mass planting (M)	Elegant colors, interesting shrub form

[42] *Carolina Home Gardener*

Familiar Name	Catalog Name	Best Exposure	Uses and Leaf Size	Special Features	Familiar Name	Catalog Name	Best Exposure	Uses and Leaf Size	Special Features
Spirea	*Spirea*	Sun	Garden, mass planting (S)	Graceful form, early flowers	Yaupon holly	*Ilex vomitoria*	Sun to light shade	Woodland garden, background, hedge (S)	Gray bark, red berries
Large Evergreens (6'–12')					*Large Deciduous Shrubs (6'–12')*				
Anise tree	*Illicium*	Light shade	Specimen, garden (L)	Fragrant bark and leaves, fresh green color	Beauty bush	*Kolkwitzia*	Sun to light shade	Garden, mass planting (M)	Graceful form, delicate coloring
Camellia	*Camellia japonica*	Shade to light shade	Specimen, garden, espalier, planter (M)	Spectacular winter and spring flowers, glossy foliage	Chaste tree	*Vitex*	Sun to light shade	Specimen, garden (M)	Midsummer blue flowers
Camellia	*Camellia sasanqua*	Shade to light shade	Specimen, garden, espalier, planter (M)	Fall flowering, glossy foliage	Crape myrtle	*Lagerstroemia indica*	Sun to light shade	Specimen, garden (S)	Picturesque form, summer flowers, silver bark
Chinese holly	*Ilex cornuta Burfordi*	Sun to light shade	Hedge, specimen, base planting, garden (M)	Glossy leaves, heavy red berries	Deutzia	*Deutzia*	Sun to light shade	Garden background (M)	Early pink or white flowers
Elaeagnus	*Elaeagnus*	Sun to light shade	Background for large shrub garden (M)	Fragrant fall flowers	Euonymus (winged)	*Euonymus alatus*	Sun to light shade	Garden, specimen (M)	Red fall coloring, bark
English laurel	*Laurocerasus officinalis*	Sun to light shade	Base planting, hedge, garden (L)	Large leaves, dense growth	Forsythia	*Forsythia*	Sun to light shade	Garden, specimen, mass planting, espalier (M)	Yellow flowers, graceful form
Euonymus	*Euonymus*	Shade to light shade	Base planting, shrub garden (M)	Glossy foliage, orange berries	Fringe tree	*Chionanthus*	Sun to light shade	Specimen, woodland garden (L)	Fragrant white flowers
Everblooming jasmine	*Jasminum floridum*	Sun to light shade	Shrub garden, informal espalier (S)	Graceful form, yellow flowers	Lilac	*Syringa*	Sun to light shade	Specimen, planter, garden (M)	Fragrant flowers
Indian azalea	*Azalea indica*	Shade to light shade	Woodland garden (M)	Fine color in large quantities	Native azalea	*Azalea nudiflora*	Shade to part shade	Woodland garden (M)	Delicate pink flowers
Leatherleaf viburnum	*Viburnum rhytidophyllum*	Shade to light shade	Specimen, garden (L)	Unusual leathery leaves	Pearlbush	*Exochorda*	Sun to light shade	Garden background (M)	Early white spring flowers
Perny holly	*Ilex Pernyi*	Sun to light shade	Specimen, garden (M)	Prickly leaves, fruits	Rose of Sharon	*Althea*	Sun to light shade	Garden, espalier (M)	Late summer flowers
Photinia	*Photinia*	Shade to light shade	Hedge, base planting, garden (L)	Copper-colored new growth	Saucer magnolia	*Magnolia soulangeana*	Sun to light shade	Specimen, garden, planter (L)	Interesting form, early pink flowers
Pyracantha	*Pyracantha*	Sun to light shade	Espalier, garden, specimen (S)	Lavish red and orange berries	Scotch broom	*Cytisus*	Sun to light shade	Mass planting, garden (S)	Prolific blooms, green stems, graceful form
Schipka laurel	*Laurocerasus schipkaensis*	Sun to light shade	Base planting, hedge, garden (M)	Glossy leaves	Snowball	*Viburnum*	Sun to light shade	Specimen, garden (M)	Snowy white flowers
Tea olive	*Osmanthus*	Sun to light shade	Base planting, hedge, garden (M)	Leaf form, fragrant flowers	Star magnolia	*Magnolia stellata*	Sun to light shade	Specimen, garden, planter (L)	Unique form, starlike white flowers, blooms early
Tree box	*Buxus arborescens*	Shade to light shade	Shrub garden background, base planting (S)	Fine-textured foliage	Sweet-Breath-of-Spring	*Lonicera fragrantissima*	Sun to light shade	Woodland garden (M)	Winter fragrance
Wax-leaf ligustrum	*Ligustrum lucidum*	Sun to light shade	Hedge, base planting, garden (M)	Glossy leaves, compact growth	Weigela	*Weigela*	Sun to light shade	Shrub garden, mass planting (M)	Floriferous, graceful form
Wax myrtle	*Myrica*	Sun to light shade	Planter, garden, background (S)	Shrub form, bark and fruit					

SOURCE: The preceding list is based in part on information found in R. Gordon Halfacre, *Carolina Landscape Plants* (Raleigh, N.C.: Sparks Press, 1971). This book contains useful descriptions of more than two hundred shrubs, trees, vines, and ground covers grown in Carolina gardens.

An Introduction to Garden Design [43]

Leaf Size and Texture in Garden Design

It is especially important in planning an all-shrub garden, whether shady or sunny, to consider the size and texture of the leaves, particularly those of the evergreen varieties.

A basic formula for the proportion of leaf sizes to use might be as follows:

1 part large bold leaves:
Loquat, leather-leaf viburnum (*Viburnum rhytidophyllum*), mahonia, photinia, English laurel (*Prunus laurocerasus* var. *officinalis*), pittosporum (*Pittosporum tobira*), rhododendron, aucuba

1 part medium-sized leaves:
Camellias, Chinese and American hollies, ligustrum, osmanthus, pieris, cleyera (*Cleyera japonica*)

2 parts small-leaved shrubs:
Boxwood, azalea, Japanese holly

Texture is also important in design, and it is achieved in several ways. Combinations of sizes such as those listed above create texture by contrast and accent. Leaf colors and the way in which the leaves are attached to their stems are a part of garden texture. Motion contributes to texture; observe the interplay of green and silver in the wind-tossed silver maple (*Acer saccharinum*) or the aspen tree (*Populus tremuloides*). Their shadows and highlights weave an everchanging pattern of textures. Sunlight on the waxen leaves of the Burford holly reflects a glossy texture, and much light is absorbed and lost in the dark green depths of the small-leaved boxwood.

Form is also important to texture, as witness the bold upward thrust of the yucca (*Yucca aloifolia*), the candle-form of the redhot poker (*Kniphofia uvaria*), and the lacelike delicacy of the maidenhair fern (*Adiantum pedatum*). Fantastic textures may be observed in nature. Analyze the textures of a stand of rhododendron seen against a backdrop of hemlocks (*Tsuga* spp.), or study a bit of moss clinging to the crevices of a weathered rock. These are the ways to create textural interest in the home garden.

Shrub Flowering Sequence

Satisfying gardens, large or small, contain shrubs for blooms at different seasons of the year. Select from the following ones those best suited to the size and growing conditions of your garden.

January–February

As might be expected, the cold months of January and February provide the leanest offerings. However, there are surely no more distinctive flowers in any month than the chartreuse blooms of the mahonia that open in January.

The winter honeysuckle is not as elegant as the mahonia, but the perfume of its small creamy flower has earned it the name "Sweet-Breath-of-Spring."

A third January flowering shrub worthy of note is the winter jasmine. The small, bell-like yellow flowers wreathe the bright green stems for several weeks during winter's olive drab. Poor pruning practices have made this shrub unpopular. If all old wood is removed each year after flowering, the winter jasmine will maintain its best qualities.

By the middle of January the silver buds of the pussy willow (*Salix discolor*) need only a few hours indoors to become furry catkins. The pink French pussy willow is an especially appealing forcing subject.

Carolina Home Gardener

Throughout January and February the two deciduous magnolias, the white star magnolia (*Magnolia stellata*) and the pink saucer magnolia (*Magnolia soulangeana*, often called the tulip tree), bloom between periods of freezing temperatures.

The winter camellias (*Camellia japonica*), also subject to the same winter-weather vagaries as the magnolias, may supply a few spectacular blooms throughout January and February.

March–April–May

During the spring quarter season of the year, the number of evergreen and deciduous flowering shrubs, as well as trees, increases to a yearly high with shrubs overlapping each other in their flowering sequence. If winter temperatures have been on the mild side, the Kurume azaleas may bloom as early as March, though April is more normal for them. More independent of the weather are the hardier early spring shrubs. These are the flowering quince, almond, spirea, forsythia, flowering fruit trees, and the evergreen pieris.

In late April and early May the garden scene is gay and fragrant from the blossoms of the Scotch broom, deutzia, lilac, pearlbush, mock orange, viburnum, weigela, kolkwitzia, and the mid-season azaleas.

June–July–August

The flowering plenty of spring lingers on through June with the blooms of the macrantha azalea, the native Rosebay rhododendron, the coral red blooms of the pomegranate (*Punica granatum*), and, in gardens southeast of Greensboro, the fragrant and beautiful gardenia or Cape jasmine (*Gardenia jasminoides*).

As the summer weather warms to the season, the hibiscus (*Hibiscus coccineus*), althea, hypericum, oak-leaf and peegee hydrangeas, rose, vitex, and crape myrtle provide a colorful background for the summer annuals.

September–October

September and October mark the onset of a long flowering period for two of our large evergreens, the osmanthus and elaeagnus. Although their flowers are tiny, their wonderful perfume can fill the entire neighborhood. The fall-flowering sasanqua camellia has no fragrance, or very little, but it is the pièce de résistance of the fall garden as far as shrubbery is concerned. Quite frequently the earlier varieties begin blooming by Labor Day and flower intermittently into December.

November–December

By late November and early December the early winter camellias (the japonica varieties) begin to open. Among the best of these early varieties are September Morn, Dikagura, High Hat, Morning Glow, Arejisha, Mrs. K. Sawada.

There are, of course, several midwinter camellia varieties, but in our area it is safer from the standpoint of weather damage to select either from the early group listed above or the late winter group, which includes Finlandia, Blood of China, Herme, Sara Frost, Flame, Elegans, Flame Variegated, and Leucantha. Over the years I have occasionally had camellias for the decoration of my Christmas dinner table, and, most years, enough intermittent picking of flowers to keep my spirits up.

Judging by the difficulty we now have in finding locally grown camellias, some gardeners must feel that our uncertain weather is too much of a hazard. Personally, I consider camellias good garden subjects if only for their shining dark green leaves. Properly grown, it is a handsome shrub; the flowers that escape the frosts and freezes can be deemed a bonus. In coastal and more southerly gardens, camellia blossoms are not damaged as frequently by fluctuating temperatures as they are in the immediate vicinity of Greensboro and westward.

Shrub Flowering Calendar in My Garden

My small garden allows me a limited number of varieties of mostly intermediate-size shrubs (3'–5') and a few larger ones (6'–8'), which must be kept in bounds by strict pruning. My list of shrubs and their approximate flowering dates might be of help in making preliminary choices for a small garden.

Approximate Flowering Date	Variety
January	Mahonia, star magnolia, winter jasmine
February	Forsythia, star magnolia, camellia, winter jasmine
March	Flowering almond, forsythia, pieris, camellia
April	Viburnum mariesi, Kurume azaleas, snowball, kerria
May	Deutzia, rhododendron, weigela, azaleas (Kaempferi, Glen Dale hybrids, gumpos)
June	Azaleas (gumpo, macrantha varieties)
July	Hibiscus, crape myrtle, althea
August	Hibiscus, crape myrtle, althea
September	Althea, crape myrtle, osmanthus, sasanqua camellia
October	Camellia (sasanqua), osmanthus
November	Camellias (japonica) (if winter is mild)
December	Camellias (japonica) (if winter is mild)

How to Select Healthy Shrubs

Inexperienced gardeners are often in doubt as to what a healthy shrub (or tree) should look like. This lack of knowledge sometimes results in impulse buying from roadside stands or other places where plants of inferior quality may be offered for sale. In recognition of this problem, the horticultural extension specialists of North Carolina State University have prepared a leaflet called "A Buyer's Guide" to inform the public on points to look for in purchasing nursery stock.

This is how a healthy plant is described: select "an exceptionally healthy, vigorous plant which is well-shaped, heavily branched, and densely foliated." These down-grading factors should be noted:

Canes or Trunks: Weak or poorly formed; excessive scarring; poor graft unions not healing properly; branches poorly distributed.

Foliage: Leaves of improper shape, size, texture, and color; excessive chlorosis (loss of green color) as a result of mineral deficiency or other causes; excessive insect or other mechanical leaf injury.

Root System: Container-grown stock: plant loosely established in container or root-bound (tight in can); large roots growing out of container. Balled and burlapped stock: plant loosely established in ball; ball containing added soil or soil loosely held by the plant roots; ball poorly or loosely tied; ball containing too few roots; ball too small or shallow.

Experience is required for expert plant selection, and with the above points in mind, buy carefully; in due time good quality plants may be recognized at a glance.

Trees in Landscape Design

The Treeless Lot: Without question trees are the keynote of the garden design; without their magic alchemy a lot is never a garden. And if you should have the misfortune to find yourself living on a treeless lot, trees should be planted as soon as possible.

The placement of trees is a simple matter; they should be planted where they are needed for shade, windbreaks, screens, and the general enhancement of the house and garden.

The choice of trees is a more complicated matter. They are long-term investments, slow to grow, and, one hopes, long-lived. Considerable study and thought should preface their selection.

Garden design experts differ on the number of trees a lot should have. John A. Grant, West Coast architect of note, feels that four trees, two of medium size and two small, are plenty for a lot measuring 60' × 120'. Furthermore he feels that the four should be placed so that there will be no overlapping branches at maturity. Other designers, notably Sylvia Crowe, feel that climate should dictate the density of tree plantings, and probably most southern gardeners would agree. It is generally agreed among most landscape designers that all tree choices should be in scale with the size of the house and lot and that their form, longevity, and adaptability should be in accord with the existing site.

Thinning the Wooded Lot: Any tree is valuable if there is only one on the lot. Therefore, the value of trees depends on the quantity as well as the variety, and it is only when there are too many that selection becomes a problem. When choices must be made, those to be retained are selected according to their variety, health, position in the yard, and to some degree what additional smaller plants you plan to combine with the trees in the final garden composition.

In removing surplus trees from a heavily wooded lot, make it a gradual process by removing a few each year until all undesired ones are out. Many new homeowners have found to their sorrow that where all undesired ones came out at one time, many of the remaining ones died later. This loss can be reduced by the few-at-a-season approach, which does not create such a rapid environmental change for the remaining trees.

In the Carolinas we prize most highly the hardwood trees because these are the slowest to grow and generally the most long-lived. In this category the outstanding ones are the white oak (*Quercus alba*), post oak (*Quercus stellata*), willow oak (*Quercus phellos*), and pin oak (*Quercus palustris*), the American beech (*Fagus grandifolia*), cucumber magnolia (*Magnolia acuminata*), black gum (*Nyssa sylvatica*), hickory (*Carya ovata*), the sugar maple (*Acer saccharum*), and the Norway maple (*Acer platanoides*).

Where evergreen trees are desired, the evergreen magnolia and the native holly are my first choice. The evergreen live oak (*Quercus virginiana*) is hardy as far north as Greensboro and southward. In smaller gardens the Carolina cherry laurel (*Prunus laurocerasus* var. *caroliniana*), Burford holly, photinia, yaupon, and ligustrum may be pruned to a single trunk and will eventually make very handsome evergreen trees in scale with the size of the garden.

Faster-growing trees include the American white ash (*Fraxinus americana*), American elm (*Ulmus americana*), cork-bark elm (*Ulmus alata*), thornless honey locust (*Gleditsia triacanthos*), small-leaved linden (*Tilia cordata*), tulip tree, also called the tulip poplar (*Liriodendron tulipifera*), hackberry (*Celtis*), sweet gum (*Liquidambar styraciflua*), and the softwood maples—the silver maple (*Acer saccharinum*) and the red maple (*Acer rubrum*). The Chinese elm (*Ulmus chinensis*), willow (*Salix* spp.), and red and silver maples are the least desirable of the fast-growing trees because the fast growth typical of these varieties results in brittle wood that is easily damaged by wind and ice storms. The sweet gum and sycamore (*Platanus occidentalis*) are attractive trees, but their seed balls are a littering nuisance on the lawns and seem to fall the year around.

In spite of the losses from the southern pine beetles, plenty of pines (*Pinus* spp.) remain, and although they are not as long-lived as the hardwoods, there are no more beautiful trees in America. The tall and stately specimens supply high, light shade for growing many of our choicest shrubs to their happiest and most luxurious perfection. Camellia-azalea gardens find the conditions provided by pines exactly to their liking. A pine-shaded garden has the advantage of being self-mulching, and the decaying needles help in the maintenance of the required acid soil for the best growth of these evergreen shrubs. Young pines are also excellent screens for use where fast growth is desired. As they grow older, however, their lower limbs are gradually shaded out by their tops so that their use as hedges, screens, or background material cannot be depended upon indefinitely.

Native cedars (*Juniperus virginiana*) are plentiful and deserve a wider use than they receive as garden subjects. I find a good deal of prejudice against this tree which I am at a loss to understand. One or two in a garden provide needed accent; a larger quantity is likely to produce an uneasy feeling in the observer for their strong conical shapes constantly draw the eye upward.

Both the Carolina hemlock (*Tsuga caroliniana*) and Canadian hemlock (*Tsuga canadensis*) grow in the wilds of cooler, higher elevations of North and South Carolina. Their satisfactory use in the garden decreases as one moves eastward in both states. In the piedmont areas of both states, however, both these hemlocks are successfully grown, especially when there is some light shade available from other trees.

An Introduction to Garden Design

Size Classification for Some of Our Recommended Trees

Small (under 25'):
American holly, Cassine holly, crab apple (dwarf types), dogwood, fringe tree, hawthorn (*Crataegus*)—native varieties preferred to English hawthorns (*Crataegus oxyacantha*)—redbud, serviceberry (*Amelanchier laevis*), yaupon holly

Medium (25' to 40'):
Birch (*Betula*), buckeye (*Aesculus*), catalpa (*Catalpa*), cherry (*Prunus*), crab apple (*Malus* spp.), ginkgo (*Ginkgo biloba*), goldenrain tree (*Koelreuteria paniculata*), hornbeam (*Carpinus*), live oak, plum (*Prunus*), silverbell (*Halesia carolina*), sourwood (*Oxydendrum arborea*), yellowwood (*Cladrastis lutea*)

Large (over 40'):
Ash, hackberry, honey locust, linden (*Tilia*), magnolia (*Magnolia grandiflora*), maple, pin oak, pine (*Pinus* spp.), sweet gum, tulip poplar, water oak, willow oak

The Addition of Bedding Plants

The shrub and tree garden is recommended for those who have interests other than gardening to occupy their leisure time and are satisfied with a presentable home setting for their own enjoyment and that of the neighborhood. For those of us who are interested in plants for themselves, the variety,

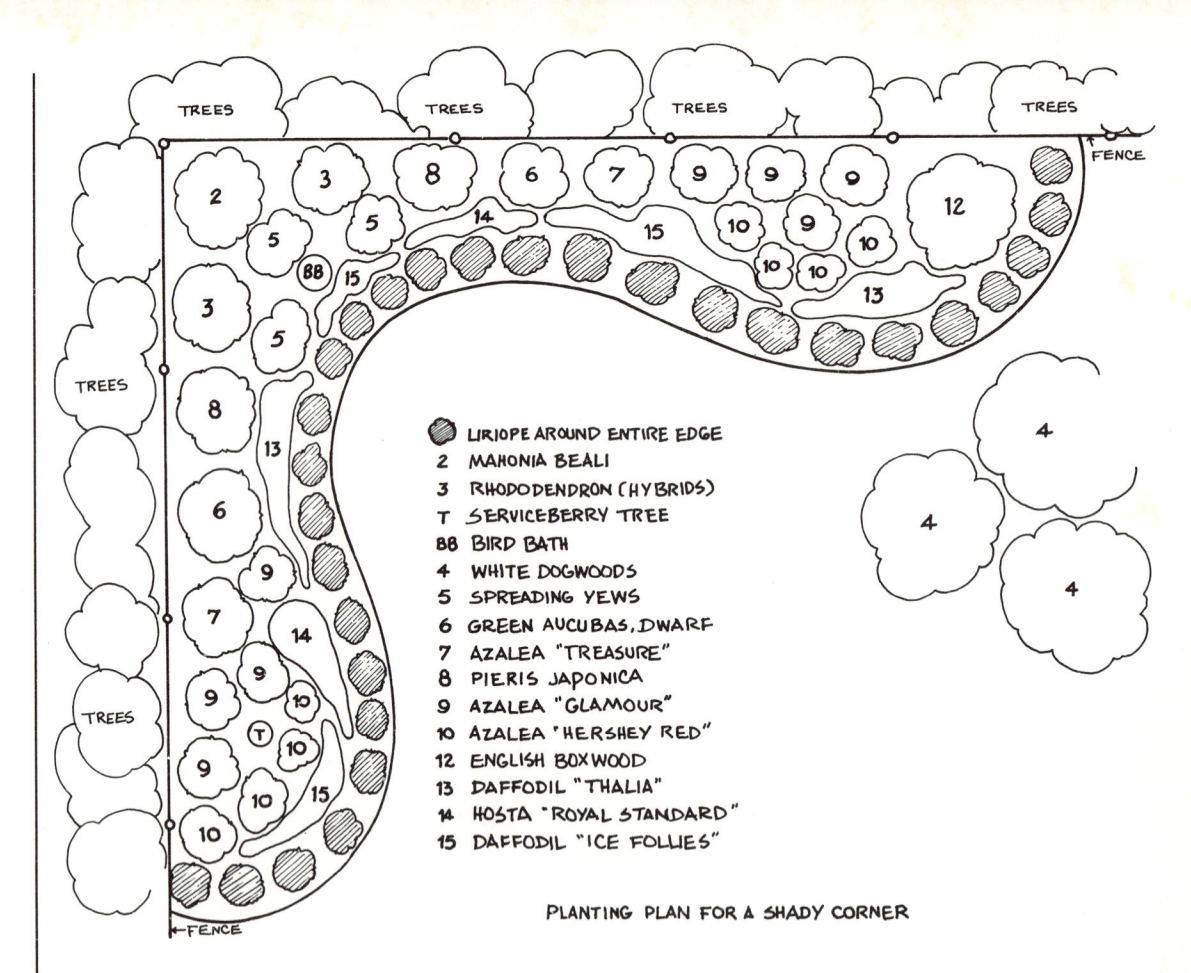

PLANTING PLAN FOR A SHADY CORNER

- LIRIOPE AROUND ENTIRE EDGE
- 2 MAHONIA BEALI
- 3 RHODODENDRON (HYBRIDS)
- T SERVICEBERRY TREE
- BB BIRD BATH
- 4 WHITE DOGWOODS
- 5 SPREADING YEWS
- 6 GREEN AUCUBAS, DWARF
- 7 AZALEA "TREASURE"
- 8 PIERIS JAPONICA
- 9 AZALEA "GLAMOUR"
- 10 AZALEA "HERSHEY RED"
- 12 ENGLISH BOXWOOD
- 13 DAFFODIL "THALIA"
- 14 HOSTA "ROYAL STANDARD"
- 15 DAFFODIL "ICE FOLLIES"

Carolina Home Gardener

colors, and forms of annuals, biennials, and perennials make these plants the next logical addition to the basic shrub garden.

A Closer Look at Bedding Plants

Of the three groups of bedding plants—annuals, biennials, and perennials—the perennials, because of their relative longevity, are most important. Perennials are evergreen or herbaceous plants that usually live three years or longer in the garden. Herbaceous perennials will have their tops killed by frosts and freezing weather, but they will grow again from the roots with the return of warm weather. The number of herbaceous perennials greatly outnumbers the evergreen varieties, but since the herbaceous ones have the disadvantage of creating a vacant spot while they are dormant for the winter, I make a definite effort to use as many evergreen perennials as I can for the sake of the garden's winter appearance.

Pictures of and visits to gardens in cooler climates may create disappointments for Carolina gardeners. In compiling a list of perennials for your own garden, be cognizant of the fact that, because of our hot, humid summer weather and the ups and downs of winter temperatures, such choice perennials as *Delphinium grandiflorum*, lupin (*Lupinus polyphyllus*), astilbe, primula, and doronicum (*Doronicum caucasicum*) may turn out to be a poor investment.

1. Ageratum.   2. Alonsoa.   3. Sweet alyssum.   4. Argemone
5. Asperula.   6. Amblyolepis setigera.

An Introduction to Garden Design

A List of Some of My Favorite Perennials
(Those marked E are evergreen)

Variety	Time of Bloom	Sun	Shade
Armeria (*Armeria splendens*) (E)	Spring	x	
Aspidistra (*Aspidistra lurida*) (E)	Foliage plant		x
Aster (*Aster*)	Fall	x	
Bearded iris (*Iris germanica*)	Spring	x	
Bergenia (*Bergenia cordifolia*) (E)	Spring	x	x
Boltonia (*Boltonia asteroides*)	Fall	x	
Candytuft (*Iberis sempervirens*) (E)	Spring	x	x
Christmas rose (*Helleborus niger*) (E)	Winter		x
Chrysanthemum (*Chrysanthemum* spp.)	Summer, fall	x	
Columbine (*Aquilegia*)	Spring	x	x
Coral-bells (*Heuchera sanguinea*) (E)	Spring	x	x
Day lily (*Hemerocallis*) (Semievergreen)	Summer	x	x
Dianthus (*Dianthus deltoides* and *D. plumarius*) (E)	Spring	x	
Evening primrose (*Oenothera perennis*)	Summer	x	
Hardy begonia (*Begonia evansiana*)	Summer		x
Hosta (*Hosta*)	Summer		x
Japanese anemone (*Anemone hupehensis*)	Fall	x	x
Lenten rose (*Helleborus orientalis*) (E)	Spring		x
Liriope (*Liriope muscari*) (E)	Summer	x	x
Loosestrife (*Lysimachia punctata*)	Summer	x	x
Oriental poppy (*Papaver orientale*)	Spring	x	
Peony (*Paeonia lactiflora*)	Spring	x	x
Plumbago (*Plumbago* spp.)	Fall		x
Sedum (*Sedum* spp.)	Summer	x	x
Shasta daisy (*Chrysanthemum maximum*)	Summer	x	
Spiderwort (*Tradescantia* spp.)	Summer		x
Spring phlox (*Phlox divaricata*)	Spring	x	x
Summer phlox (*Phlox paniculata*)	Summer	x	x
Thermopsis (*Thermopsis caroliniana*)	Spring	x	x
Thrift (*Phlox subulata*) (E)	Spring	x	
Virginia bluebell (*Mertensia virginica*)	Spring		x

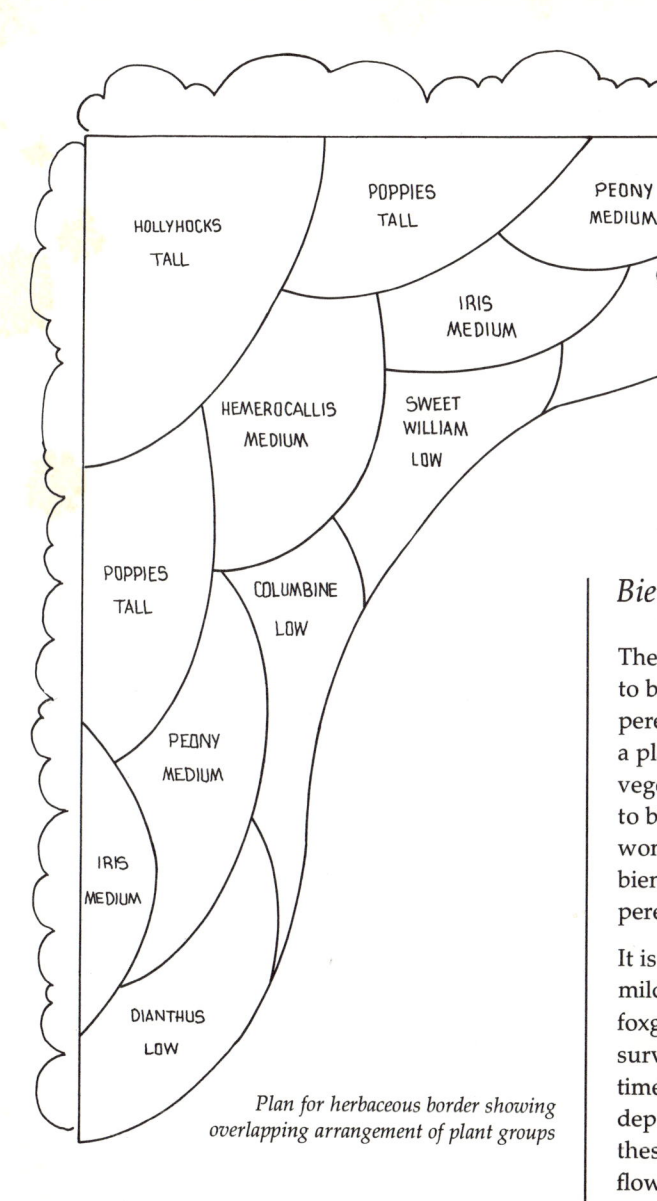

Plan for herbaceous border showing overlapping arrangement of plant groups

Biennials for the Garden

There are instances in which it is a bit difficult to be sure whether a plant is a biennial or a perennial. The popular definition of a biennial is a plant that needs one growing season to make vegetative growth and a second growing season to bloom. Then it is supposed to die. In the wonderland of Carolina gardens, some so-named biennials may survive and bloom as long as many perennials.

It is a common occurrence, when winters are milder than usual, to have the biennial hollyhocks, foxgloves, sweet williams, and sweet rockets survive and bloom the second, and even third time, around. In spite of this, such behavior is not dependable, and it is safer to grow new plants of these varieties each season to maintain the best flowering quality.

In addition to the hollyhock (*Althaea rosea*), sweet william (*Dianthus barbatus*), foxglove (*Digitalis purpurea*), and sweet rocket (*Hesperis matronalis*), there are these additional biennials for southern gardens: pansy (*Viola* spp.), Canterbury bell (*Campanula medium*), English daisy (*Bellis perennis*), forget-me-not (*Myosotis sylvatica*), wallflower (*Cheiranthus cheiri*), California poppy (*Eschscholtzia californica*), Shirley poppy (*Papaver rhoeas*), and larkspur (*Delphinium cultorum*).

All require a season for vegetative growth before flowering; the survival of some varieties to bloom a second year, as noted above, depends on the weather.

Many biennials are sturdy enough to be sown directly in their permanent sites in late summer or autumn. Among these are the larkspur, honesty,* and poppy. Other biennials—the pansy, foxglove, hollyhock, sweet william, etc.—should be planted in containers in midsummer to late summer to be grown under protected conditions until the plants are large enough to be transplanted to outdoor beds in late fall or early spring.

---

*Although honesty (*Lunaria annua*) is sometimes classified as an annual, two growth seasons are required for it in the Carolinas.

An Introduction to Garden Design [51]

Flowering Annuals

Annuals are plants that can be started from seeds; they grow, bloom, and die all in one short season, usually the summer. The large family of annual plants contains such easy-to-grow favorites as the marigold, zinnia, scarlet sage (*Salvia splendens*), nasturtium (*Tropaeolum majus*), and many more (see list of annuals on pages 72 and 80).

Perennials, biennials, and annuals all have a place in the garden, and when designing new gardens, it is my practice to reserve small areas in and out of the middle and foreground areas of the shrubbery planting for a few choice members from each of the three groups.

In my own garden, I rely greatly on that long-flowering biennial, the pansy, for great masses of color throughout the spring months. In fact, over the years I have replaced the relatively short-term, low-growing biennials—such as wallflowers, English daisies, and forget-me-nots—with pansies, which often are in bloom by Christmas and continue well into May. Pansies supply fresh, continuous color while such garden members as bulbs, azaleas, and early perennials make their brief splash and fade. There is no other bedding plant, in my opinion, so worthy of its space and cost as the pansy.

The pansies in my garden are followed with such summer replacements as the self-seeding cleomes (*Cleome spinosa*), vincas (annuals), and impatiens, to which some summer annuals such as bedding begonias, marigolds, ageratum (*Ageratum houstonianum*), and dwarf snapdragons are added to supplement the summer and fall perennials. The combination is satisfactory and one that I have spent many years perfecting.

Wild Flowers Are Also for Gardens

A wild-flower garden has been defined as one in which plants native to the vicinity grow. The "vicinity" this book envisions covers a region with a mind-boggling number of native plants that have evolved over eons of adaptation to a wide range of altitudes, from sea level to mountain high, and to equally diverse soil, temperature, and drainage conditions. The result is a number of wild-flower varieties said to be second only to the state of California and ranging in character from Canadian to tropical.

In his classic volume *The Natural Gardens of North Carolina*, B. W. Wells writes that the state's native plants fall into eleven distinct types of vegetation associated with and dependent upon the elevation, soil, drainage, and climate of the area. He lists these plant communities, beginning at the sea and proceeding westward to the mountains, as follows: (1) The dune or upland seaside community, (2) salt marsh, (3) fresh-water marsh, (4) swamp forest, (5) aquatic vegetation, (6) shrub bog, (7) grass-sedge bog, (8) sandhills, (9) old-field community, (10) great forest, (11) boreal or high mountain forest.

From Plenty to Extinction

As is the case with wild flowers and all other natural resources, there is an urgent need to educate, protect, and conserve. Because of ruthless land-clearing practices, erosion, construction, and injudicious collecting, many once beautiful stands of native plants have been lost to us forever. Growing these plants in the garden and teaching more responsible attitudes toward land usage might save what is left of our priceless wild-flower heritage, but time is running out.

The Gardener's Responsibility

Before introducing wild flowers into your garden, take the time to learn about their needs, and if you cannot meet them, neither conservation nor your own garden will be served.

Observe with care where wild flowers are growing naturally. Is it shady, sunny, or half-and-half? Damp, boggy, or dry? By a brook, woodland edge, or dense forest floor? These are your guideposts; follow them.

It is wise, when selecting wild flowers, not to stray too far from the area in which you live. Since there is much overlapping of the eleven plant zones, you will find generous variety in all parts of the Carolinas. But to try, for example, to grow the beautiful sandhill lupine (*Lupinus diffusus*) in the hard clay of Guilford County is a total waste of plant and energy. Likewise, the fabled Venus's flytrap has a short life expectancy in most areas of the state other than its native coastal zone.

Wild-Flower Sources

North Carolina Garden Clubs and the North Carolina Wild Flower Preservation Society have compiled a list of 144 species of native plants in danger of extinction, and these are now protected by law. Plants on this list can be legally collected only in areas that have been designated as development, roadway, or reservoir sites. Additional varieties not on the list should be collected sparingly if the stand is large. Where the stand is sparse and few plants are established, none should be taken from it. Conservation needs are better served by learning to grow your own wild flowers from seeds or buying plants from nurseries that propagate their own.

Wild Flowers in the Shade Garden

Gardeners with wooded lots often think that wild flowers are their best hope for garden-making. With no wish to dampen their enthusiasm, let me suggest that growing small wild flowers in competition with large established trees is in every way as demanding as growing any other type of plant under the same conditions. Generous quantities of organic matter must be supplied regularly as well as extra water and food.

Designing with wild flowers is no less difficult than designing other styles of gardens. As a matter of opinion, I would say that rather more than average skill is required to capture and recreate the casual and elusive charm of a natural woodland garden. Unless there is some existing landscape feature worthy of emphasis such as a spring or stream, an outcropping of rocks, or at least a stump of distinction, more conventional design might be a better choice. Of course, there are man-made features with wild-flower gardening potential such as paths, walks, pools, cascades, and rockeries. Whether the feature is natural or man-made, the wild-flower plantings should be considered within the framework of the entire garden setting, especially in an urban neighborhood.

The Sunny Wild Garden

There are a number of beautiful wild flowers that prefer the sun, but they are used in relatively small numbers compared with the shade-requiring varieties. It may be that most people who have sunny gardens prefer the showy annuals, biennials, and perennials that have been hybridized and sold as "domesticated" varieties.

Combining Wild Flowers with Other Plants

Without entering into the venerable argument as to which flowers are wild and which are tame, let me advance the thought that both types can be integrated to produce successful expressions of garden design, especially in the informal garden.

In my garden I have a case in point. In the shadiest nook of my basically sunny garden, there is a small but valued collection of a few of my favorite

An Introduction to Garden Design [53]

wild flowers. I have foam flower (*Tiarella cordifolia*), hepatica (both *Hepatica acutiloba* and *H. triloba*), Catesby's trillium (*Trillium nervosum*), which is a delicately pink variety that came from creek banks in my native southeastern county of Richmond, toad trillium (*Trillium sessile*), fragrant white atamasco lily (*Zephyranthes atamasco*), turk's-cap lily (*Lilium superbum*), Christmas fern (*Polystichum acrostichoides*), wild geranium (*Geranium maculatum*), diminutive ebony spleenwort (*Asplenium platyneuron*), and the ubiquitous "Confederate-violet" (*Viola papilionacea*). In open and sunnier dry areas of my garden, the black-eyed Susan (*Rudbeckia serotina*) and blue-eyed grass (*Sisyrinchium angustifolium*) contribute seasonal color and interest, while among the crevices of a loosely laid rock retaining wall, the dainty bluet (*Houstonia caerulea*) has made a home for itself.

For those who have an enduring love for wild flowers, and there are legions of us in the South, there is a place in every garden, in sun or shade, for a few wild flowers. Interest, space, and suitability should dictate the variety and numbers.

The following is a list of the wild flowers that in my experience lend themselves most agreeably to garden uses. References at the end of this book will yield additional information.

Some Wild Flowers for Shade:
Alum-root (*Heuchera americana*), beebalm (*Monarda didyma*), bleeding heart, bloodroot, Canada wild ginger (*Asarum canadense*), Christmas fern (also other native ferns), columbine, great Solomon's seal (*Polygonatum commutatum*), hepatica, Jacob's ladder (*Polemonium caeruleum*), mottled wild ginger (*Asarum ariofolium*), small Solomon's seal (*Polygonatum biflorum*), spiderwort, trillium (*Trillium grandiflorum* or snow trillium is one of the showiest), trout-lily, violet, wild hyacinth (*Camassia scilloides*)

Wild Flowers for Sun:
Aster (*Aster grandiflorus*), baptisia (*Baptisia australis*), black-eyed Susan, butterfly weed (*Asclepias tuberosa*), goldenrod (*Solidago odora*), moss pink (*Phlox nivalis*), Spanish bayonet (*Yucca*), thermopsis

Evergreen Wild Flowers:
Galax (*Galax aphylla*), ginger, hepatica, oconee bell, pipsissewa (*Chimaphila maculata*), trailing arbutus

Of special interest to wild-flower gardeners is the winter issue (1974) of the *American Horticulturist* magazine. The entire issue is devoted to articles on preserving, growing, and landscape gardening with native species.

Oliver J. Stark, botanist at Bowman's Hill Preserve, Washington Crossing Park, Washington Crossing, Pa., has contributed an impressive chart containing the main habitat requirements and design characteristics of more than three hundred native plants suitable for wild-flower gardening. Copies of this issue (vol. 53, no. 5) may be purchased for $2.50 from the American Horticultural Society, Mount Vernon, Va. 22121.

Don't Overlook the Big Natives

The true character of a woodland garden is more strongly established by the presence and arrangement of native trees and shrubbery than it is by the small flowers beneath them. Recognizing that perhaps a majority of the shade trees in Carolina gardens are native, indispensable, and usually taken for granted, let me remind you of a few of our choice native flowering trees. If you fail to have at least one or two from this group, acquire some by all means; they are as valuable to the formal garden setting as they are to the woodland and informal garden.

They include the redbud, dogwood, fringe tree, Carolina silverbell, sourwood (which was honored a few years ago with the Medal of Merit by the British Royal Horticultural Society), the serviceberry, the native hawthorns (*Crataegus Crus-galli* and *Crataegus apiifolia*, better known perhaps as the cock-spur thorn and the parsley haw), and last, but surely the most regal of the small evergreen trees, the American holly.

The Native Shrubs

Elsewhere I have extolled the beauty of the winterberry and the possum-haw holly, and I would also like to mention the nine species of deciduous azaleas that grow as native plants in the Carolinas. These, in addition to sweet shrub (*Calycanthus floridus*), leucothoe (*Leucothoe Catesbaei*), rhododendron, evergreen yaupon, and mountain andromeda (*Pieris andromeda*), are among the best of several native shrubs suitable for the home garden.

Native Plants Protected by Law in North Carolina

Wild Flowers:
Aaron's rod (*Thermopsis villosa*), bird's-foot violet (*Viola pedata*), bloodroot (*Sanguinaria canadensis*), blue dogbane (*Amsonia tabernaemontana*), cardinal flower (*Lobelia cardenalis*), columbine (*Aquilegia canadensis*), dutchman's-breeches (*Dicentra cucullaria*), gentian (*Gentiana* 9 spp.), ginseng (*Panax quinquefolium*), ground cedar (*Lycopodium* 10 spp.), hepatica (*Hepatica americana* and *H. acutiloba*), jack-in-the-pulpit (*Arisaema triphyllum*), lily (*Lilium* 6 spp.), lupine (*Lupinus* 3 spp.), maidenhair fern (*Adiantum pedatum*), may apple (*Podophyllum peltatum*), monkshood (*Aconitum* 2 spp.), orchid (*Orchis* 55 spp.), pitcher plant (*Sarracenia* 4 spp.), sea oats (*Uniola paniculata*), shooting star (*Dodecatheon*), Shortia, oconee bells (*Shortia galacifolia*), Solomon's seal (*Polygonatum* 2 spp.), trailing arbutus (*Epigaea repens*), trillium (*Trillium* 10 spp.), Venus's flytrap (*Dionaea muscipula*), Virginia bluebell (*Mertensia virginica*), walking fern (*Asplenium*)

Shrubs and Trees:
American holly (*Ilex opaca*), flowering dogwood (*Cornus florida*), fringe tree (*Chionanthus virginicus*), hemlock (*Tsuga canadensis* and *T. caroliniana*), leucothoe (*Leucothoe* 4 spp.), mountain laurel (*Kalmia latifolia*), redbud (*Cercis canadensis*), red cedar (*Juniperus virginiana*), rhododendron (*Rhododendron* 3 spp.), white pine (*Pinus strobus*), wild azalea (*Rhododendron* 9 spp.)

Garden Club of South Carolina Conservation List of Wild Flowers, Shrubs, and Trees

(NOT TO BE PICKED)
Wild Flowers:
Bloodroot (*Sanguinaria canadensis*), columbine (*Aquilegia canadensis*), closed gentian (*Gentiana Andrewsii*), fringed gentian (*Gentiana crinita*), Indian pipe (*Montropa uniflora*), lady's slipper (*Cypripedium* spp.), rose mallow (*Hibiscus moscheutos*), trailing arbutus (*Epigaea repens*), Virginia bluebells (*Mertensia virginica*), yellow fringed orchid (*Habenaria ciliaris*)

Shrubs:
Atlantic azalea (*Rhododendron atlanticum; Azalea atlantica*), Cassine holly (*Ilex Cassine*), yaupon holly (*Ilex vomitoria*), flame azalea (*Rhododendron calendulaceum; Azalea calendulacea*), fringe tree or grandsir greybeard (*Chionanthus Virginica*), mountain laurel (*Kalmia latifolia*), pink rhododendron (*Rhododendron punctatum*), pinxter flower (*Rhododendron nudiflorum; Azalea nudiflora*), stewartia (*Stewartia malachodendron*), rhododendron (*Rhododendron maximum*)

Trees:
American holly (*Ilex opaca*), flowering dogwood (*Cornus florida*), redbud (*Cercis canadensis*)

Grasses:
Sea oats (*Uniola paniculata*)

(TO BE PICKED SPARINGLY)
Wild Flowers:
Bird's-foot violet (*Viola pedata*), ground pink (*Phlox subulata*), liverwort (*Hepatica triloba*), marsh marigold (*Caltha palustris*), spotted wintergreen (*Chimaphila maculata*), spring beauty (*Claytonia virginica*), sweet white violet (*Viola blanda*), trillium (*Trillium* spp.)

NOTE: Wild-flower growers will find much help and pleasure in a book called *Wild Flowers of North Carolina*, by William S. Justice and C. Ritchie Bell. This book contains four hundred full-color photographs and descriptions of wild flowers, trees, shrubs, vines, herbs, and weeds common to the Carolinas and surrounding southern states. Also of interest is James W. Hardin, *Guide to Literature on Plants of North Carolina*, Agricultural Extension Service Publication no. 66 (Raleigh, N.C.: Agricultural Extension Service, 1971).

Herbs Are for Both Kitchen and Garden

It may be more than coincidence that today's gardener, remembering that herbs and spices led to the discovery of this country more than four hundred years ago, is experiencing a rebirth of interest in the age-old culture and use of herbs.

Herbs as a group are relatively simple to grow; they are ornamentally a credit to the garden and most useful in turning lackluster foods into gourmet delights. Growing and using fresh herbs, like one's own tomatoes and cucumbers, soon relegates the commercially produced varieties to second choice.

Herbs are classified as annuals, biennials, and perennials, and most varieties are readily grown from seeds, cuttings, or root divisions, using the same basic growing methods as those used for ornamental bedding plants.

Herbs may be grown in containers, special bedding areas, or integrated with the ornamental garden where their interesting foliages and flowers are a distinct addition. Growing sites should be located as close to the kitchen as possible for harvesting ease. Sunny, well-drained areas are preferable, and soils should be enriched with organic matter.

Begin with two or three of your favorite herbs and add to the list as space and interest dictate. To help you in getting a start, I have compiled a list of several of the most commonly grown herbs with some cultural suggestions and a brief evaluation of their ornamental possibilities as members of the pleasure garden.

Harvesting and Curing Herbs

Fresh, young leaves can be gathered and used any time in the herb's growing season, but if you wish to harvest the surplus for yourself and friends, keep in mind that the flavor is best when the herbs are collected at the peak of flavor, cured, and stored.

Generally speaking, the herb is at its peak of flavor when it begins to bloom, and flavor is best preserved with rapid drying. Some gardeners dry herbs where the air circulates freely and the room can be darkened to preserve as much of the green color as possible. Slow drying damages flavor, turns the leaves dark, and permits the growth of molds. Some herb growers prefer to spread their herbs thinly on cookie sheets to dry in the electric oven set at the lowest heat. The door should be left ajar and drying requires two to three hours. (The pilot light of the gas oven is enough to permit drying without additional heat.) When leaves are thoroughly dry, place in metal or opaque glass containers and close tightly to preserve the flavor. Label all containers.

Chives

Dill

Herbs

(Key to Classification: A—Annual, B—Biennial, P—Perennial)

Name	Cultural Suggestions	Ornamental Qualities
Basil (A)	Sow seeds in early spring	Purple bronze leaves, lavender flowers, 30″
Chamomile (A)	Sow seeds in early spring	Delicate fine leaves, daisylike flowers, 12″
Chives (P)	Slow to germinate, recommend dividing old plants, sun or part shade	Onionlike leaves, beautiful lavender flowers, 12″
Coriander (A)	Sow seeds in April in sunny, moderately fertile soil	Delicate leaves, pinkish flower, seeds become fragrant in drying
Dill (A)	Sow seeds fall or spring in full sun	Stake plants for wind protection, 4′
Fennel (B)	Sow seeds in April	Looks much like dill
Lavender (P)	Sow seeds in April or make cuttings, add some lime to growing soil	Three varieties, all have purple flowers, good ornamental, 3′
Lemon balm (P)	Sow seeds early summer in sun	Very ornamental, do not permit self-seeding, 3′
Marjoram (P)	Start seeds in early April indoors, transplant in late May to outdoor beds	Gray foliage, 15″
Mint (P)	Grow from cuttings or divisions	Because of rapid, pervasive growth, plant in a tub
Parsley (B)	Sow in early spring or fall in well-prepared beds, thin for best growth, germination slow—three or four weeks	Lush and curly dark green foliage, handsome plant
Rosemary (P)	Sow seeds indoors in early April or make cuttings	Large plant with unusual narrow, two-color leaves of great fragrance, 6′
Sage (P)	Seeds or cuttings in early spring	Shrubby with gray green leaves, bluish flowers, 2′
Summer savory (A)	Seeds or cuttings in early spring	Yellow to red flowers, 18″
Tarragon (P)	Cuttings or divisions of root	Outstanding as ornamental, 2′
Thyme (P)	Sow seeds in early spring, add lime to growing soil	Creeping variety excellent for rock gardens and walks, taller type good foreground edger, 1″–6″
Yarrow (P)	Sow seeds in early spring or divide old plants	Excellent for garden or making flower arrangements, 2′

Putting the Garden Together

In the foregoing pages I have suggested that gardens be located in the private areas of the property, and I have recommended that this private garden area be enclosed and framed by a hedge or structure such as a wall or fence. Some attention has also been given to the shrubs, bedding plants, trees, and other plants suitable for garden making. Now it becomes necessary to decide on the shape and size of the garden, the arrangement of plants, and the choice of colors.

Basically garden layouts are formal or informal in nature.

Formal Garden

The formal garden is made up of straight lines and geometric forms, a style best suited for level land. Plant balance in these beds is actual or symmetrical, meaning that the same plants and the same numbers are used in each segment of the garden.* This style of garden design is not as popular as it was fifty years ago, but in spite of this it is an easier style of design for the beginner than the currently popular informal garden. Maintenance for both styles of gardens is about equal.

*English poet-gardener Alexander Pope described the formal garden, which he disliked, in these words:
    . . . Each alley has a brother
    Half the garden just reflects the other.

A simple example of the formal garden could be a square area with four beds of equal size that are grouped around a central focal accent such as a sundial, bird bath, or piece of statuary. Each of the four beds would be planted identically.

There are many variations of the formal garden design, and I have been pleased to observe a renewal of interest lately in formal garden design by owners and builders of colonial and Georgian styles of houses to which this garden style is so well suited. A trip in springtime to Colonial Williamsburg will show you why, since many of their small gardens are formal, charming reminders of the English gardens the homesick colonists had left behind.

Informal Garden

The informal garden is one characterized by free-form, curving outlines and should be used on hilly, uneven terrain, with the lines of the garden following the natural curves of the land. A fine example of the beauty of natural contouring may be observed in the Carolinas where knowledgeable farmers have learned how to prevent the erosion of their topsoil by soil terracing and row contouring. Note how their soil terraces flow in and out with the curvature of the land. This is what you should try to emulate in the informal garden layout.

When I am contouring a garden on rolling land, I find it is most helpful to use a pliable hose (a rubber one is best) to mark the flowing lines of the curves, and I always strive for a few deep and flowing rhythmic contours, rather than short, choppy, squiggly scallops.

Plant balance in the formal garden is actual and symmetrical, but in the informal garden, balance is visual and asymmetrical. It is achieved by playing groups of different plant materials against each other. As an example, I often use three deciduous dogwoods on one side to balance one evergreen pine tree in another section of the informal garden. Asymmetrical balance is seen at its finest in the Japanese garden where plants, stones, gravel areas, or such garden features as a stone lantern, a bridge, or a water basin are played against each other for subtle and sophisticated balance.

The informal garden is more difficult to design than the formal, but it is a style more in harmony with our modern, casual way of life, and with study and observation, it is a style within the reach of the amateur.

The Garden Size

The size of the garden beds should be in proportion to the total size of the lot. A proportion of approximately one-fourth to one-third of the total private area is not too large for a combination of trees, shrubs, and bedding plants.

It is helpful to think of the backyard as a large outdoor room and approach it as you would a room with four walls. If it is a small room, less furniture (garden plants) can be accommodated, and most furnishings (plants) would be smaller in scale. Clutter (small, isolated beds) should be omitted in order to have as much unbroken carpet space (lawn) as possible. Because of the initial cost and subsequent maintenance, most garden beds are too small rather than too large. Again, it might be best to start a planting with shrubbery (background) and plan eventually to add the bedding plants if your interest indicates such a move.

Plant Arrangement

Regardless of the formality or informality of the garden design, the plants themselves can be arranged informally. As a matter of fact, with the passage of time, formal, balanced plant arrangements become less and less formal. The famous Middleton Gardens of South Carolina are an excellent example.

In all gardens, plants should be arranged so that they can be seen from as many viewing points as possible. Obviously this indicates the need for planting the tallest plants at the back of the garden and working to the foreground with decreasing sizes. In order to achieve the softly blending natural look that one can observe in the most beautiful informal gardens, heights (as well as textures) must blend in overlapping patterns from back to front.

Instead of straight unbroken lines of tall plants, intermediate plants, and small plants, a few plants from each group must be dropped back into the ranks of the other. There should be low plants intermingled with intermediates, and intermediates repeating the performance with the tallest varieties. Here and there, to vary the skyline silhouette of the garden, a tree should be introduced or a shrub of taller height than its companions.

Take the time to study a natural wooded area in the distance. You will observe the silhouette rising and falling in a natural pattern; fine-textured pines blending with the large leaves and bold form of the sourwood and the green lace elegance of a willow oak are complementary and in harmony with each other.

Man-made examples of plant arrangements can be observed in every garden of note throughout Carolina communities and elsewhere. When you visit such places, have firmly in mind that you are going to study the size and style of the garden, the numbers and placement of each type of plant material. Look beyond the color, which is only transient, and examine the skeleton and framework. The answers are all there if you learn to see them.

Color in the Garden

Flower arrangers who cut stems to exact lengths and fret about such matters as analogous and monochromatic color harmonies may feel that I take the matter of color much too lightly. I have struggled through those stages myself, but after some years of observing the compatibility of outdoor colors, I have concluded that precise and exact color schemes in the garden are not only difficult to achieve but largely unnecessary in view of the fact that colors appear vastly different in the outdoor environment.

Flower arrangements have the greatly limiting boundaries of four walls. Indoor light is also different, both day and night. Shadows and shifting winds are mostly absent, and the color scheme of the house decor is of paramount importance.

It is so much more fun to work with outdoor color, at least it is for the gardener. Nature combines her colors with a bold and lavish hand. Blue and purple flowers have gay centers of orange and yellow; bluebirds have muted gray and red to go with their basic blue, and in the iridescence of the rainbow, the reds, oranges, yellows, blues, and violets blend in perfect harmony side by side.

An Introduction to Garden Design

In a garden setting all color exists in a blended and refined harmony. Brilliant colors are subdued and muted by the space colors of blues and grays and by the pink, orange, and red of the changing skies. Earth colors vary as well, yet all are warm, serene, and delicately veiled in gossamer haze and mist. There is never a clash in nature's palette.

The final choice of color should be the gardener's own, and since I like best the mass bouquets made in the Colonial Williamsburg manner, which employs many flower forms and colors, it follows that I also like many forms and colors of flowers in my own garden. These suggestions on color choices might be helpful in selecting your own chromatic scheme.

1. Select one basic color to be used in fairly large quantities and distribute it throughout the entire garden. Such repetition of color produces sequence, movement, and rhythm as the eye naturally moves from one color grouping to another of the same color.

2. Use white flowers and pastels generously with groups of strong colors. White enhances all color and acts as a peacemaker where there might be incompatibility. White, blue, and basic green are the garden's cooling colors, a matter of importance in our hot summers. Yellow, orange, and red are warm colors. Cool them off with white.

3. For wider range in the selection of bedding-plant colors, plant a number of white- or pastel-flowered trees and shrubs in the background. A stronger color such as that of an orange red flowering quince might spoil an entire color scheme of more delicate hues.

4. White, yellow, and pastels can be seen at greater distances than reds, blues, or purples. Magenta is a difficult color for most gardeners.

Spring is the season that produces the only really jarring color clash of the year for me, and this is the fault of gardeners, not the season. The magenta or lavender pink of the redbud is a fearsome sight combined in a garden with orange red quince, bright yellow forsythia, and salmon pink dogwood. I suggest that white dogwood and white flowering quince could be combined with any of the other plants, but that something should be omitted. White dogwood and pink dogwood? Yes. White dogwood and redbud? Yes. White dogwood and red quince? Yes. White dogwood and forsythia? Yes. I can think of no way to have all these plants in the same garden without a clash, so I would suggest you pick the combination you like best.

Landscaping the Farm Home

In rural areas, the entire acreage is the setting for the home, and neatness and cleanliness are surely the most important aspects of any rural beautification program. Of paramount importance is the absence of signs, billboards, and ramshackle structures along the roadside approaches. Well-tended, open fields, and thriving woodlands are part and parcel of an attractive rural home.

At the home site proper, tidiness is doubly significant. A background of tumbledown, unkempt outbuildings, falling fences, and rusting, unused farm machinery can spoil the effect of the most imposing farmhouse. Service areas and structures should be kept in the best state of repair possible both for the sake of beauty and economy.

Plant screens of evergreens (large hollies, pines, privet, laurels, and even magnolias, are excellent) in the large yards that usually exist around farmhouses wherever they are needed to separate dwellings from service areas.

Fruiting trees are particularly appropriate for ornamental uses in rural sections. One gnarled and picturesque apple tree can give more authentic atmosphere to a country home than a dozen hitching posts, wagon wheel entrances, or concrete elks eternally stuck about a yard.

Only limited quantities of evergreens are needed in base plantings unless, of course, the house has an unsightly foundation. Space-requiring deciduous shrubs (crape myrtle, deutzia, lilac, quince, and forsythia) are at their best around rural homes. However, these are more effective if planted in groups along the boundaries between yard and field than when haphazardly dotted about as specimen plants all over the yard.

For vines nothing is as handsome as the grape, with clusters of plenty to adorn them in their proper season. Gourd vines (*Cucurbita pepo*) are handsome ornamentals, too, and the dried gourds make fine homes for the birds, establishing an air of rural peace and serenity unmatched by all the factory-built birdhouses in your catalog.

Where additional shrubbery and flowers are indicated, those native to the area should be planted if the growing conditions provided are suitable for their needs. In general, it is infinitely preferable to maintain the atmospheric identity of the community in which you live by also selecting most of your lawn trees from those that are native to the area. (The resort towns of Southern Pines and Pinehurst, N.C., have heavy plantings of native holly, long-leaved pines, and native dogwood, and these give a character and feeling of belonging unmatched by exotic varieties.)

Self-seeding annuals and biennials such as larkspur, cornflower, poppy, Drummond phlox, cockscomb (*Celosia argentea*), and a host of others are excellent additions to the rural garden scheme where there is usually plenty of space available for their proper growth.

Above all else the country gardener should not copy the city garden. Keep your larger area natural, neat, uncluttered, and clean. Having all that wonderful space makes you a gold-plated plutocrat, and don't you forget it!

Design and Garden Maintenance

"To keep a garden the way you keep yours must require a lot of help or most of your time," a visitor remarked to me recently. Let me hasten to reassure you. The only helper I have, indoors or out, is a husband who can turn his hand to whatever needs doing.

Even if we wanted to we could not spend all of our time in our own garden. The reason, simply stated, is that we work for a living. For the present and many years past, we have earned our livelihood as landscape contractors and in the designing and maintenance of gardens not our own. With the time left we have kept our own house and garden, raised a daughter, traveled, camped, fished, and sewed.

I believe that the amount of time we give our own garden could be managed by any working couple who enjoys gardening as a hobby. Our small plot produces not only flowers, but vegetables and fruits as well. We also have a small rose garden that we find worth its care. Both pride and curiosity underly my efforts to be as self-sufficient a gardener as possible. Most of my plants are propagated from seeds, cuttings, and divisions on the premises, and composting loads of neighborhood leaves maintains the garden's fruitfulness.

Keeping to the Basics

If I lacked the enthusiasm and energy for such a diversity of gardening activities, I would eliminate the bedding flowers, roses, and vegetables that take fully half my gardening time. To make a setting for my house as attractive as possible with the least amount of work, I would plant my garden space and house foundation with a selection of slow-growing evergreens suitable for the soil and exposure, add some deciduous shrubs of interest, and finish the job with a few shade and flowering trees, planted where needed on a green, uncluttered lawn.

Plant Selection and Maintenance

Bedding Plants: Annuals and biennials require the highest maintenance of all the plant groups. Replacement twice a year is needed for continuous bloom, and constant care is required by way of removal of faded flowers, feeding, watering, and weeding. Concentrate bedding plants in fewer areas to simplify care and reduce their numbers by substituting such sturdy perennials as peonies, iris, and day lilies.

Roses: No other group of plants requires as much care as roses, and the individual must decide if they are worth it. Weekly sprayings can be less troublesome by combining the fungicide and insecticide into one spray. A single spray mixture in a six-gallon hose-gun applicator will cover approximately twenty-five roses, so you might save work by keeping your rose garden to that number, and by all means plant all your roses together.

Evergreen Shrubbery: Avoid too many exotic, unproven varieties and adhere mainly to area-tested, slow-growing types best suited to your own garden soil and exposures. Group together shrubs of similar growth requirements such as camellias, azaleas, and rhododendrons.

Hedges: Avoid extensive hedging that must be pruned often to maintain a formal appearance. Replace these with loose, informal hedges that require less pruning. Espaliered forms are also high-maintenance items; replace with vines.

Naturalized Areas: The work-saving aspects of the naturalized area have been greatly exaggerated.

Island beds of azalea, juniper, liriope, or the more conventional ground covers, such as ivy, periwinkle, or pachysandra, require weeding, watering, spraying, and other special attention to keep them presentable. In addition, the naturalized area is frequently an amoebalike blob without rhythm, proportion, contouring, or aesthetic relationship to the land or structural features such as walks, drives, or the house itself.

Grass is without question the most satisfactory and easily maintained of all ground covers, and it is worth the extra attention required to grow it in the more difficult sites where naturalized areas are often resorted to as the solution. Problem areas of insufficient light for grass may be vastly improved by the removal of low-hanging tree branches and the thinning of boughs from the crown of the tree. If extra watering and feeding are required, as they usually are in such problem spots, they are equally necessary for all ground covers, grass or otherwise. In all areas where grass is grown, avoid narrow strips and cul-de-sacs where the mower cannot be freely used.

Garden Structures and Maintenance

Walks: Clipping grass around individual flagstones or other types of stepping stones is an odious task that can be greatly lightened by laying walks of solid construction. Better still, avoid laying unnecessary walks or those that are more circuitous than needed. A straight line is the shortest distance—and usually the best design as well.

Garden Edgings: If the entire garden is planted as one large unit, fewer edgings of any type will be needed. For the exposed sides however, an edge of such structural materials as bricks, blocks, hardwood logs, railroad ties, treated boards, metal strips, or synthetic fiber strips can serve to define the garden contours, retain the soil, and exclude unwanted grass.

My own garden has a dual-purpose edging of weathered cinder blocks laid crosswise to the garden edge to form an eighteen-inch walk. From the standpoint of design, I felt this arrangement was preferable to breaking my small lawn area with numerous walks. It works very well. The blocks were underlaid with heavy black polyethylene strips that aid greatly in holding back the pervasive runners of the Bermuda grass which threaten to overrun the fescue in our sunny lawn.

Mowing Strips: If the bed edger is to serve also as a mowing strip to save hand-edging, it must be set flush with the ground level to permit one of the lawn mower wheels to roll on its surface. Such an edging looks attractive but does not function as efficiently as a taller edging for restraining grass and retaining soil.

Fences: If maintenance cost and labor are the major factors in choosing the enclosure, avoid those that must be painted. Use, rather, those of natural, weather-resistant woods. Ideal enclosures for low maintenance are of brick, stone, or metal.

How to keep the area at the base of the fence neat and well-groomed is a problem, regardless of the style of fencing. If only grass is growing at the fence base, herbicides may be helpful if carefully used. Having had some rather unpleasant experiences with the far-reaching and unexpected results of using herbicides, I prefer to keep my fences neat the hard way, clipping by hand.*

The problem is much simpler where hedges or garden boundaries exist along the fence line. Strips of black plastic anchored and covered with mulch will choke out, or at least hinder, the growth of most of the extraneous plant materials.

Regular Care and Maintenance

A point often overlooked in the average maintenance program is the importance of a sustained, regular routine of gardening chores. For example, a little pruning done now and then throughout the year eliminates the need for the yearly amputation ordeal, and the year-around appearance is much better for it. Weeding is another case in point. In fact, with the number of garden activities that could and should be done the year around, there is no need for the garden to be a burden at any time (see Garden Calendar, pp. 27–32.)

Other than the planting seasons of early spring and fall, I have many days when I do nothing at all in my own garden. Those, to me, are the ones I think of as my lost days.

*Small rechargeable battery-powered grass shears are a good tool for performing this chore.

Part Three
A Year in My Garden

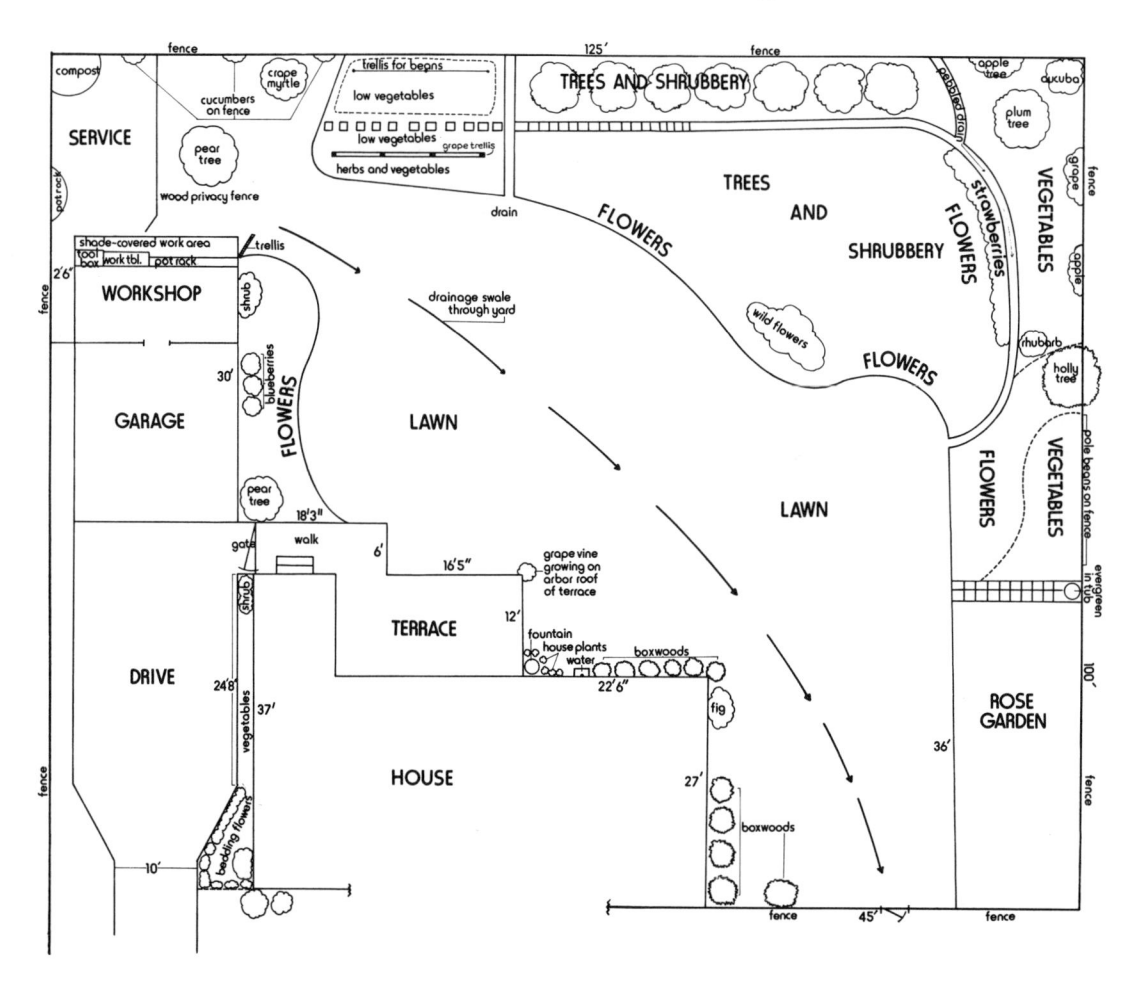

A plan of the author's garden

My Approach to Gardening

In the first two parts of this book I have concerned myself with the tools and techniques of gardening and the artistic use of plant materials in garden design. This third section, "A Year in My Garden," is a personal accounting of the month-by-month activities that make up the year's work in my own private garden. In this recounting, I have placed some emphasis on the following:

1. The ways and means of growing a variety of flowers, fruits, and vegetables in a small area. A list of these plants is included. Keep in mind throughout that most of these plants grow in a single integrated garden unit in the backyard of our lot of one-third acre.

2. The recognition that gardening is a continuous, overlapping, and even repetitive process. Such necessary details as weeding, planting, watering, and pruning are indeed continuous and overlapping, but so is the enjoyment of the growth process and the harvests of flowers and food.

3. An awareness of the importance and indispensibility of the weather in the gardening partnership.

4. The need for self-sufficiency in gardening, both for the sake of the budget and the gardener's self-esteem.

5. The expression and sharing of my own unbounded pleasure with gardening as my way of life.

Plants in My Garden
*(Numerals after names indicate the number of varieties; * denotes native plants.)*

Annuals:
African marigold (*Tagetes erecta*), begonia, Browallia, calendula, cleome, cornflower, Drummond phlox, French marigold (*T. patula*), geranium, impatiens, ornamental peppers, snapdragon, sweet alyssum, vinca (*Vinca rosea*)

Biennials:
Honesty, pansy

Bulbs:
Agapanthus or lily-of-the-Nile (*Agapanthus umbellatus*), anemone (spring), atamasco lily*, colchicum or fall crocus (*Colchicum autumnale*), crocus (*Crocus biflorus*), daffodil (*Narcissus* spp.), Dutch iris (*Iris xiphium*), gladiolus (*Gladiolus* spp.), glory-of-the-snow (*Chionodoxa Luciliae*), Hall's amaryllis (*Lycoris squamigera*), hyacinth (*Hyacinthus orientalis*), milk-and-wine lily (*Crinum* spp.), scilla (*Scilla hispanica*), snowdrop (*Galanthus nivalis*), snowflake (*Leucojum vernum*), spider lily or lycoris (*Lycoris radiata*), turk's-cap lily*

Ground Covers:
Ajuga 2, ivy 2, pachysandra, periwinkle 2

Perennials:
Ageratum, anemone (fall), aspidistra, bellflower, black-eyed Susan, blue-eyed grass*, candytuft, canna 2, chrysanthemum 4, coral-bells, day lily 7, dianthus 2, dutchman's-breeches*, English daisy (species), evening primrose, ferns* 5, foam flower*, ginger lily (*Hedychium coronarium*), globe thistle (*Echinops exaltatus*), green-and-gold*, hardy begonia, hen-and-chicks (*Sempervivum tectorum*), hepatica, iris 4, Italian arum (*Arum italicum*), loosestrife, lupine, peony, phlox (spring and summer types), plumbago, polemonium*, primula, sedum 4, spiderwort, strawberry geranium (*Saxifraga sarmentosa*), trillium* 2, violet* 3, Virginia bluebell*, wild ginger*

Roses:
Climber, floribunda, hybrid tea, polyantha, single

Shrubbery
(E—Evergreen; D—Deciduous):
Althea D, aucuba 3E, azalea 5E, boxwood 4E, camellia 2E, cherry laurel E, cleyera E, crape myrtle D, daphne E, deutzia D, elaeagnus D, euonymus 2E, fatshedera or tree ivy E (*Fatshedera lizei*), flowering almond D, forsythia D, hibiscus D, holly E, kerria D, ligustrum E, mahonia 2E, nandina E, osmanthus 2E, photinia E, pieris E, poet's laurel or Alexandrian laurel E (*Danae racemosa*), red-stemmed dogwood D, rhododendron E, schipka laurel or schip laurel E (*Prunus laurocerasus* var. *schipkaensis*), star magnolia D, viburnum 2D

Trees:
Ash D, Callery pear D (*Pyrus Calleryana*), cherry D, crab apple D, dogwood D, holly E, iron-wood D, magnolia E, maple D, pine E, redbud D, sweet gum D, sycamore D, tulip poplar D, willow oak D

[64] Carolina Home Gardener

Vegetables:
Beet, bell pepper (*Capsicum frutescens*), broccoli, cabbage, Chinese cabbage, collard, corn salad, cucumber, endive, field pea, garden pea, Irish potato, lettuce, lima bean, okra, onion, salad greens (mixture of turnip, mustard, and kale), snap bean, squash, Swiss chard, tomato
NOTE: Corn is omitted for lack of growing space.

Fruits:
Apple, blueberry, fig, grape, pear, plum, strawberry

Vines:
Carolina jessamine, clematis, climber rose, climbing hydrangea (*Hydrangea petiolaris*), red honeysuckle* (*Lonicera sempervirens*)

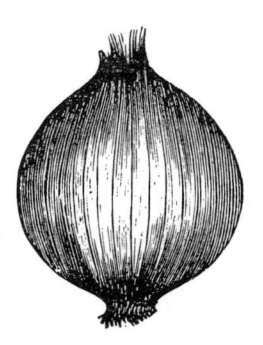

January

Making Cuttings for Summer

The first of several crops of cuttings for bedding begonias and geraniums (*Pelargonium*) used as summer bedding plants in my garden is always made in early January. To make these cuttings, the long shoots or stems are removed from large plants being over-wintered in the house. These stems, three or four inches long, are broken from the parent plant at a leaf joint, and the leaves from the lower half of the stem are removed with a single-edged razor blade or sharp knife to avoid crushing or bruising the tender stems. These stems, several to a glass, are put in water and set in sunny, warm windows.

Some of the cuttings will root and others will not, but they continue to bloom during the rooting period to make a bright note in the winter kitchen or other rooms. Several weeks are usually needed for root formation, and as soon as the roots are an inch or so long the cutting can be transplanted to containers of well-drained potting soil, usually by mid-February or early March. After being pottted, they must remain in the warmth and sunshine indoors until late April and planted outdoors about 1 May.

Begonias of the fibrous-rooted type (*Begonia semperflorens*) are among the most versatile of summer garden plants and they thrive in part shade or full sun. Each plant produced at home is worth at least a dollar to the garden budget. The process of removing the long stems from wintering begonias and geraniums in January is also quite beneficial to the parent plant since it serves as a needed pruning. In fact, this pruning should be done regardless of how the trimmings are used.

House Plants

Growing house plants is an entire gardening subject in itself, and in January, I practice it in a small way. The tending of a few potted plants helps to relieve the tedium of winter when spring seems so far away. A majority of my house plants are stationed outside or planted in beds by the first of May, and they do help substantially with the furnishing of my summer garden.

When I was young and lived on larger grounds, I had a spacious greenhouse in which I grew thousands of plants for fun and profit. I enjoyed it a great deal, but it was hard work, very confining, and such dedication for me is past. I now have found an excellent substitute—a 4′ × 6′ window greenhouse attached to the east window of my bedroom. Although especially designed heating elements are available for these solar window units, I make do with the warmth of the sun in the mornings and the heat that leaks through the window from my bedroom in the afternoons and at night. Only on very cold nights is it necessary to burn a light bulb inside the greenhouse to hold the temperatures at a safe level. When the temperatures are in the low teens, my bedroom window is opened two or three inches to provide extra warmth. I also add a blanket to my bed on such nights.

A Year in My Garden [65]

Feeding, spraying, watering, turning, and grooming can be done from inside the bedroom, and each day the ventilator on the greenhouse top must be opened, if only for a short period during the warmest hours of the day, to permit a change of air. By March it is safe to leave the ventilator open most of the day. In early to mid-April the plants come out for a few days of protected hardening off in the sunny side of my open garage. By the last of April or first of May, they reach their final planting destinations—the open beds, planters, and hanging baskets.

These small window greenhouses may be used in two ways: first, solely for the beauty of flowering plants through the winter (since plants must have plenty of space to flower properly, very few plants can be accommodated in this limited space); the second use is for storage of cuttings and old plants with their tops cut back severely, both designed for the summer garden. I use my unit for both purposes, happy to settle for a few blooms and some help with the summer garden. Each season I store a few large old plants that have been cut back severely to save space and several small cuttings of geranium, begonia, fern, wandering Jew, Boston daisy, ageratum, and lantana. Even the cuttings produce a few flowers, and each floret is appreciated in January.

Where to Locate the Window Greenhouse

Frequently the question is asked as to which side of the house is best for a window greenhouse. Such things as existing trees and other buildings influence such a choice. Everything being equal it is my opinion that an east window is the best exposure in this region. A south window would certainly be a warmer place and cactus hobbyists might prefer this, but for the uses I make of it, the east window is fine. Each gardener should decide what to grow and locate the unit as advantageously as possible.

This January my greenhouse held thirty pots. I used green plastic containers filled with loamy soil mixtures to minimize the weight as much as possible. The thirty containers filled three shelves, but more shelves could be added if the grower limits the heights of the plants to six inches or less. For a mixture of plant sizes such as I store, three shelves is the best arrangement.

Fully half the thirty pots contained geranium cuttings made in the fall before frost. In addition to the cuttings, some of the old geraniums and bedding begonias were lifted from the summer garden at the same time and potted several to the pot. Of course, it was necessary to cut the old plants back severely, both the tops and the roots, to accommodate several in one container.

These plants received no food and scant watering through January. There was little room for top growth in the window greenhouse, and in a state of suspended animation, they held on to the thread of life until late winter when more food and water could be given in preparation for warmer weather and subsequent planting outside.

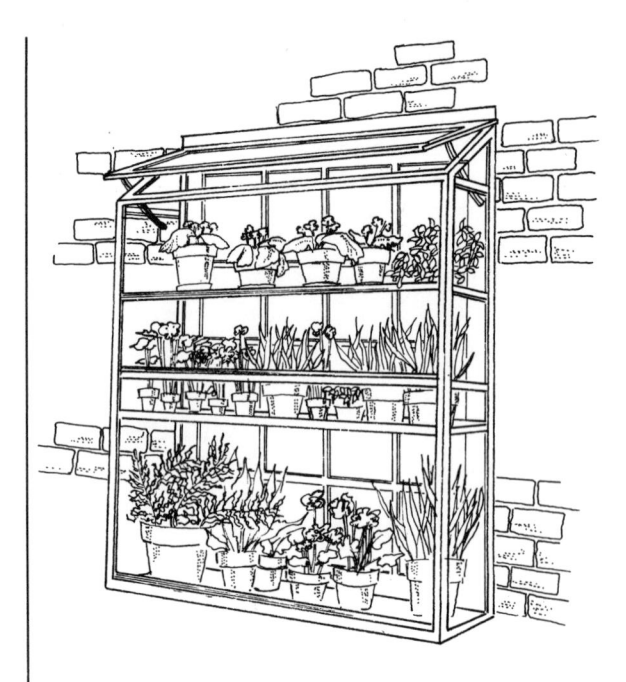

Cineraria Trial

Each year something new is tried in the greenhouse unit. This year it was the cineraria (*Senecio cruentus*), a potted plant said to prefer cool weather for blooming and much admired on visits to England where it is grown in large numbers. The cineraria seeds were sown indoors in an empty egg carton in early March. They germinated readily and thrived in the cool spring weather, but summering presented a problem.

Cinerarias require several months of vegetative growth before flowering but do not like hot weather. In May I placed the potted small plants outside in the shade of the north side of the house.

They sulked a bit through July and August, but they survived.

By Thanksgiving, the March-sown seeds began to bloom in the window greenhouse, and I have never seen more exciting colors. They continued in bloom throughout the winter, a most satisfactory reward for my efforts.

To summarize my experience with the window greenhouse unit, I would say that it is an excellent and inexpensive way to preserve the propagation stock of the more costly summer annuals such as begonia, geranium, Boston fern (*Nephrolepis exaltata*), fuchsia, lantana, wandering Jew, and Boston daisy—and, when the space permits, to try a new plant or two now and then. But without some means of providing additional heat, it is too cold in January and February to germinate the seeds of warm-weather crops such as tomatoes, marigolds, bell peppers, and the like.

Two Indoor Favorites

Before finishing my comments on indoor gardening for January, I would be remiss if I failed to mention two house plants that have been foolproof and eminently satisfactory under indoor winter conditions.

In my living room during the winter I have had a dwarf orange (*Citrus taitensis*) for ten years, and it might have reached the ceiling five years ago except for the annual drastic pruning that it receives each spring. Almost any day of the year, and particularly in winter, this plant can boast all stages of typical citrus growth—fragrant blossoms, small green fruits, and golf-ball-size golden ripe oranges. Other than quarterly feedings each year and an occasional spraying for mealy bugs, its only requirements are plenty of sunshine and water.

The second house-plant favorite is a spathiphyllum (*Spathiphyllum patinii*), a tropical member of the arum family. Long-lasting, spathelike white flowers are borne above a cascading rosette of lustrous dark green leaves a foot long and half as wide. As the flowers mature, the white is replaced with chartreuse coloring fully as beautiful as the white. Like the miniature orange tree, the spathiphyllum requires copious amounts of water, but it absolutely cannot tolerate direct sunlight. If you are fortunate enough to find a spathiphyllum, have patience with it as two or three years may be needed to achieve the finest quality and size. However, it is handsome at all stages, and when it begins to flower it is indeed a floral spectacular.

Both the orange and the spathiphyllum summer outdoors in their containers, the orange in full sun and the spathiphyllum in deep shade—like the floor of the densest jungle whence it came.

A Plus for January

One of the outstanding pleasures of January indoors is the perusal of the new seed catalogs that fill the mailbox at this season. Many contented hours can be spent reading about the new introductions, cross-checking old varieties for availability and prices, and finally, making up the new year's order. I had a moment of private amusement when I realized that my first check of January was addressed to a seed company. Happy New Year!

Looking toward a time when food may not be as plentiful as it is today, this year's seed order contained more food items than usual. I ordered four dwarf fruit trees, two apples and two pears, to use where I once would have planted dogwoods, crab apples, or redbuds.

Fruiting apples, pears, cherries, and plums are in every way as beautiful as their nonfruiting ornamental counterparts. Dwarf sizes are better than standard sizes for the small city garden. True, some spraying will be necessary to insure fruits, but the dwarf types are readily reached with hose applicators, and if you fail to get the spraying done, wormy apples are better than none.

Do some research before selecting fruit varieties. Keep in mind that at least two trees of a variety are needed for good yield. Dwarf sizes vary, too, according to the rootstock used for grafting. Unfortunately, the extremes of spring temperatures in this area make peaches an uncertain crop. If space is limited, omit peaches in the colder parts of the Carolinas.

In addition to the fruit trees, I ordered rhubarb roots. Rhubarb is a perennial vegetable with very handsome ornamental leaves, making it an attractive addition to the vegetable garden or the perennial flower border. My Faithful Helper assures me he doesn't like rhubarb; he also admitted he has never eaten any. I thought I would offer it as a new type of apple pie. He will eat anything in a crust.

Too Early for Seed Planting

By the end of January the winter-weary gardener begins to feel an implacable itch to plant some tomatoes and zinnias to germinate on the kitchen window sill. Such efforts are premature and usually wasted. If indeed these seeds manage to germinate, they are apt to grow poorly by becoming tall, spindly, and unable to undergo the shock of outdoor planting later on.

Unless you have a warm greenhouse or special growing lights, restrain your impulse at least until the first to the fifteenth of March to plant seeds of warm-weather plants. Remember that tender summer crops such as tomatoes, peppers, marigolds, and zinnias will grow very little until the earth is warm enough to sustain ground temperatures throughout the night. This overnight warmth seldom arrives before the first of May in the upper reaches of piedmont North Carolina, although it is earlier in the coastal and southern zones of the two Carolinas. For the piedmont the odds are better than fair that tomatoes planted in early May to outside beds will be ready for eating about as early as those you struggled to start in the kitchen in January and February.

Outdoor Gardening in January

A mid-January feeding is due some of the spring-flowering bulbs planted in the fall of the previous year or years. Daffodils, crocus, snowdrops, snowflakes, and glory-of-the-snow are up by this date and some are ready to bloom. They need food for the rapid growth they make at this season. A nitrogenous fertilizer is best, and I used 8-8-8 chemical fertilizer, about two to three heaping tablespoons to each bulb. Where tops were not yet in evidence, I scattered the fertilizer in about the same amounts over the surface of the bedding areas.

As for tulips, if you grow them, they will not be showing above ground at this time. Wait another month and feed them a lower nitrogen food. A 5-10-10 fertilizer would be adequate. I do not believe in investing much money in tulips for this area. Even in my old garden where the drainage was perfect, I seldom had any tulips the second year. In this poorly drained present garden, tulips rotted the first year and I had no blooms at all. It appears that our Carolina climate is unsuited to their growth cycle and temperature needs. Except for some of the hardy species tulips (*T. Clusiana, Fosteriana, Kaufmanniana,* and others), I feel that tulips are a poor investment.

I have been relieved to find that daffodils, snowdrops, scillas, and snowflakes have survived the wet conditions of my new garden far better than tulips.

Weeded Garden

Chickweed (*Stellaria*), henbit (*Lamium*), dock (*Rumex patientia*), and other winter weeds grow lustily in January—and February—and March. On one of the warm days in January, I attended to clearing these weeds from the bedding plant areas where the mulch never seems to restrain them. The most efficient tool I have ever found for this weeding chore is a snub-nosed, kitchen butcher knife cut down to a three-inch blade. Between your thumb and this sturdy blade, the weeds come out easily. Dig below the surface to get the parsniplike root of the dockweed; otherwise, the tops continue to grow forever.

Groomed the Iris

The outer leaves of established bearded iris continue to turn brown and die throughout the winter, and seemingly the year around. In January, on a warm day, I removed these leaves that may harbor harmful diseases and insects. Such foliage is always assigned to the trash can for removal from the premises. The beds looked better for the cleaning.

Replanted Winter-Heaved Plants

Small bedding plants that may not be firmly established are often pushed out of the ground by the alternate freezing and thawing of the soil. Through January (and February) I checked pansies, columbine, and coral-bells after each such period of weather and pressed the roots back into their proper position.

Restored Mulches

Winter winds blow willfully through January to drift the mulches into corners and away from the plants where they are needed for protection. I restored the mulch twice during January.

Planted Shrubs

Evergreen and deciduous trees and shrubs may be planted in January (and later) when the ground is workable. Two hollies and a forsythia were planted in my garden during January.

Divided Day Lilies

Dividing and replanting day lilies may also be done in January or later throughout the early spring. I prefer January for this chore when the tops are at maximum dormancy; dividing is needed about every three years, although it is safe to divide more often if additional supplies are desired.

The division of day lilies requires more muscle than skill. In my garden it is done by putting a spade through the center of the plant and prying out approximately half of the clump. The uprooted half is then cut in half, or in quarters if the size permits.

Old and very large clumps should be lifted out in their entirety and subdivided into four or eight pieces. Each subdivision must have both roots and growing buds. Plant two to three feet apart in improved soil and water immediately after planting.

Food Gardening in January

A gardening chore that I always do in late January is the annual pruning of my grapevines. In my small garden I have four vines: a purple Concord, a white Niagara, and two scuppernongs.

Four vines will not a vineyard make, but they are enough to supply fresh table grapes and jelly and juice for winter. No fruits I have ever grown are less trouble. The vines are also quite ornamental and may be used where any vine is needed if there is space and ample sunshine.

Pruning should be done when the vines are at their greatest dormancy, theoretically in January or February. However, cold and warm weather alternate so regularly in this area that I suspect there is never total dormancy. At any rate, I pruned in January, as I have in all the years past, and although some sap spilled from the cuts, it has never appeared to damage the yield. There are several methods of pruning grapes illustrated in books on the general subject of pruning. I prune most simply by removing some of the oldest wood and shortening the small branches remaining on the newer canes to lengths of twelve to eighteen inches. The grapes are borne on these short stems.

In Case It Snows

There was no snow in January, but there should have been. We had snow in December and we may have some in February or later. (It snowed 25 March.)

Regardless of the date, as soon as the snowfall is over, shake the drifts from boxwoods and azaleas. These two shrubs are quite brittle and easily damaged by the prolonged weight, and it is both safe and easy to dislodge the snow immediately after it falls. If you are unable to get this done before the branches are locked into a frozen drift, leave them alone for natural thawing. Dislodging fresh snowfall from one's shrubs is a wonderful excuse to get out into the snow. A person in her twilight years may feel that making a snowman or snowballs is a bit undignified, but it is perfectly proper to venture out to check on the welfare of the garden. How enchanting to find the most staid of the plants gowned in sparkling jewels and snowy ermines!

Goodby January

I could not write finis to January without a word of pride that I trust another gardener can forgive. On 10 January, still green and growing some on warm days, were the salad makings planted along a warm west wall.

The buttercrunch lettuce (one of the Bibb lettuces), Chinese cabbage, and green onions planted last September were still alive and perfectly edible.

To these three ingredients I added home-grown tomatoes and turnips stored in the refrigerator and slivers of green bell peppers from the freezer. A complete tossed salad from my own garden in January!

Tomatoes stored for this length of time (they were gathered green last October on the night of the first frost) are not tasty by vine-ripened, summer-tomato standards. However, they are fully as acceptable as those purchased on this date at the supermarket.

Summary of Garden Activities for January

1. Made cuttings of begonias and geraniums
2. Tended house plants
3. Grew cinerarias
4. Checked new catalogs; ordered seeds and plants for spring
5. Fed bulbs
6. Weeded garden
7. Groomed iris beds
8. Replanted frost-heaved bedding plants
9. Restored and replenished mulches
10. Planted shrubs
11. Divided and replanted day lilies
12. Pruned grapes
13. Ate fresh salad makings from outdoor garden

Flowers of January

Camellia, Christmas rose, crocus, flowering quince, mahonia, pansy, saucer magnolia, star magnolia, Sweet-Breath-of-Spring, winter jasmine

February

The tempo of gardening accelerates sharply in February, especially if there are several warm days scattered along through the month to tempt one outdoors. On such days there are shrubs and trees to plant, feed, and prune; seeds to sow; and a host of the miscellaneous chores that fill the days of the gardener.

Seed Sowing for February–March

To know which seeds should be planted at this time of the year, it is necessary to understand that there are two basic classes of both flowers and vegetables: those that grow and mature in the cool-weather seasons of the year (spring and fall) and those that must have the warmer temperatures of summer to grow and mature. According to my records, more vegetable than flower seeds are planted in February and March.

Cool-Weather Vegetable Planting Schedule

Vegetable	Outdoor Planting Dates
Beets*	15 Feb. to 1 March
Broccoli*	15 Feb. to 1 March
Cabbage*	15 Feb. to 1 March
Chinese cabbage	1 Sept. to 15 Sept.
Corn salad	15 Feb. to 1 March
Endive*	15 Feb. to 1 March
Garden peas	15 Feb. to 1 March
Lettuce*	15 Feb. to 1 March
Mustard, kale, turnips*	15 Feb. to 1 March
Onion sets*	15 Feb. to 1 March
Potatoes, Irish	1 March to 15 March
Radishes*	15 Feb. to 1 March

*Fall crops should be planted 1–15 Sept.

Cool-Weather Test Plantings

To learn the rhythm of the seasons in gardening, I would recommend that the beginner make a trial run of three easy-to-grow, cool-weather crops such as lettuce, mixed greens, and onions. (Mixed greens are mixtures of turnip, kale, mustard, and others.)

Prepare outside planting areas according to directions given elsewhere in this book. Select a site that is well drained and receives five or more hours of sunlight during the growing season of the crops you wish to plant.

Prepare two areas about 40 inches square. This will grow two pounds of onion sets and enough lettuce for four people, provided you gather bottom leaves from the lettuce instead of cutting the whole plant at once. A space 3' × 5' is ample for a mixed-greens bed since such a bed should be harvested regularly to maintain continuing new growth. To cover the greens and lettuce seeds, sweep the surface of the planting bed lightly with a leaf broom, or water gently to settle the seeds to the needed growing depth. If you want some table turnips large enough to amount to anything, plant these seeds thinly in rows a foot apart and separate from the greens mixture.

Onions are best grown by beginners from "sets" that are really little bulbs. Plant as you would any bulb—that is, to a depth three or four times the length of the bulb. Onions are planted in lazy-man style in my garden. With the edge of the hoe a shallow trench three or four inches deep is laid open. The bulbs are dropped in with about an inch between each bulb. I never worry about how they fall. There is no way for growth but up, and the tops get to the surface eventually regardless of the slight detour. The trench is then refilled and the soil tamped gently with the bottom of the hoe. This small effort supplies our table with tender green onions in fall, winter, and spring. Four pounds of onion sets a year, two pounds planted in the fall and two more in the spring, will supply onions for four. Since they store poorly, I make no attempt to save any for curing.

If growing space is in short supply, poke some onion sets here and there among the spring flowers and bulbs. Onion leaves are attractive and the onions can be pulled as needed without any disturbance to their elegant neighbors. Be sure you know which foliage is which, however. I sent a member of my family out to bring in fresh onions, and she brought back a handful of my finest Dutch iris—an understandable mistake when you think about their similarities. A few buttercrunch lettuce plants in the flower border are fully as ornamental as sweet williams or English daisies, and if no other room is available for them, by all means grow them together.

My February Seed Trials

No season passes in my garden without some small experiment in search of easier and better methods of growing. This year I tried planting seeds of lettuce and endive indoors and outdoors on the same date: 15 February. According to my records, both plantings were ready to eat at the same time.

Seeds of broccoli, cabbage, Drummond phlox, and calendula were sown for indoor starting on the same date. More about these later.

Beginner's Trials

Cornflowers and sweet alyssum are perhaps the easiest of all the annuals for beginners to try. Prepare and sow outside beds according to the directions given earlier for lettuce and mixed greens. Thin as needed. Cornflowers require considerable growing space since one plant will grow two feet high and almost as wide, if the soil is well prepared. Sweet alyssums vary a little in height according to the variety but are usually about six inches for both height and spread.

Using Cool-Weather Annuals in the Garden

Throughout the years I have relied heavily on some of the cool-weather annuals to supplement the garden in a special way. Calendula, cornflower, Drummond phlox, larkspur, and poppy seeds sown directly to the surface of beds in the fall—where daffodils, hyacinths, and tulips have been freshly planted—will germinate in the fall, grow a bit through the winter, and be tall enough to bloom at the time in late spring when the bulbs have completed their flowering. At this stage they are excellent both as color replacements and as a camouflage for the ripening bulb foliage that one must suffer through if the bulbs are to produce flowers again another year.

Cool-Season Flower Seed Planting Schedule

Cool-Weather Annuals*	Outdoor Planting Dates	
	15 Feb. to 1 Mar.	15 Sept. to 30 Sept.
Alyssum, sweet	x	
Calendula	x	
Cornflower	x	x
English daisy	x	
Forget-me-not	x	
Larkspur	x	x
Pansy		x
Phlox, Drummond	x	x
Poppy, California and shirley	x	x
Portulaca (*Portulaca grandiflora*)	x	
Sweet pea (*Lathyrus odoratus*)	x	
Wallflower		x

*There are other cool-season annuals, but this group has performed best in my garden.

NOTE: Some biennials are included with the annuals since their growing requirements are the same.

Cornflowers, phlox, poppies, and larkspur are prolific self-seeders as are certain of the varieties from the group of hot-weather annuals. The four listed above have become as pestiferous as weeds in some of the grain fields of the state. In a well-ordered garden, however, I can't imagine that this self-seeding habit would become a nuisance.

Lessons from Self-Seeding Plants

A gardener can learn a good deal by observing the self-seeding behavior of plants. Where these varieties grow to maturity and drop their seeds in early summer, the new plants usually germinate by fall or during the fall. Unless the winter is quite severe, many of the sturdiest of these seedlings will survive to bloom in the spring as earlier and better specimens than the gardener usually gets from hand sowing.

Emulate this timing by sowing some of these hardy seeds in the fall. If they fail to survive, plant some more in March. Regardless of when they are planted, if a crop once survives to seed-scattering maturity, the chances are it will never be necessary to replant the same varieties again. Thinning may be necessary, or removing the seedlings that pop up in unwanted spots, but pulling out the undesirables is as simple as weeding.

Generally speaking, the behavior of these cool-weather plants varies widely from season to season depending on the temperatures and the rainfall. Last December the weather was balmy and warm on several days throughout the month. There was also a five-inch snowfall. On one of the warm days I sowed cornflower seeds over a bed of daffodils. By February, they were three to four inches high and growing very well.

In February there were also self-sown seedlings of last summer's cleome and sweet alyssum coming up here and there in the garden beds. Following the warmest January in twenty-four years, they were not unexpected. Subsequent freezing spells killed the lot, but there were more later to take their place, germinating at the correct time for survival.

To summarize, be prepared for all sorts of behavior when you work with cool-weather self-seeding annuals. By all means learn to identify the seedlings of each variety; use and enjoy them. They are nature's free gift to the gardener.

Flower Gardening in February

The begonia and geranium cuttings made in early January and put in water to root responded well, and by mid-February three-fourths of the number had a full component of roots and were ready for transplanting into potting soil for further growth.

The transplanting stage is most critical for both begonias and geraniums. The stems are tender, succulent, and full of water. At this point they are highly susceptible to root rot. One measure of extra sand should be added to the potting soil for rapid drainage, and watering should be done as sparingly as possible until new top growth signals that all is well at the root level.

House Plants Need Help in February

By February many house plants have had too much of indoor conditions and they look it. A few are so poorly, in fact, that they may not survive. Their chances for survival can be increased by some extra care at this time. Examine each plant patiently and remove dead or dying leaves and stems to allow more air and light to penetrate to the healthy remaining parts. Long, leggy growth should be removed as a pruning measure. Stocky, compact plants can be kept that way only by periodic pinching of the terminal buds from the tallest branches. Use these for cuttings, if desired.

Last year's begonias from which my January cuttings were taken have produced lush new growth. What a fine addition they will make to my hanging baskets come May.

On 15 February I fed all the potted plants with a water-soluble fertilizer made especially for house plants. This feeding will be repeated at three-week intervals until time to put them outdoors.

The pet dwarf orange tree mentioned earlier developed a severe infestation of spider mites before I realized it. On a sixty-degree day, it was taken outside, washed with the hose, dried thoroughly by sun and air, sprayed top and bottom, and brought indoors before sundown. This should hold it until summer.

And the Weeding Goes On

Chickweed, henbit, dock, wild onion (a black-sheep member of the *Allium* family), and other weeds can take over a garden in February if left alone. A few minutes of regular weeding off and on will keep them under control. Pick a pleasant time of the day, get a low stool, basket, and weeding tools, and sit down to work at a leisurely pace. It is a perfect time for some long, lazy thoughts about unimportant things. While you work you may hear some sounds long unheard drifting by on the wind. A dove mourns sweetly in the distance, or your friendly neighborhood chickadee may light on a limb above your head to ask what you are up to now. I guess I really like weeding.

Pruning Done in February
(More pruning will follow in March, and April, and May, and June)

Nandina: Removed tall canes only.

Mahonia: Removed tall canes only.

Boxwood: Removed winter-damaged branches; top-thinned heaviest specimens and cut back long branches of American and Korean boxwoods to maintain a loosely rounded shape.

Japanese Maple: Thinned out a portion of the twiggy top growth to allow better air and light penetration.

Rose (climbers and hybrid teas): Removed only dead canes killed by winter weather; heavy pruning must wait until the last of March for the hybrid teas, late June for climbers.

Ligustrum Hedge: Cut back long branches to one-half their length to induce greater compactness.

Azalea: Removed dead and broken branches only.

Crape Myrtle: Removed some surplus side growth and cut back top branches lightly.

Althea: This plant is trained as an espalier against a brick wall; all branches that confused the formal fan pattern were removed.

Fertilizing Done in February

Pansies: The fall-planted pansies make their greatest growth from February to 1 May. To get the best floral showing, I fed each plant a heaping tablespoonful of 8-8-8 fertilizer on 1 February. (They were already in bloom and had bloomed intermittently since the new year.)

Evergreen Shrubbery: My evergreens were not as lustrous green as I would like, so all received a portion of cottonseed meal in addition to 8-8-8 fertilizer this month.

Deciduous Shrubbery: All received an application of 8-8-8 according to their size.

Small Trees: Surface fed with 8-8-8 fertilizer.

Large Trees: My Faithful Helper bored holes with the electric auger for feeding our five large trees; amounts of 8-8-8 fertilizer distributed according to size.

Bedding Plants: All perennials, ground covers, and vines received their first feeding of the year; 8-8-8 was used.

Lawn: Fescue (*Festuca*) lawn fed with 8-8-8. (Fescue variety: Kentucky 31)

Summary of Garden Activities for February

1. Planted in outdoor beds the seeds of lettuce, endive, and garden peas

2. Planted indoors in egg cartons the seeds of cabbage, broccoli, lettuce, endive, Drummond phlox, and calendula

3. Transplanted rooted begonias and geraniums from water to small clay pots

4. Groomed, sprayed, pruned, and fed house plants

5. Weeded garden

6. Pruned evergreens

7. Fertilized all shrubbery, trees, bulbs, bedding plants, and lawn

Flowers of February

Camellia, candytuft, crocus, daffodil, flowering quince, forsythia, pansy, saucer magnolia, snowdrop, Sweet-Breath-of-Spring, star magnolia, winter jasmine

March

It must be part of a master plan that the flow of spring sap in the plant world coincides with a complementary flow of energy in the gardener. A majority of my gardening springs have been blessed with a generous portion of this miraculous adrenalin. This year was no exception. In early March, I was also endowed with an equal measure of good intentions, but I failed to get everything done in spite of them. The "undones" must wait for April.

Vegetable Gardening in March

More Seeds of Cool-Weather Vegetables: Beets, turnips, and onion sets were planted outside during the warm weather of early March, and they all germinated within a week. (In cooler temperatures, we had eighty degrees plus that week, the time would have been longer.)

Transplanted to Outdoor Beds: The small four-to-six-leaved seedling cabbage and broccoli plants sown to indoor peat pots in February were transplanted outside.

Provided Daily Watering: During the first ten days of March the following were watered daily: freshly sown seeds of beets, turnips, and onions; newly transplanted cabbage and broccoli plants; small lettuce and endive plants sown outside in February.

Daily waterings are usually unnecessary at this time of the year. This March, however, the weather was clear and rainless for ten days, and the temperatures were in the eighties. Under such conditions all small plants and seedlings yet unestablished require additional watering. A few hours of drying out can destroy the time and labor of several weeks. Weather is always the arbiter of gardening, and the successful gardener must be in tune at all times with weather conditions. Beds of established plants such as pansies and bulbs should also have some extra water during such periods of unusual warmth and dryness, but they would not require daily watering.

Planted Seeds of First Warm-Weather Vegetables

At mid-March seeds of tomato, cucumber, squash, and bell pepper were planted, two to four seeds per peat pot, to be started indoors. (Without the help of the window greenhouse, the planting of these seeds would have been postponed until 1 April.) In the even temperatures of the utility room all the seedlings germinated in five days except the peppers, which are always slow to sprout.

As soon as the seeds had germinated, I moved them to a sunny window in a cooler room to slow their growth rate. Seedlings grown too fast are never as stocky and strong as they need to be for survival. Each day the tray that held the seedlings was turned around to force the plants to grow in a vertical rather than a leaning pattern. On sunless days, I made room in the window greenhouse for the tray in order to insure uniform progress.

Watering was done as sparingly as possible throughout the first two weeks of growth, as too much moisture may cause molds or rots to develop.

No day passed without two or three inspections of these seedlings. Only a passing glance is needed, and it may be the difference between failure and success during this critical period.

If This Is Too Much Trouble

If the care of small plants which I have described above seems too much trouble, you may want to join the people who bought small tomato plants at the local garden stores about the same time I planted my tomato seeds. When I commented to a salesman about the doubtful wisdom of planting greenhouse-grown tomato plants outside in March, he replied quite frankly, "Yes, it is much too early, and I keep saying so, but they buy them anyway. No doubt I will be able to sell them replacements later on." He did. There were three heavy frosts in April.

A Year in My Garden

Flower Gardening in March

Fed House Plants: It may seem paradoxical to feed house plants and at the same time pinch back the tips of the new growth, but I did it.

Warmer spring weather brought on rapid new growth so that the plants needed extra food. With at least six more weeks before outside planting time, continuous pinching was in order to prevent weak and leggy growth. As is my custom, some of the longer prunings were put into water glasses to root, a part of the continuing process of maintaining ample garden supplies throughout the season.

Fed the Pansies: Several heavy rains and one snow have fallen since the pansies had their February feeding. To sustain them during this period of rapid growth and flowering, I fed them moderately with a side dressing of 8-8-8 fertilizer, taking care to hose off any accidental residues from the leaves immediately after feeding. (Past records indicate that I usually feed pansies lightly as often as three or four times from February to May.)

Cut the Tops of Liriope and Christmas Ferns: It is important that the old leaves of liriope and Christmas ferns be removed in early March (or late February) to make room for the new year's growth. Since the new liriope leaves and fern fronds are beginning to grow by March, a delay in the cutting may injure the new growth. Liriope leaves are tough and leathery, and the best tool I have found for their cutting is a pair of scissors that has been retired from sewing duties.

Added Some New Shrubbery: Five late-flowering azaleas were planted as replacements for the poorest existing specimens of some of the early-flowering Kurumes on the premises. One Gumpo, two Kaempferis, one Macrantha, and a Glen Dale hybrid may help to insure some azalea flowers in spite of the late frosts of spring.

Other shrubs added were several dwarf yaupon hollies to serve as a low hedge; six roses, including the climber Golden Showers, a photinia (for its coppery pink new leaves in the spring), and a couple of dogwood sprouts donated by a neighbor.

Indoor Seeds Planted: Seeds of the Christmas pepper were planted at the same time to share the tray and treatment of the tomatoes, squash, cucumbers, and bell pepper seeds. The ornamental pepper requires a long growing season, but its glowing red fruits are featured in my fall garden along with dwarf chrysanthemums in my favorite autumnal colors of gold and crimson. As frost dates approach in the fall, a few of the best Christmas pepper specimens can be potted for use indoors until well after the Yule holidays.

Planted Outdoors (late March) Seedlings: Calendula and Drummond phlox that had been started indoors in February in peat pots were planted outdoors.

Divided Some Perennials: Spring phlox, ajuga, hosta, and liriope were mainstays in my former shady garden. They have done so well in my new, mainly sunny garden that I divided some of my old clumps in March and filled some of the areas in need of replenishing. These are truly versatile perennials, and any list of my plant favorites would surely include this foursome.

Removed Faded Blooms from Daffodils and Other Bulbs: The removal of these spent blossoms serves a two-fold purpose. First, it directs the plant energy that would be spent in the formation of seeds to the formation of next year's bloom, which is developing in the bulb underground. Secondly, the removal of the faded flower improves the looks of the garden.

A word of warning at this point. The foliage of the bulb must be left intact until it can be lifted easily from the bulb. Where growing conditions are good, this time is from May to early July. It is the one disadvantage of bulb culture. Brown, ripening bulb foliage is no asset to any garden, but many growers feel that bulb blooms are worth this period of unsightliness. This problem can be mitigated somewhat by sowing fast-growing, cool-season annuals (Drummond phlox, poppies, etc.) among the bulbs for cover during the ripening of the bulb leaves. It is my own practice to use bulbs in the background areas of the garden and among shrubs where they are relatively unobtrusive during their ugly-duckling days.

I suppose I should comment at this point that faded pansy blooms should also be removed to prolong their flowering. Indeed they should, but I plant these flowers by the hundreds in my garden, and the task of keeping the dead blooms removed would be monumental. I don't do it, and I am happy enough with the performance of my pansies. After all, I don't plant them to last all summer as I have other uses in mind for the spaces they occupy.

The Bugs That Grow in March

Another little-noted but important consequence of the unseasonably high temperatures of January and early March came to my attention during a routine garden inspection in late March. The boxwood leaf miners and the holly leaf miners were growing rapidly, and an earlier hatching of these pests than usual seemed certain unless cold weather returned and remained for the duration of the early spring season. These two leaf miners are among the most damaging enemies of the American boxwood and the American holly tree. English boxwoods are less susceptible to miners although I have occasionally seen infestations on the English boxwood.

How to Identify Leaf Miners

The boxwood and the holly miners are not identical although they have a number of common characteristics and control methods are the same. Miners spend a great part of their life-span of a year in fattening themselves on the plant juices of their helpless hosts, safely hidden between the upper and lower layers of the leaf surface.

Inside their leafy fortresses, miners are invisible and impregnable. No surface sprays can reach them, but a sharp-eyed gardener can detect their presence by the tiny brownish ridges and bumps on the boxwood leaves and by the discolored blotches and serpentine tunnels or trails on the leaves of they holly. With the thumbnail break the leaf and lift the top layer of leaf tissue from the bottom layer. The boxwood miner larvae (worms) are bright yellow and no larger than a coarse hair, but they were wiggly and full of pep in late March. A holly leaf can be opened the same way, but the larva of the holly miner is brown, bug-shaped, and lethargic.

Following a sufficient amount of warm weather, both the boxwood and the holly leaf miners will break through the leaf tissues and emerge as gnat-sized flies. The box miner fly has bright orange wings, and I have seen them swarming around boxwoods, busily laying the eggs for another crop. The holly miner fly is dark brown and is less conspicuous at the flying stage of its life.

Control Methods

For years the accepted control method has been the application of such insecticides as DDT, Lindane, Malathion, Isotox, and others. If these are applied at the proper time, they are effective. However, since the hatching period depends on the weather, it is difficult for the average gardener to know exactly the best spraying date. And often, when the timing is accurate, a hard rain will fall immediately after the spray is applied and most of the repellent benefits are washed down the drain.

Try Systemic Insecticide

For several years there has been available a granular systemic insecticide that I think does a much better job than any of the usual sprays. It is applied to the surface of the soil around the root system and watered into a solution. The chemicals are absorbed by the roots and carried to every leaf on the plant. When the leaf miner gets a snootful of this potion, that is all.

Three years ago I recommended the use of systemic insecticide to a Winston-Salem gardener whose extensive collection of American boxwoods was dying from years of unchecked miner infestation. Recently I saw the boxwoods again, once more luxuriant and beautiful. I have had equally good results with systemics on the holly leaf miner, the columbine leaf miner, and the iris borer.

As a matter of fact, systemic granules are recommended by the manufacturers for control of a wide range of chewing and sucking insects. However, it is a highly toxic substance and very expensive, and I personally limit my use of it to the four insects listed above.

Late February and early March are best for application to holly and boxwood; early April for iris and columbine. Be extra careful to use it exactly as instructed on the container label.

An Ounce of Prevention

One of the most valuable preventive sprays for many common insect pests is a dormant and growing-season oil spray that should be applied in February or March when the growing season for both plants and pests is just beginning.

Many ornamentals (roses, evergreens, and deciduous trees and shrubs) as well as fruit trees provide winter quarters for a multitude of harmful insects. An oil spray properly timed can break the life cycle of the pests. Apply with a hose applicator when temperatures for twenty-four hours are between forty and seventy-five degrees. Scales, whiteflies, mealybugs, mites, aphids, etc., have a distinct aversion to an oil spray. It is both safe and easy to apply.

Beware the Ides of March

After all that balmy weather of early March, we had our comeuppance. Temperatures fell to twenty-six degrees on three consecutive nights: 12 March, 13 March, and 14 March.

Now and then I grow a little weary of our crystal-ball weather forecaster who feels that the only bad weather is the kind in which he can't play golf. At forty minutes to midnight he pipes up cheerfully to say, "It's going to freeze tonight, folks. Be sure to protect your tender vegetation." If only I could! With a whole hillside of azaleas showing color, there is little that can be done to protect the flowers.

For light frosts at thirty degrees, covering is quite beneficial, but at twenty-six degrees, it is freezing cold in or out of the covers. One of the local experts suggested burning lights under the covers. I decided he must be joking. If so, it wasn't very funny. What really hurts is to see azaleas cold-blighted for the third consecutive spring. At my age I am running out of springs.

It is surely as good a time as any to suggest that the gardeners in this area, where spring is a sometime thing until early May, should plant azaleas that bloom later in the season than some of those we are now using. The first azaleas introduced into this area were the Kurume types, early spring bloomers that flourish farther south with such well-known names as Snow, Coral Bell, Hinodegiri, Hino-Crimson, Pink Pearl, and others. Many Carolinians think there are no other kinds and are still planting them by the thousands every spring. With average weather, these Kurumes usually bloom the first two weeks in April. The unseasonably warm weather of this spring had my Kurumes showing color when the cold blasted them on 12 March.

Bearing in mind that our average late frost date in this region is around 20 April, it is no wonder that we seldom get a decent showing from these early-bird azaleas. There are a number of equally beautiful later-blooming azalea varieties that could be used in place of the early varieties, and as I mentioned earlier, I am changing to the later ones as fast as I can afford it.

There is also a wide range of color and flower forms among the later-blooming groups of Kaempferi hybrids, Satsuki hybrids, Macranthas, and Glen Dale hybrids. Visit your local nurseries when some of these varieties are in bloom and select the ones that please you most. It would certainly relieve much of the anxiety we suffer at this time of the year.

Gardeners often worry unnecessarily about the welfare of some other hardier garden subjects during early spring cold snaps. Pansy blooms are damaged by frost and low temperatures, but the plants are not, and new, fresh blooms will soon replace the cold-damaged ones. Daffodil and snowdrop blossoms were unhurt by the twenty-six-degree weather, but the remaining blooms of the star and saucer magnolias were demolished. However, we had already enjoyed most of their blooms during the first warm days of March. New tender growth on flowering crab apple, weigela, and kerria was burned, but later growth quickly covered the burned portions. Small cabbage, broccoli, calendula, and phlox plants set outside earlier came through with flying colors.

Summary of Garden Activities for March

1. Planted *outside* seeds of beet and turnip, and onion sets

2. Transplanted *outside* small plants of broccoli, cabbage, calendula, and Drummond phlox

3. Planted *inside* seeds of tomato, cucumber, squash, and pepper

4. Fed house plants and pansies; made additional begonia and geranium cuttings

5. Pruned liriope and Christmas fern; cleaned dead wood from magnolia and hybrid tea roses

6. Planted dogwood, holly, photinia, roses, and clematis

7. Divided perennials: ajuga, liriope, hosta, and spring phlox

8. Mourned the cold-damaged blooms of the early azaleas; planted some later-flowering varieties

9. Removed faded blossoms of daffodils and snowdrops

10. Applied systemic insecticide to holly trees, boxwoods, and iris

11. Applied Volck oil spray to evergreens, deciduous shrubs, trees, and roses

Flowers of March

Apple, candytuft, Carolina jessamine, cherry, Dutch iris, flowering almond, forsythia, glory-of-the-snow, honesty, hyacinth, pansy, pear, pieris, primrose, scilla, snowdrop, spring phlox, Virginia bluebell

April

The April flower garden is apt to have its full quota of surprises. Plants that I had forgotten about planting pop up, and, of course, nature does quite a bit of gardening on her own, showing a distinct preference for the best-prepared beds. Volunteer seedlings of dogwood, phlox, violet, and the Virginia bluebell came up all over, and the pink trillium flowered after a two-year abstinence.

A rare old bulb, known hereabouts as the hoop-petticoat daffodil (*Narcissus bulbocodium*), finally bloomed, although a little late, to remind me of the cherished gardening friend who shared this and other plants, as well as her extensive garden lore, with unstinting generosity for all her lifetime. Few Greensboro gardens are without at least one memorial from the garden of Salene Chrismon.

A camellia from my old garden, which I had given up for lost, spunkily sent forth a few tentative buds to test its new environment. Perhaps it will yet survive. Under the brown-leaf mulch, a couple of the bedding begonias survived from last summer. The winter wasn't as cold as I thought, but April is too early to uncover the tender green shoots. But enough of April euphoria; it takes more than adjectives and memories to keep a garden growing.

The Spring Rose Clinic

On 1 April the roses received their spring checkup. I had planned it for 25 March, but on that day we had a five-inch snowfall. It melted immediately, and as far as I could tell did no more damage than a benign spring shower. In spite of the poor drainage endemic to this lot, all the roses survived the winter. I feel confident that planting them three or four inches above ground level must take the credit. With lower planting levels, many had died the previous winter, drowned, no doubt.

Pruning is always based on the vigor of the individual; strong growers with several canes were cut most severely, with the weaker plants having only the dead and diseased wood removed and the tops pinched off of the remaining canes. Tree paint was then applied to all the cuts the size of a large nail or larger. This protection helps to prevent the destructive rose borer from entering the center of the freshly cut stems, and it is a good idea to apply it throughout the season when roses are cut for the house or pruning is done for the late summer blooms.

Fertilizing and spraying ended the rose clinic for April. I hasten to add that roses should be sprayed earlier than the first of April. Aphids, blackspot, and mildew—three of the rose's worst enemies—begin to affect the plant as early as the first of March. Spraying programs should begin at that time.

Flower Exodus
from the Window Greenhouse

The begonias, geraniums, ferns, wandering Jew, and other plants that had wintered in the window greenhouse were hastily removed on 1 April when the temperature inside reached ninety-five degrees. (Outside temperature was eighty-five degrees.) Knowing that there would be more frost, these plants were placed with the cuttings, seedlings, and plants that had been coming and going in the garage since 1 March. Naturally, one of the cars had to "rough it" outside for the duration. I can't think how one gardens without a sunny southern-exposed garage. Sure enough, on 9 April our yo-yo weather dropped to twenty-eight degrees, a record low for the date, but everything in the garage survived.

Annual Flower Seed
for the Summer Garden

Without a greenhouse or cold frame, 1–15 April is really soon enough to plant indoors the seeds of fast-growing annuals such as zinnia, aster, marigold, scarlet sage, and the like. And, when I am too busy to plant these seeds by the middle of April, I just wait another two weeks and plant them outside in the beds where they are to grow. Considering the unsettled nature of our early spring weather, the blooming time for both methods will be about the same.

Growing Your Own

Many gardeners prefer to buy already grown plants from the nurseries and gardening centers. For me, it is a matter of pride as well as economy to grow my own. Some of us still have this heritage of self-reliance, and it is a part of ourselves well worth passing on to younger gardeners. Any one, regardless of generation, who has missed the excitement of watching a seedling breaking from the brown bondage of the seed shell, or a cutting making roots as a separate and independent plant, has not known the full reward gardening can offer.

The savings made possible by growing one's own plants are by no means inconsiderable, and if I were to buy ready-grown all the plants I use in a year of gardening, I would be obliged to curtail my gardening more than I would like.

Still another advantage of growing your own has to do with convenience. Where pansies and spring bulbs comprise a big portion of the spring bedding plants, they usually must occupy the bed space until mid or late May. By this date, many of the choicest summer annuals have already been sold out at gardening centers. Growing your own plants insures against this contingency and permits growing the varieties that are most interesting.

During the spring of 1974 I recorded the plants produced in my window greenhouse and elsewhere on the premises. The numbers are correct and my estimate of their value conservative.

Window greenhouse:	40 early vegetable plants	$10.00
	35 geraniums	35.00
	25 begonias	18.00
	3 large hanging baskets	30.00
Annuals planted outside:	50 (flowers)	10.00
	25 (late vegetables)	5.00
3 rooted rosebushes		10.00
	Total value	$118.00

My total figure does not include the divisions made of existing hostas, day lilies, liriope, ajuga, and other perennials already in the garden, nor the dozens of volunteer seedlings of annual vinca, cleome, and impatiens that were used to fill any gaps.

April Flower Addenda

Peony: By mid-April the peonies are twelve to fifteen inches tall; staking should be done at this stage to protect the developing flower from weather damage later on. For those who exhibit peonies, remove all side buds as soon as they appear and retain only the central terminal bud.

Easter Lily (Lilium candidum): Plant gift Easter lilies outside in a sunny, well-drained spot as soon as they have faded and frost danger is over. Lift from the pots with the dirt ball intact and plant to a depth of six to eight inches. These fragrant white lilies will grow, multiply, and bloom for many more springs—but not again at Easter. Once outside, they resume their normal time schedule.

Gladiolus, Dahlia, and Canna: April and May are planting times for these plants, whether purchased new or stored from last year's garden. Gladioli are excellent cut flowers but poor garden subjects; their blooms are short-lived in the garden and their foliage is scanty and rather awkward. If space is available, relegate them to a cutting garden. Several plantings can be made at biweekly intervals until July to supply a succession of flowers.

The large-flowered dahlia requires more growing space than is usually available in the small garden. However, the dwarf single-flowered forms are more satisfactory in bedding areas than zinnias. They flower over a longer period, the colors are varied and beautiful, and they are less subject to mildew. Dahlias of all types are readily grown from seeds started in the spring. After the first growing season in the garden, their tuberous roots may be dug in the fall and stored for future use.

Cannas, especially some of the older varieties, survive the winters in all but the coldest Carolina gardens. Old ones may be divided and new ones planted in April or May. Elephant's-ear (*Colocasia antiquorum*) is also planted in late April and May.

Chrysanthemum: By mid or late April new growth develops at the base of old chrysanthemums that grew in the garden the previous year. As soon as the new shoots are three or four inches high, lift the entire clump, remove the new sprouts, reset in improved soil, and discard the remains of the old plant. When new mum varieties are wanted, small plants may be had from gardening centers by April or earlier. New plants (or divisions of old plants) may be planted as late as mid-June. It is well to remember that in this area mums may be had for early, midseason, or late flowering. Avoid the latter since frost usually blackens the flowers just as they are opening.

Over the years I have grown many chrysanthemums from seeds. Sow them in early March or April and treat them as you would any other annual seeds. They are as easy, but not as fast, to grow as zinnias. The Korean mixture of chrysanthemum seeds contains an exciting range of colors, but they require considerable growing space. Other types of mums such as decoratives, spiders, anemones, and spoons may also be seed-grown.

For limited space, the cushion is perhaps the most suitable chrysanthemum form, although there is considerable variance in the size of the cushions, some being quite tall. Among my favorites are the Masterpiece cushion mums, an introduction from a nursery firm in Ohio. Several from this group begin to bloom by 1 July and continue until frost. The color range is excellent and the forms varied. A white button variety called Baby Tears is as diminutive and dainty as its name implies. It is one of the regulars in my summer garden.

So many new chrysanthemums are offered each year that it is often quite difficult to find a particular named variety. To be sure that I have Baby Tears and other favorites each year, I protect the old plants through the winter and make subdivisions from them in the spring.

A Year in My Garden [81]

(*A chrysanthemum footnote:* Cloud Nine, a recent new addition to the Masterpiece line of chrysanthemums, performed brilliantly on its first trials in my garden. The ivory white, incurved blooms were four to five inches across without disbudding. The plants were bushy, dark green, and about one and a half feet tall. The flowers opened early in the fall and lasted for weeks thereafter. One trial, of course, is insufficient to judge winter hardiness, or to guarantee its future performance, but on the first time around it was for me, in every way, the most magnificent chrysanthemum that it has been my good fortune to grow.)

April Vegetable Gardening Chores

As previously noted, the window greenhouse, emptied hastily of its winter occupants by the unseasonably high temperatures of 1 April, did not remain vacant. The flourishing peat-pot-sown seedlings of tomato, cucumber, squash, and pepper planted in March were transplanted to four-inch clay pots and placed in the window greenhouse to take full advantage of the extra warmth and light available there. It was a good move; three weeks later the squash plants were blooming, the tomatoes twelve inches tall, and the cucumbers were fanning about hunting for a place to climb.

This was on 21 April, still too early in this area to plant tender vegetables or flowers in the open garden, but I decided to take a chance. Sure enough, on the subsequent dates of 24 and 25 April we had heavy frosts.

Emergency Measures

By twilight of both nights the garden looked like a Gypsy enclave. Old bedspreads, folding chairs, baskets, burlap bags, and paper sacks covered most of the hill as I attempted to protect the tender vegetables just planted, the blooms of strawberries, and grapevines, the tender young growth of the Irish potatoes, and several geraniums that had been planted earlier. All survived.

At this point I would comment that Irish potatoes must surely be the tenderest of all the cool-weather vegetables. During April their fresh green tops were damaged three times on frosty nights. Yet, thanks perhaps to the four-inch layer of mulch heaped around each plant, the frost-bitten surface growth was quickly replaced from below each time, and I harvested a fine crop in June.

Trouble with the Broccoli

The frost of early April nipped the broccoli a little as well, but no permanent damage resulted. A far more injurious and quite unexpected damage was sustained from a flock of vitamin-hungry sparrows. Fully half the leaf surface was devoured before I figured out what was going on. A heavy spraying of Sevin dust made the leaves less attractive, and the plants finally recovered to produce fine large heads followed by many juicy lateral heads of edible size.

April Cutworms and the Tomatoes

Since many tomato plants are planted in late April, perhaps this is a good time to call attention to a prevalent enemy of young tomato plants, the cutworm. This pallid, unattractive grub lurks near the surface of the ground in spring (and later) and has been known to fell an entire row of tomatoes in a single night. Most often this damage is fatal, although I have had a few plants to survive and grow from lateral buds that had been left at ground level in the planting.

A simple protective collar can be devised by removing the bottom from a quart-sized food container of cardboard, plastic, or metal. Slip this collar over the tomato plant, pressing the bottom an inch or two into the soil. Since cutworms work only at the surface, this simple method is quite effective. The collar can be removed fifteen days or so later, although I often leave mine and use them as funnels for watering during dry weather.

[82] *Carolina Home Gardener*

April Weeding

By the end of April, the final load of topsoil distributed about the premises in late winter was beginning to divulge its true character. Cockleburs, ragweed, and nut grass were sprouting by the legion. Only a Pollyanna would say that she was thankful to have these instead of Johnson or Bermuda (or wire) grass, but I agree with her.

A question I receive frequently is where to get good topsoil. There is very little left and only a fool would part with it. Any topsoil that is relatively free of clay chunks, rocks, roots, and noxious weeds will usually mix with various forms of organic matter to make a good growing medium with the addition of fertilizer. The color has little to do with the quality of the soil; porous, friable red dirt is equally as good as most of the so-called "rich" dark soil so popular with the layman.

Always discuss the soil quality with your prospective dealer before he delivers it, and go to have a look at it beforehand when possible. Request porous, relatively clean soil, and buy it with the understanding that the load may be refused unless it is of reasonable quality.

Make it clear that an absence of Bermuda, Johnson grass, and chrysanthemum weed is also a criterion of acceptable soil. If you inadvertently get one or more of these plant pests in your topsoil, fall on each piece that rears its ugly head and ferret out every root fragment. Unless you do, you may as well start looking for another garden elsewhere.

A Confession Is Made about My Vegetable Garden

Although I have had a good deal to say over the preceding pages on the subject of growing vegetables, I think it is time to confess that I do not have a vegetable garden, at least not in the conventional sense of the term. Until I moved this last time, I had always had a vegetable garden, and I had firmly expected to have another at my new house, a neat secluded little area with rows as straight as dies and partitioned subdivisions for herbs, asparagus, and strawberries. In fact, a plot 50' × 30' was carefully set aside for this purpose on the plot plan of the property.

But alas for some of my best-laid schemes—it turned out that most of the surplus water from the two lots above passed through this spot. To slow down the speed of the rainwater and to save the rest of the lot from erosion, my prospective garden plot became a part of the permanent lawn.

Unwilling to make any radical changes or sacrifices in the layout of the ornamental garden, I decided to do whatever I could to integrate flowers and vegetables in the same areas without damaging the appearance of the ornamental garden. Instead of the neat rows of vegetables I had visualized, individual plants of tomato, squash, pepper, eggplant, and cucumber are placed here and there among the flowers. Since only a few vegetable plants of these varieties are needed to fill the needs of my family of three, their presence in no way detracts; in fact, most observers do not see them at all until they are pointed out.

Since my entire backyard is fence-enclosed, maximum use is made of vertical spaces. Pole snap beans and climbing limas cover sections of fencing, as well as cucumbers (which delight to climb), garden peas, "espaliered" tomatoes, dwarf fruit trees, and grapevines. These food plants contribute greenery, varied foliages, and some color in their season.

The Sun-Trap Garden

I am especially proud of an area that I call the sun-trap garden. This mini-garden is a 2' × 20' strip of land that lies between the west wall of the house and the driveway. In the summer the unshaded west wall would fry an egg save for the problem of gravity. In the winter the area is totally frost-free and the ground temperatures warm. What this narrow strip of land produces is nothing short of fantastic. Something for the table grows there the year around, camouflaged from public view by a clump of shrubs and flowers at the front corner of the house.

Last summer, for example, pole lima beans climbed a neat, nearly invisible poultry-wire trellis to a height of ten feet. They grew so lustily that several prunings were needed throughout the summer to keep the vines from obstructing the roof ventilator. This thick, leafy wall cover shaded the kitchen, holding temperatures to a more comfortable level without the constant use of the air conditioning. From it we had ample lima beans for the table and twelve pints extra for the freezer. The final fillips this mini-garden provided were the unbelieving faces of the neighbors when they saw me picking beans from the top of a step-ladder.

By the middle of September the spent lima vines came down, and the wire trellis was stored in neat cylinders for next year. The land was reworked with additional compost and fertilizer, and the seeds of Chinese cabbage, lettuce, and onion (sets) were planted for harvesting through January.

In mid-February, following another cultivation and replenishing of compost and plant food, seeds of more lettuce and endive were planted for the spring salad makings.

By May, we were back where we started: the planting of more lima beans.

A Year's Production Record

From this sun-trap garden and all the odd spots planted throughout the premises, I kept last year's record of what was canned, pickled, and frozen from the produce grown on the lot.

- 29 pints string beans
- 7 pints squash
- 13 pints cucumber pickles
- 65 pints tomatoes
- 12 pints lima beans
- 12 pints field peas
- 7 pints bell peppers

Total 145 pints

No record was kept of what was consumed from day to day and given away.

Getting the Most from Limited Space

Getting the maximum yield from a limited space depends on the quality of the soil preparation, faithful feeding, watering and spraying, and a knowledge of crop continuity. Individual spots for tomato, pepper, squash, etc., must be dug deeply and filled with a loamy mixture of friable topsoil, compost, and fertilizer. The quality of the prepared soil should be much akin to potting soil. Fertilizer should be applied lightly at approximately three-week intervals, or oftener if heavy rains intervene.

The spraying that must be done for certain vegetables will not harm the flowers. On the contrary, it is often quite beneficial. Because of the frequent spraying required for the roses, no vegetables are grown in their vicinity. Systemic insecticides are omitted entirely during vegetable-growing season and are, in fact, never used in areas where any residues might eventually wash down to vegetable plots. If all the instructions provided by the manufacturer of garden sprays are followed faithfully, there is little likelihood of danger in growing food and flowers in proximity to each other.

Crop Continuity

Which crops should follow other crops is a knowledge best gained through experience. My own crops vary each year to some degree as I try out new vegetables and discard a few old ones. I have kept a sample continuity record to serve as a starter. After two or three seasons, you will be able to devise a succession of crops to suit yourself.

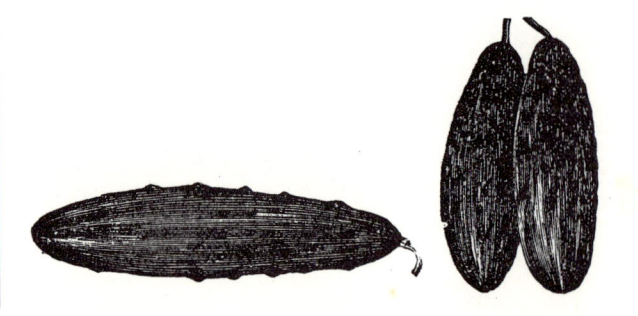

Crop Continuity

Area	Crop	Date Planted
1	Garden peas and onions (sets)	20 Feb.
	Followed by:	
	Sweet pepper (plants)	10 May
	Eggplant (plants)	15 May
2	Turnip (seeds) and broccoli (plants)	3 Mar.
	Followed by:	
	Pole lima and bush lima beans (seeds)	15 May
3	Cabbage and broccoli (plants) Beet (seeds)	1 Mar.
	Followed by:	
	Okra and Swiss chard (seeds)	4 May
	Collard (plants)	14 Aug.
4	Squash and cucumber (plants)	21 Apr.
	Followed by:	
	Okra (plants) and snap beans (seeds)	1 July
	Melon (seeds)	10 June

Area	Crop	Date Planted
5	Garden peas (seeds)	1 Mar.
	Followed by:	
	Pole snap beans (seeds)	11 May
6	Salad greens (seeds)	1 Mar.
	and Irish potatoes (divisions)	15 Mar.
	Followed by:	
	Melons (seeds)	10 June
7	Lettuce, endive, corn, salad greens (seeds)	15 Feb.
	Followed by:	
	Pole lima beans (seeds)	11 May
	Followed by:	
	Onion (sets), lettuce, Chinese cabbage (seeds)	15 Sept.
8	Tomato (plants)*	21 Apr.
	Field peas (seeds)*	11 May

NOTE: In mountain areas, delay spring planting two weeks; plant two weeks earlier in the fall. In the eastern coastal section, plant two weeks earlier in the spring and delay fall planting by two weeks.

*Although tomatoes and field peas were the only crops planted in area no. 8, early crops such as lettuce, garden peas, greens, or onions could have occupied the same spaces if they had been needed.

Summary of Gardening Activities for April

1. Transplanted peat-pot seedlings to four-inch clay pots of tomato, cucumber, squash, and pepper, and placed them in window greenhouse for the additional heat and sun available there

2. Put geranium, begonia, fern, etc., from the window greenhouse in the open garage for a hardening period

3. Became impatient with the weather and planted tomato, cucumber, squash, pepper, and some of the geraniums outside in late April

4. Subsequently covered these and other tender vegetation on three separate nights from frost; all came through safely except the early azalea blooms; not bad for the season

5. Weeded!

6. Pruned, painted stems, fed, sprayed, and mulched the rose garden

7. Divided and replanted divisions of liriope, day lily, ajuga, hosta, and chrysanthemum. Added some new trial chrysanthemum plants

8. Staked the peonies and planted my Easter lily gift outside

9. Planted stored dahlias and gladioli corms

10. Enjoyed to the fullest the unfolding of spring

Flowers of April

Ajuga, azalea, blue phlox, candytuft, Carolina jessamine, clematis, crab apple, daffodil, dianthus, dogwood, honesty, iris, kerria, lupine, pansy, primula, redbud, scilla, spiderwort, trillium, viburnum mariesi, Virginia bluebell

A Year in My Garden [85]

May

May marks the beginning of summer weather in this area, and from the hosts of flowers and vegetables that require warmer temperatures to complete their growth cycles, the gardener can select the plants of most appeal.

Summer-Flowering Annuals

From records of annuals grown in my garden over the years, I have chosen the following favorites. Both seeds and small plants of these varieties can be planted safely outside by the month of May.

Warm-Weather Annuals:
(*Small seeds; should be started in containers.
**Self-seeding varieties.)
Ageratum, amaranthus (*Amaranthus bicolor*), aster, begonia*, Browallia, castor bean, celosia** coreopsis (*Coreopsis lanceolata*), cosmos (*Cosmos bipinnatus*), flowering tobacco (*Nicotiana alata*)**, four o'clock (*Mirabilis jalapa*)**, gourd impatiens**, love-in-a-mist (*Nigella damascena*)**, marigold, morning glory (*Ipomoea purpurea*), nasturtium, petunia*, portulaca**, scarlet sage, snow-on-the-mountain (*Euphorbia marginata*)**, stock (*Matthiola incana*), strawflower (*Helichrysum bracteatum*), summer cypress (*Kochia scoparia*), thunbergia (*Thunbergia alata*), vinca (*Vinca rosea*)**, zinnia

For the Beginner

From the varieties listed above, an easy threesome for the novice might be castor beans, zinnias, and marigolds. The seeds of all three are relatively large in size and can be easily grown when planted in soils of average quality directly to the outside bed where they are to grow.

May and the Hanging Basket

May is also the month to bring out the hanging baskets that are now enjoying another turn in a long history of popularity. Current books and magazines are rife with information about container growing, including the hanging-basket varieties. However, for the gardener who has bedding room to grow in, hanging baskets are only a grace note to the major garden theme.

How Many Are Enough?

It is possible to overdo this garden accessory, and the number that may be used effectively depends on the space, the existing structures, and garden accessories. Understandably, apartment dwellers and others with limited growing areas should make free use of hanging and container gardening generally. The constant care these plants demand in this artificial environment will doubtless keep their numbers within the limits of good taste.

Types of Baskets

There are many styles of hanging containers available, from the costly, finely detailed ceramics to the flimsiest plastics. My own favorite type is a sturdy wire variety painted dark green and lined with burlap, sphagnum, or the lovely green mosses from the woods. Such a container is too discreet to overpower the floral contents, plants thrive acceptably therein, and the basket can be reused in future seasons. Plastic containers are at the bottom of my list.

What to Grow in a Basket

Plant selections for baskets depend to a large degree on the amount of sunshine they will receive. In the sunniest spots such plants as sedum, cactus, and certain succulents do very well. For half-and-half exposures, ivy-leaved geranium (*Pelargonium peltatum*), petunia, and such annuals as lobelia (*Lobelia erinus*), thunbergia, nasturtium, marigold, Browallia, and the annual vinca bloom satisfactorily, but they are so short-lived that it is well to keep some spares waiting in the wings to serve as replacements. Where exposures are shady to partly shady, many types of begonia, coleus, impatiens, fern, variegated vinca (a green and white form of *Vinca major*), wandering Jew, fuschia, hosta, liriope, and ivy will grow with colorful profusion.

In fact, any plant that sprawls or crawls a bit is a potential candidate for a hanging basket, and it is stimulating to try new and different plants as subjects. Personally, I like well-filled baskets made of a combination of plants suited to the exposure. Some thought should be given to achieving interesting combinations of foliage and flower sizes, shapes and textures. After all, a hanging basket is a flower arrangement and as such is subject to the same elements and principles.

Caring for the Hanging Basket

During the clear summer days I find that my hanging baskets must be watered daily. This excessive amount of water leaches the fertilizer from the soil so rapidly that it is necessary to apply new fertilizer every ten days. Water-soluble plant food such as that used for other potted plants is used according to the strengths suggested on the container. A layer of sphagnum or wood moss placed as a mulch on the top of the container helps some with water conservation.

By frost time in October the baskets are emptied; the ferns, hostas, and other perennial plants stored in soil for wintering; and the baskets are saved for another year. Considering the extra dimensions one can achieve through the proper choice, planting, and placement of hanging baskets, they are, like roses, worth all the trouble.

May in My Flower Garden

Flowers in bloom in May were numerous and varied. Robust perennials such as the iris, peony, and lupine created a voluptuous and lavish effect unsurpassed at any other season. Several of the late-flowering Gumpo azaleas in pink and white added their own special charms, the roses bloomed well, and the flowers of the hybrid clematis were the largest I ever had.

I was also especially happy with the performance of the calendulas and Drummond phlox that I had started from seeds back in February. The yellow and gold calendulas were taller than I had remembered, growing to a height of more than two feet. Except for their airy lightness such height might have been out of place in the garden foreground where I had planted them. With their faded flowers kept cut, the calendulas and phlox were in bloom through May, June, and July.

Alas for the Pansies: By the middle of May the pansies were spent, leggy, and weary from continous blooming since January, and I pulled them out without regrets. Replacements for the foreground areas they had occupied were some test dwarf snapdragons sent for trials, geraniums and bedding begonias that had over-wintered indoors (including those rooted in January), divisions from several favorite chrysanthemums that survived the winter outdoors, and several new dianthus plants called Persian Carpet.

Planning for Late Summer: May is my favorite month to make the soft or greenwood cuttings of bedding begonia, geranium, coleus, dianthus, impatiens, and candytuft. Regardless of the current supply of these plants on hand, extra ones are always needed before the summer ends. A few stems of the first growth made in early spring were put in clay pots of sharp sand, three or four stems from each variety, watered, and set in a shaded, protected spot outside. I water as sparingly during the rooting process as possible to avoid decay of the succulent stems most summer cuttings have at this season. No covering is used for these cuttings for the same reason.

Rose Cuttings: The month of May is also the best time to make rosebush cuttings, although they may be made anytime throughout the summer. There are legal restrictions against propagating patented roses, but for those no longer covered by the patent rights, propagation by cuttings is simple and easy.

Rose cuttings may be made from the stems of the first rose blossoms of the spring. Cut a stem ten to twelve inches long and discard the terminal three or four inches. From this point, rose cuttings are handled in precisely the same manner as the azalea and other evergreen cuttings described elsewhere, with the following exception: by late summer, if the rose cutting shows vigorous top growth, the fast-growing rose may be transplanted to a permanent site in the garden. It is not unusual for a rose cutting made in May to have blooms on it by frost. It is a good idea to stake a home-rooted rose for the first year until firm root anchorage is achieved.

A Year in My Garden [87]

Fertilizing in May: Garden plants, both flower and vegetable, grow lustily in May and June, using up their food as fast as a growing boy. During early May I fed all the bedding plants and vegetables on the premises. Azaleas developed a yellowish cast to their leaves, usually the sign of a depletion of their iron supply, which happens as a result of their rapid spring growth. A foliar spray of iron chelate applied with the hose gun was the cure.

Grooming in May: The greater the flower show one has in spring, the more the cleaning up that follows. Faded blooms of candytuft, lupine, peony, calendula, and clematis required removal every other day. I also cut the seed stems from the blue spring phlox and Virginia bluebells and scattered them among the shrubs and bedding areas where they will self-seed for another year. They are both most obliging in this respect. By late May the leaves of the daffodils were brown and unsightly, but their hold was too strong for safe removal. Where they stood in foreground areas of the garden, I folded the leaves in a clump and tied them loosely. It helped somewhat.

Pruning in May: All the evergreens grew prodigiously throughout May, and although they had received their heavy annual pruning earlier in the spring, I made the rounds pinching off the tip-ends of the subsequent new growth of the Chinese and Japanese hollies, camellias, azaleas, photinias, ligustrums, osmanthus, and the rest. Such tip-end pinching will be a continuous, summer-long process but so easily done that no tool is needed other than a resolute thumb and forefinger.

A Problem with Mildew: The wetness of early spring set the stage for a severe case of mildew on the roses. The Phaltan spraying failed to stop it so I consulted with local members of the American Rose Society about the problem. They suggested a white powder called Benlate, which finally checked the trouble. Mildew is uncommonly stubborn, and I allowed it to get a foothold by not beginning my spraying program by the first of March. At the first signs of it in your own garden, consult your county agent or local members of the American Rose Society—or any neighbor who grows good roses.

The Summer Vegetable Garden

A goodly number of gardeners of my acquaintance bypass the cool seasons entirely and wait for the warm summer weather of May to plant their one and only vegetable crop.

For these, as well as the more provident gardener who also plants a cool-weather crop, there are plenty of summer vegetables from which to chose. The list below contains my favorites.

Warm-Weather Vegetables, Outdoor Planting Dates 1 May to 15 May:
Corn*, cucumber*, eggplant, field pea, lima bean*, melon, okra, pepper (sweet or hot), snap bean*, Swiss chard*, squash*, tomato*

*Later plantings may be made at intervals for continuous harvesting.

NOTE: For additional vegetables and planting dates, request a copy of George R. Hughes, *Garden Manual,* Agricultural Extension Service Publication no. 122 (Raleigh, N.C.: Agricultural Extension Service, 1973).

Test Plantings: For a first effort, try the seeds of tomato, cucumber, and string bean, all of which may be planted directly in the beds where they are to grow by the first of May.

Four healthy tomato plants will supply a family of four with some left over. I usually plant six, however, to allow for providential losses. By all means use only wilt-resistant varieties. Allow five or six feet of space for each plant. If your tomatoes don't fill it, your soil was not properly prepared.

Many gardeners are surprised when I suggest planting tomato seeds directly outdoors. Perhaps it will reassure you to know that commercial growers plant acres of tomatoes in this manner, and, in your own garden, you may have plenty of volunteer seedlings to grow without any help from you after one crop has matured and dropped some seeds. (Ready-grown plants are, of course, standard gardening-center items.)

Three cucumber vines will supply plentiful amounts if fed and watered properly. According to last year's records, I grew fifty pounds of cucumbers from three hills (mounds of soil) and finally stopped counting before the harvest ended.

A twelve- to fifteen-foot row of string beans is enough for a family of four unless it is one of the family's favorite dishes. Pole beans properly framed will yield far more than bush beans.

May in My Vegetable Garden

Seed Planting: Seeds of beet, Swiss chard, watermelon, cantaloupe, and okra were planted in my garden in early May. The okra seeds had a twenty-four-hour soaking period before planting to loosen their tough seed coats. In mid-May second crops of squash, cucumber, tomato, and lettuce were planted. I tried a new idea with the lettuce. Instead of planting them in beds, I sowed wide-topped clay pots thickly with Bibb lettuce seeds. They grew quickly in strong indirect light and off the ground safely away from cutworms and other denizens of the underworld. Harvested as needed, the pots supplied tender, crisp lettuce leaves of excellent flavor until the first of August. Apartment dwellers please take note.

The early May okra planting failed to fare so well. The seed germinated well enough, but snails ate every vestige of green as fast as it grew, and my metaldehyde baits didn't faze them. I planted seeds three separate times, and finally, in a fit of frustration, I sowed okra in peat pots and raised them up to six-inch stalwarts before putting them in the ground. It worked, too, but the okra was a month late reaching the table.

Seeds of pole, snap, and lima beans and my favorite crowder peas were delayed in planting until nearly mid-May because of wet and cold weather. These four varieties germinate very poorly under such conditions, and I waited until the temperatures were a bit more favorable. By that time it was dry and warm, and extra watering was in order.

Special Vegetable Chores: All tomato plants had a pair of stout stakes in place by mid-May, and weekly tying was needed to keep the fast-growing branches in place. All vegetable crops also received a side dressing of 8-8-8 fertilizer during May.

Meanwhile—in the Kitchen: A harvest of cool-weather crops brightened the menus. We had cabbages (one head weighed five pounds), broccoli, beets, onions, lettuce, turnips, squash, new potatoes, garden peas, and strawberries. Everyone should plant an early garden!

Summary of Garden Activities for May

1. Planted and installed eleven hanging containers on terrace, garden walls, and under grape arbor

2. Removed faded blossoms regularly following the prolific flower crop of May

3. Removed pansies and replaced with summer annuals, being careful to leave some space for the self-seeding vincas and impatiens already up and growing in May

4. Made cuttings of roses and bedding plants for late summer replacements

5. Fed roses, bedding plants, and vegetables; applied iron chelate to azaleas

6. Tip-pruned all evergreen shrubbery making rapid new growth

7. Battled mildew (on roses) and slugs (on okra)

8. Planted Swiss chard, okra, melons, and second crops of beets, squash, cucumbers, tomatoes, and lettuce

9. Staked tomatoes

10. Harvested broccoli, beets, onions, lettuce, turnips, squash, new Irish potatoes, garden peas, and strawberries

Flowers of May

Atamasco lily, begonia, Boston daisy, calendula, clematis, cornflower, day lily, Deutzia, dianthus, Drummond phlox, evening primrose, foam flower, geranium, iris, late azalea, loosestrife, lupine, marigold, pansy, peony, petunia, rhododendron, rose, snapdragon, spring phlox, summer phlox, trillium

June

When the volunteer seedlings from last year's crop of cleomes, impatiens, and annual vincas pop out all over the place, I know that summertime has come. Actually, a few seedlings of these plants germinate in warmish spots from April on, but they are only harbingers for the hordes that grow in June. Over the years I have come to depend more and more on these "freebies" for color supplements to the summer garden. All three varieties are self-cleaning as well as self-starting, requiring little of the constant grooming needed to keep roses, geraniums, dahlias, and the like in flowering condition. With a minimum of care cleomes, impatiens, and vincas bloom from summer to frost.

A Year in My Garden [89]

Cleome (Spider Flower)

Cleomes provide a tall, airy background flower, growing in moderately fertile soil, to a height of five feet or more with proportionately horizontal branching. The leaves are large, deeply lobed, and lovely; the flowers are delicate and orchidlike.

Cleomes are available in colors of pink, rose, purple, yellow, and pure white. For background effects, I prefer the pink or the pure white, which are available under the varietal names Pink Queen and Helen Campbell respectively. For the sake of maintaining pure color as long as possible, I plant only one color and pull out any seedlings of poor color as soon as they show. Cleomes transplant easily and can be shifted anytime from where they are in surplus to where they are needed.

There are some disadvantages connected with this flower, as one might anticipate. The plant is somewhat coarse in effect if too many are allowed to grow; they have a slightly unpleasant odor; and they will take over the entire garden unless diligent removal of the surplus is practiced.

Impatiens (Patience or Sultana)

Impatiens has been a summer standard in shady and partly shady gardens as long as I can remember. The plant scientists have had a field day with this plant. The results are available in the seed catalogs and nursery centers today. There are dwarf, medium, and tall impatiens; variegated colors; a range of solid colors with every hue of the rainbow; and even a new yellow, aptly named Tangerine. Flower forms vary, too, from single to fully double flowers that resemble an open rose. After a few years of free and easy cross-breeding in the garden, there will be all sizes and a veritable rainbow of pastels, and here and there a pure white one to enhance the deeper colors.

Although impatiens, unlike cleomes and vincas, prefers some shade, I have noted that it tolerates as much as four hours of sunshine quite well, especially if the soil is well prepared and water is generously supplied. Like the cleome and vinca, impatiens transplants readily, and I have shifted large plants in full bloom quite successfully by providing some shade for a few days to allow new roots to grow.

Vinca (Annual Periwinkle)

Beginning gardeners are surprised to learn that there is an annual periwinkle that is quite unlike the more familiar perennial ground-cover periwinkle that is evergreen and produces rather inconspicuous blue or white flowers in early spring.

The annual vincas are excitingly different, especially the white-flowered varieties. In fact, I may be somewhat prejudiced against the pink, rose, and red flowering vincas; to me they appear faded and washed out compared to the cool, pristine quality of the white. I am especially partial to an all-white variety called Little Blanche and another white with a rose center listed by the trade as Little Bright Eyes. Producing, as they regularly do, hosts of large flowers nested in a wealth of lustrous green foliage, they are as refreshing as a tall cool drink on a hot afternoon. Masses of these white vincas are used in the foreground areas of my summer garden, and although they are a little later coming into flower as volunteer seedlings than the cleome and the impatiens, they are worth the slight delay.

To get a start of vincas in your own garden, it might be better to buy the first half dozen plants or so from a commercial source. Seeds of vinca, unlike cleome and impatiens, are a little more difficult for the beginner, and with a few plants you can start the self-seeding cycle with less trouble.

Other Self-Seeding Annuals

In addition to cleome, impatiens, and vinca, there are several more self-seeding annuals of garden value. Among these are flowering tobacco, noted for its many colors and surpassingly sweet fragrance, the cool green and white snow-on-the-mountain, four o'clock, nigella (so delicate of foliage and unusual in flower form), and the gay and colorful portulaca. The self-seeding plants from this second group, as well as the cleome, impatiens, and vinca, produce satisfactory flowers for several seasons from volunteer plants. (The double portulaca reseeds as single-flowered blossoms, but the singles are more attractive than the doubles.)

Although I have limited my discussion to a few of those that I consider the most valuable warm-weather self-seeding annuals, many other additional annuals will reseed under proper growing conditions. This characteristic is not an unmixed blessing. Certain highly hybridized annuals such as the petunia, marigold, zinnia, and celosia, for example, produce markedly inferior volunteer seedlings both in form and color. These varieties should be grown from fresh, commercially produced seeds each year, and their subsequent progeny should be discarded along with the crabgrass.

Two Self-Seeding Perennials for the Summer Garden

The self-sown annual seedlings of cleome, impatiens, and vinca are the main augmenters of my summer garden, but I also value highly the contributions of two perennials that also self-seed satisfactorily. These are the native rudbeckia, affectionately known as the black-eyed Susan, and the hardy begonia.

Black-eyed Susan: There are several rudbeckias, both wild and domesticated, but I have found none so appealing as the piquant black-eyed Susan. They may be seen in many rural areas growing on the margins of fields and along the roadsides throughout the Carolinas. Just one seedpod from the wilds, broken up and scattered in the garden, can put you in business for life with the black-eyed Susan. Small plants must have a year of growth before reaching flowering size, and they can be transplanted wherever they are wanted.

Plants in my garden grow to a height of four feet, and the charm and gaiety of the hundreds of yellow flowers with their black shoe-button eyes dancing on their sturdy stems elicit many admiring comments from my garden visitors.

Winter-Hardy Begonia (Begonia Evansiana): The perennial begonia is surely the aristocrat of the whole self-seeding colony. It is, as far as I know, the only begonia we have that can consistently survive our outdoor winters, grow again from the old bulb or corm left in the ground, and renew itself with seeds, powder-fine, scattered by the winds. Best adapted to the shady garden, these plants will begin to appear in warmish spots as early as April and be large enough to begin to bloom in late June. They flower until frost. Growing to a height of two feet or more, they produce bold and handsome leaves with deeply crimson undersides. The flowers are airy and a true begonia pink.

Humusy, uniformly moist soils are best suited to the needs of the begonia. Where it is lacking, the plant may have some difficulty getting established. Where these growing conditions prevail, one planting will insure a continuous supply for years to come with ample surplus to divide with other gardeners.

My garden practice is to plant begonias among the foreground azaleas in combination with the Virginia bluebell. The bluebells are also self-seeding. They bloom very early in the spring, and the tops soon turn yellow and disappear, leaving the space for the coming of the begonias that have been there all the while. Together they are a truly happy and congenial garden twosome.

June in My Flower Garden

Beetle-Bother: To be sure, it was not cause for celebration, but the first Japanese beetle of the season was sighted in my garden on 11 June. For six weeks thereafter I waged continuous warfare against what proved to be the heaviest infestation I have seen in the ten or fifteen years since the first appearance of this pest in our region. My most unobservant neighbors even noted the presence of, and damage from, the hordes of metallic green beetles, and no wonder. During the ten-day peak period of their activities, the air above and the grass below buzzed with swarms darting about in all directions.

Favorite Beetle Fare: For the uninitiated, the Japanese beetles do not eat everything, but their tastes are too diversified for the comfort of the gardener. Among their first preferences are the blooms and leaves of the rose; if roses are unavailable, they will dine on the althea, hollyhock, hibiscus, flowering almond, crab apple, clematis, certain azaleas, Japanese holly, maple, willow oak, sycamore, dahlia, crape myrtle, petunia, and more.

I would also like to add at this point that, in spite of the claims from some quarters that the geranium and the marigold are beetle deterrents, the beetles apparently had not been told, for they ate those flowers too. It is entirely possible that I drove them to it; I sprayed everything else—and finally sprayed geraniums and marigolds as well. By late July the main beetle crop had had its day, but a few lingered on throughout August and into the month of September.

What to Do: An insecticide called Sevin, which may be applied as a powder or spray, is the best and safest control method I have found for the Japanese beetle. The 50 percent wettable powder form applied as a spray lasts for several days unless there are rains that wash it off. A dash of dishwashing detergent will add to the tenure of the spray.

Incidentally, I am pleased to have finally a word of praise for the raucous blue jays and starlings. They came, along with a pair of brown towhees, to help with my beetle problem. The larger jays and starlings gulped the scratchy beetles down one-to-a-bite fashion, but the smaller towhees needed to peck the beetles into smaller bits before they could eat them. I can never recall having seen this bird behavior before.

In the rose garden the Japanese beetle shows a distinct preference for the yellow, white, or cream-colored roses. It would be interesting to know whether this is because these lighter colors are more visible or whether they are chosen for their flavor.

June's Brighter Side: By June the garden was brilliant with the fresh, vivid beauty of bedding begonias and geraniums rooted in January, and the volunteer seedlings of cleome, impatiens, annual vinca, and sweet alyssum. In addition, the two perennial self-seeders, the black-eyed Susan and the hardy begonia, were also up and beginning to show color. Perhaps if everything grows well these plants will smother the crabgrass that makes its own move by June.

Care for the Chrysanthemums: The last batch of rooted chrysanthemums that arrived late were planted in early June. Those planted in April had their tips pinched for the second or third time, depending on their rate of growth. Most cushion chrysanthemums are self-branching and require little if any tip-pruning. Taller varieties, however, require three pinchings from April to 1 July at growth intervals of five or six inches. Unless this is done, a straggly, thin plant will result. At the same time the pinching is done, apply a light side dressing of a balanced fertilizer (8-8-8 will do). Water copiously throughout the growing season.

Final Feeding for Trees and Shrubs: During the last week of June, I gave the trees and shrubs their final feeding for the year. In general all the evergreens maintained a luxuriously dark green through their main growing season this year. I am confident that the cottonseed meal applied in conjunction with the 8-8-8 fertilizer in February is responsible. The azaleas, however, required additional iron chelate throughout the summer to maintain a healthful green.

June among the Vegetables

Summer vegetable crops as well as flowers have their full share of preying insects that eat and multiply their kind to the maximum during the summer months. Beans, grapevines, fruit trees, and other food plants received equal time with the flowers from the Japanese beetles. Thanks to Sevin, which I used on vegetables as well as flowers, I was able to hold the damages to a minimum. The beetle invasion was not the end of the insect story, however. Ground-dwelling insects, flying insects, and even the birds attacked the okra, beans, gourds, and peas.

When plantings are as limited in size as mine, such invasions cannot be tolerated. Having experienced the same problems before, I brought out my accumulation of nylon nets, discarded window screens, and poultry-wire guards to discourage the birds. Some Snarol and chlordane helped with the ground worms and slugs, and the Sevin saved us from the assortment of flying insects. Discouraging as it may seem, all concentrated in a paragraph or two, we still had a good crop.

Watering in June: By June the rainy weather of early spring has usually ended, and the droughts of summer are just around the corner. This June was no exception. To reduce the cost and labor of constant watering, I applied double or triple layers of newspapers to the surface around tomatoes, cucumbers, peppers, eggplants, bean rows, and wherever I could squeeze them in. On top of the papers I placed a layer of ground leaves and a light sprinkling of pine needles for anchorage and newsprint camouflage. Black polyethylene is also excellent for this purpose, but the newspapers I already had. These ground-covering mulches reduce weeding, as well as watering, and provide some beneficial organic matter for the soil. I highly recommend this practice.

Summary of Garden Activities for June

1. Battled Japanese beetles, other insects, and birds for possession of flowers and vegetables; I won, but not entirely

2. Planted the last of the chrysanthemums; fed, watered, and tip-pruned the chrysanthemums planted in April and May

3. Fertilized trees and shrubbery for the last time this year

4. Applied additional iron chelate sprays to azaleas to restore and maintain their green color

5. Mulched with layers of newspapers around shrubs, tomatoes, and wherever possible to save both watering and weeding

6. Did some extra watering in late June

Flowers of June

Begonia, calendula, canna, chrysanthemum, clematis, cleome, crinum, day lily, dianthus, Drummond phlox, fairy lily, geranium, globe thistle, gloriosa daisy (*Rudbeckia hirta*), green-and-gold, hosta, impatiens, iris, late azalea (Gumpos and Macranthas), loosestrife, petunia, rose, snapdragon, spiderwort, summer phlox, sweet alyssum, turk's-cap lily, vinca (annual), zephyr lily (*Zephyranthes candida*)

July

Making Evergreen Cuttings

When an exact duplicate of the parent evergreen is wanted for the garden, the least costly way for the home gardener to get it is to make cuttings during the months of July and August. This is the season of the year when the twigs of such favorites as azalea, camellia, pieris, holly, and other evergreens are at the best stage of their development for rooting purposes.

Cuttings Supplies

What the beginner needs for making cuttings are a container, growing medium, a properly made cutting, a clear plastic bag or sheet large enough to make a tent over the container, and a frame or support for the plastic cover.

The container can be anything that will hold from three to six inches of rooting medium. For short cuttings such as those of boxwood or azalea, three inches of rooting medium is enough; for longer cuttings such as those of the camellia or rose, six inches will be needed. For a few cuttings, a clay pot of the proper depth is excellent, but seed flats, plastic containers, or cheese hoops are satisfactory.

A Year in My Garden [93]

Recipes for growing media are equally varied, but I have found that sharp sand of the type used in construction work is hard to beat. If desired, a little peat moss or compost can be combined with the sand to retain moisture. Other gardeners prefer vermiculite or light mixtures of potting soil.

Polyethylene bread wrappers, dry-cleaning bags, or plastic bought by the yard may be used to cover the cuttings. (And in case you wonder why the cuttings are so covered, it is to maintain the necessary humidity throughout the period of rooting, and to eliminate the need for most of the additional watering after the cuttings are made.)

Cuttings from azalea, camellia, holly, boxwood, and other broad-leaved evergreens should be of the wood that grew in the early spring. By July this wood is light brown in color as compared to the dark brown of old wood or the light green of the summer growth. Another helpful guide to selecting the proper wood maturity is to discard the willowy, tip-end portion of the branch and use the section that produces a sharp, snappy sound when the branch is broken.

Cutting Length

The length of the cutting depends on the growth characteristics of the parent shrub. Azalea cuttings are usually two to three inches long; camellias twice as long. Remove the leaves from the lower half of the cutting, dip the tip in a rooting hormone if you have one on hand, and insert the cutting in the rooting medium to the full length of the defoliated section. Firm the medium around the cutting and water thoroughly.

Put in cuttings sparsely enough so that they do not touch one another. Insert into the edges of the rooting medium the sticks or crossing wires that are to support the tent of plastic. Pull the plastic around and over the supporting frame and tie down securely with a string below the rim of the pot. With a sharp knife make a few slits at intervals in the plastic to allow a little ventilation.

Place the cuttings where the light is good but where no direct sunshine can penetrate. You can forget about them for four to six weeks when it will be time to check on the moisture conditions and the progress of the cuttings.

Rooting time varies considerably. Boxwoods, aucubas, and roses root rapidly as a general rule, but root formation on azaleas, camellias, hollies, etc., is erratic—or at least has proved to be so in my experience. In the past I have left azaleas and camellias in the rooting medium until spring, being careful to store them in a semiprotected place during the winter. (A "semiprotected place" might be a coldframe, sunny garage interior, or a hole in the ground covered with a discarded window or plastic sheet.) Where special rooting benches with controlled heat and misting are used, rooting is rapid and more reliable, but for the average amateur gardener the methods I have described above usually produce the plants needed.

July Weather

It can be said of our weather that it is as consistently fickle in summer as it is in the winter or spring.

To keep the record intact, a record high of ninety-seven degrees occurred on 2 July, followed by a record low of fifty-four degrees three weeks later. Throughout the month rainfall was conspicuous for its absence, with the monthly total falling well below 50 percent of the normal. Obviously such weather places quite a strain on both garden and gardener, yet experience has taught the wisdom of delaying the watering as long as possible, since once begun, it must be continued until the drought is broken.

During this year's hot, dry July, I arose very early and attended to the most pressing needs of the garden. By ten o'clock I was inside again for the rest of the day, resisting as much as I could the urge to look out on the silent suffering of my garden. After ten days of hoping for rain, watering became a matter of necessity. Everything needed water, but because of the cost of city water and the labor required to apply it, some plants received first preference.

In my garden the grass is always last on the watering list; my thought is that grass can be rejuvenated or replaced more quickly and inexpensively than trees, shrubbery, and flowers. Vegetables, too, have only a short season of growth and fruitfulness, and if they go unwatered the efforts already expended on their behalf are wasted.

"There's a Hole in the Bucket!"

Some thought should be given as to the best ways to apply the water. Trees and large shrubbery require slow, lengthy watering to achieve the necessary depth of water penetration. To save some of the time involved in this type of watering, three five-gallon paint buckets were salvaged from a construction dumping pile in the neighborhood. One hole, about the size of a pencil, was punched near the edge of each of the bucket bottoms, and the three were placed in a ring as close as possible to the tree trunks and shrubs. The buckets were quickly filled with the hose and left to soak slowly to the roots of each plant. Not a drop was lost, and while the seeping process went on, other garden activities could be pursued.

Watering the Roses and Other Plants

The rose garden received its water through a soil-soaking, perforated aluminum pipe. This ground-level watering device keeps the foliage dry and helps retard the spread of blackspot and mildew to which the roses are so susceptible in this region.

Bedding plants, small shrubs, and vegetables received their water from revolving overhead sprinklers.

Hanging baskets were watered daily and other plants on a biweekly schedule. (In normal temperatures, once weekly is sufficient.) Watering can be done in early morning or late afternoon; early morning watering allows foliage to dry before nightfall which is a deterrent to fungus infections. Water applied in the late afternoon is slower to evaporate, thus extending the effectiveness of the water applied. With so much to water, I usually watered both early and late.

Checking Mulches

Extra pine straw around each rosebush helped retain the moisture in the rose garden. Where folded newspapers had been used as mulch around shrubs and vegetables earlier in the summer, I found the soil more arid than I liked, and to save the need for additional watering, I replaced the papers that had served so well in normal rainfall with strips of black polyethylene from a roll bought from one of the gardening stores. When the strips were in place, I used a pitchfork to pierce a few holes here and there on the surface to permit water to penetrate, and covered the entire area with chopped leaves and pine needles.

Several times during the drought period I checked beneath the plastic and found the ground soft and moist each time. With polyethylene, the water cannot escape. As the moisture rises to the surface, condensation takes place on the bottom side of the plastic, and the moisture droplets fall back into the earth. When winter comes and extra moisture is not needed, the strips of plastic can be taken up for storage and reused in the next dry season.

The Beetles Liked It Hot

The Japanese beetles were even more plentiful in July than they had been in June. My one small consolation was that during the absence of rainfall the Sevin insecticide dustings lasted for days. I was cheered, too, to observe another plus for my favorite bedding begonias. The beetles shunned them completely. To thwart them still further, I cut all the buds off the roses as soon as they showed color. Although Sevin and other sprays can protect the rose foliage, I have never found anything that deters the Japanese beetle from an opening rose. During those hot, dry days I steadfastly kept in mind that by early September, when the roses made their fall showing, all the beetles would be gone for another year.

Add Summer Predators

Still other summer freeloaders enjoyed the fecundity of my ripening crops. Stem borers finally finished off the early squash and cucumber vines. I didn't really mind since we had eaten, frozen, and pickled our fill of both of these vegetables. However, with the cucumbers and squash gone, the borers moved directly to the ornamental gourd vines on a nearby fence and continued to eat.

A baby rabbit, about fist-sized, appeared in the garden in early June and resisted all efforts to evict him. Inside our snug garden fence was everything his growing appetite could wish, and our family poodle was in mortal fear of him. So, the rabbit grew fat, amiable, and confident, frisking up and down the walkways with all the grace of a small elephant. By late August we had become at least a little tolerant of him, although he ate the spring phlox down to ground level and nibbled constantly at the melon vines. We tried inviting stray dogs in and made several attempts to flush him out through one of the gates, but he foiled every try. Traps baited with all the bunny delicacies we could imagine were offered, but to no avail. If we don't get him out by pansy-planting time, there will be big trouble.

I had better luck with the birds and the ripening Concord grapes. With yards of black nylon netting, I completely enveloped the vine—or so I thought. One day I came home to find a fledgling robin caught inside and most anxious to be on his way. It took some careful handling to release him unharmed, but I managed, only to be thanked in furious bird talk from a nearby tree for at least five minutes.

Counting the Tolls of the Drought

In the last week of July following the record low temperature, there were several days of delightful weather in the high seventies, and I had the opportunity to assess fully the results of the recent heat and drought. The lima beans growing on the west wall of the house, as well as the snap beans on the garden fence, had turned yellow and dropped leaves, flowers, and fruits—their crops ended for the year. Both melons and cucumbers failed to set fruits during this period, and the blooms dropped in large numbers from my second crop of string beans. Peas, tomatoes, peppers, eggplants, okra, and chard fared better but were damaged a little. It was obvious that in spite of my faithful watering it was not the same as the manna of heavenly raindrops.

The Flower Garden in July

Because of the debilitating heat and drought through most of early July, the routine work of maintaining the flower garden fell miserably behind, awaiting a break in the weather. When the break finally arrived, I caught up with the chores.

Pruning and Related Tasks: The roses received a rather severe pruning, which is routine at this time of the year, in an effort to discourage the Japanese beetles a little and to encourage the new growth required for a good crop of fall roses. Spraying and feeding followed the pruning.

Tall branches of begonia, geranium, coleus, vinca, and cleome were pinched back to prolong their flowering. Pinched and fertilized the tall chrysanthemums for the last time this season. Pruned oldest growth from the hanging baskets to extend their flowering until frost; replaced three baskets of ivy-leaved geranium with three containing petunias to permit the geraniums to recuperate from prolonged flowering and the glare of the summer sun. Mulched the soil surface in the fresh petunia baskets with sphagnum moss to conserve moisture. Pruned, still another time, the tips of the continuing growth on all the evergreens.

During the long growing season typical of gardens in the Carolinas, these repeated light prunings should be made at growth intervals rather than by time intervals. By removing the tip-end of a stem at intervals of three or four inches, the maximum bushy growth can be achieved without wasting any of the vertical growth.

Removed faded blossom stalks from day lily, hosta, globe thistle, loosestrife, dianthus, snapdragon, and the summer phlox. These spent stalks are removed to save the energy that would be consumed in setting unwanted seeds as well as to encourage secondary flowering for many of the varieties listed. In all cases such removal is a part of the good grooming required to maintain a presentable garden.

Planting: Six well-rooted rose cuttings made in May were transplanted from their starting sand pots to a well-prepared, humusy site in the open garden. Because of the sun's intensity, these were shaded with tree branches for the first ten days after transplanting. All came through, but winter lies between July and the first rose of next spring, so let's not brag too soon.

Made cuttings of a favorite white azalea, Fielder's white, and the new delicate pink Gumpo added to this year's garden. Made cuttings of a special geranium, an impatiens that bloomed in an interestingly variegated pattern, and more coleus and dianthus. (Incidentally, by late July seedlings were up in multitudes around the new dianthus plants called Persian Carpet. I will nurture these for next summer's use and save the trouble of buying and sowing new seeds.)

Planted seeds of annual asters and marigolds, just in case they might be needed in the late fall garden, which I cherish as much as any other season of the year.

Transplanted some extra volunteer seedlings of cleome, vinca, and impatiens from where they were in surplus to fill the vacancies that always seem to occur even in the best-managed gardens. Potted some dwarf cushion mums to replace the spent geraniums in the front stoop planter.

Scattered the ripened seeds of white honesty among the areas in the middle ground of the garden beds where the smaller azaleas grow. The white honesty grows to a height of thirty inches, has handsome large heart-shaped green leaves throughout the winter, and tops its performance with great trusses of pure white flowers very early in the spring when a tallish plant is much needed in the garden. It self-seeds very well, and the silvery seed pods that remain after the seeds are removed make a charming winter bouquet.

Every gardener should have honesty—but only the white variety (*Lunaria alba*). The purple or magenta variety is a less attractive member of the family.

Staking: Tall-growing plants must have anchorage against wind and driving rains, and they should be staked before they grow too large. During late July and August, I staked and tied plants of dahlia, gladiolus, chrysanthemum, and summer phlox.

Feeding: Fertilized lightly with 8-8-8 formula all bedding plants and vegetables.

Miscellaneous: Weeded entire garden, both flowers and vegetables. Removed, at long last, the remaining daffodil and Dutch iris leaves. Noted with satisfaction the continuing flowering of the Drummond phlox and calendula, which began to bloom in early spring. Regular removal of faded flowers and occasional extra food and water can almost double the length of the flowering time of some of our bedding plants.

Admired many times the magnificent cotton-candy pink crape myrtle called Near East. In fact, the size and weight of its flower trusses may be a fault of this variety. They are so heavy after a rain that the branches are near the breaking point. Thinning potential flowering wood may be necessary when the plant gets older and larger.

And for the Vegetables, These July Chores

Some of my tomatoes reached a height of seven feet by July, and there was also too much weight, so I pruned two to three feet from the tops and thinned the remaining branches. (This growth was the result of the bushels of chopped leaves mixed with soil and fertilizer that I had applied. Two tomato plants would have amply supplied my table.)

Weeded all vegetable plantings and staked the fast-growing eggplants and peppers.

Put protective netting around ripening grapes to keep the birds from harvesting my efforts.

Fed lightly, with a side dressing of 8-8-8, plants of melons, late beans, peppers, eggplants, and cucumbers.

Discarded spent vines of squash and early snap beans and replaced them with okra started in peat pots. Made two cuttings of tomatoes to root for a chance at some very late tomatoes, although healthy summer vines, such as mine were in July, will frequently bear tomatoes until frost.

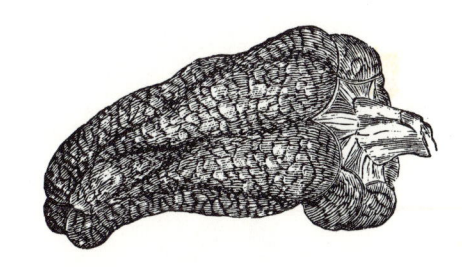

A Year in My Garden [97]

Summary of Garden Activities for July

1. Watered, watered, and watered
2. Replenished and replaced mulches
3. Fought Japanese beetles and other predators
4. Assessed the costs of the drought
5. Caught up with neglected chores

Flowers of July

Althea, begonia (annual and perennial), black-eyed Susan, Boston daisy, calendula, canna, chrysanthemum (Baby Tears), clematis, cleome, crinum, crape myrtle, dahlia, geranium, gladiolus, globe thistle, gloriosa daisy, gourd, hardy amaryllis, hibiscus, hosta, impatiens, liriope, loosestrife, marigold, nasturtium, phlox (annual and perennial), plumbago, rose, sweet alyssum, turk's-cap lily, vinca, zephyranthes

August

Years ago, when I was a farm child, our family anticipated with eagerness a special time of the year that came in late July and August. It was called "laying-by" time, and it marked the end of months of hard work in the planting and cultivating of the corn and cotton that were our main crops. It was the closest thing to a vacation that the average farm family of that era ever had, and it was close enough. We had time, at last, for family visiting back and forth and opportunities to enjoy fully the plenty of our vegetable gardens, freshly made apple cider, and luscious honey-dripping watermelons. While the younguns celebrated this rare leisure with horseplay and shouts of laughter, our elders indulged themselves in a relaxed evaluation of the year's crops, prospects for the fall harvest, and plans for another season.

My life on the farm ended in my midteens, but memories of those early days return unbidden each August, and when my inner time clock says, "This is 'laying-by' season," I slow down, eat too much of the fresh vegetables I so dearly love, and take stock of the successes and failures of my own small version of the summer's labors on the farm.

Looking Back at the Flowers

Roses: In spite of the hordes of Japanese beetles and a prolonged bout with mildews, my roses performed brilliantly this year. Faithful care, by way of feeding, watering, and better-than-usual spraying, triggered continuous vegetative growth, which in turn provided the energy required for flowering. By late August all signs pointed to a good crop of fall roses to last until frost. Remembering all the problems of poor soil and drainage encountered in my rose garden, I am filled with the satisfaction that comes from solving a problem. It is, I think, a pardonable pride.

A Word for Polyantha and Floribunda: No one admires the classical form of the hybrid tea rose more than I do, but there are two other not-so-well-known members of the rose family which are less demanding and which I use and enjoy in a special way in my own garden. These are a charming polyantha called The Fairy and a single-flowered floribunda named Betty Prior. The Fairy produces countless clusters of small baby-pink, double roses throughout the entire summer. They are as diminutive and dainty as their name implies.

The Fairy is not included in my formal rose garden of hybrid teas but is planted instead in the perennial border along with the peonies and iris. This year I added several bedding begonias in pink, rose, and red to the area where The Fairy grew. Behind this grouping I used a large pure white dahlia, and if I do say so myself, the effect was stunning. The single-flowered Betty Prior is a

[98] *Carolina Home Gardener*

distinctive two-toned pink beauty, taller than The Fairy and equally agreeable and prolific. I have placed it among the intermediate-height evergreen shrubbery as a background for bedding groups. One of my plans for another year is to make cuttings from both of these nonpatented varieties for extending their use to other garden areas.

Climbing Rose: The image of the rose-covered bower or cottage is one of the most enduring of all gardening traditions, but I am afraid my own experience with climbing roses has done little to enhance this cherished image. In my own garden, and in others under my supervision, climbing roses have been very disappointing.

In spite of past failures, I planted the pink New Dawn and the orange-blend Mrs. Sam McGredy on my garden fences two years ago. As far as vegetative growth goes, they outdid Topsy. New Dawn bloomed profusely for three weeks; Mrs. McGredy bloomed sparsely and intermittently throughout the season.

To still the loud clamor that arose from the men who mow the lawn on my side of the fence as well as that of my neighbor, I have pruned the roses constantly. Since most climbers flower only on second-year growth, I probably will have no flowers at all next year. (On second thought, I am sure I won't have any flowers next year; I shall snatch those thorny ingrates out of their beds and replace them with the evergreen Carolina jessamine vine, which is not so hostile and pervasive as the climbing rose.)

Bedding Begonia (Begonia semperflorens): In full sun or partial shade, the begonias have been magnificent this summer as in most summers past. Their neat, orderly habit of growth is ideal for bedding uses, and a mixture of white, pink, rose, and red is a superb sight. By early August the begonias had grown to somewhat leggy stature with diminishing flower quality. By pinching off the terminal stems that are three or four inches long and applying some extra fertilizer, they should last until frost in October.

Help from the Volunteers: Seedlings of cleome, annual vinca, and impatiens also continued to grow and flower throughout the summer in their customary fashion. By August, in fact, these plants, as well as some of the other summer bedding plants, had grown so much that they threatened to damage some of their permanent neighbors such as the dwarf azalea, holly, candytuft, and iris.

It is very important that such burgeoning plants be thinned or pruned enough to permit ample sunlight and air to reach the shrubs and perennials. Staking and tying tall floppy annuals may be sufficient restraint, but in case it is not, do not hesitate to remove completely any volunteer plants that have gotten out of bounds. By August the cleome, vinca, impatiens, and other annuals have already dropped ample seeds for next season's crops.

Geranium: In a final analysis, each gardener must select plants according to their performance in his or her own garden. In my garden, the geraniums have had their last summer as a member in the bedding groups. They have failed too many times under mass-bedding conditions. Early this year they developed leaf spot and stem rot, and the flowering declined as the health of the plants worsened. They failed to respond to fairly frequent prunings and sprayings, and since there are a number of new plants still untried, their spaces will be otherwise employed another year. On the other hand, geraniums have done well in the boxes, baskets, and planters, and I expect to continue their use in containers.

Camellia and Azalea: Thanks to the cottonseed meal applied in late winter and faithful watering during dry spells, my azaleas and camellias have grown well and set many buds for another season. If only the winter is kind, spring will be a splendid thing.

Obituary Item: Azalea, camellia, pieris, and rhododendron (as well as a few other shrubs) require the same growing conditions of part shade, good drainage, and acid soil. I do my best to supply these needs to plant representatives of this group, and although the azaleas and camellias flourished, the rhododendrons died. A few gardeners in this area have mastered the growing of the elegant rhododendron, but this shrub, as well as the African violet (*Saintpaulia ionantha*), has ignored my best efforts.

As for the African violet, it is beneath my scorn; but the rhododendron? Well, every garden needs a few shrubs with large, bold leaves. I shall replace the rhododendron with the more affable aucuba and mahonia.

Holly: I have two American holly trees and a hedge of the beautiful Burford Chinese holly, but neither will have the cherished red berries this year. During the time of their flowering last spring, heavy rains washed the pollen down the drains, and very little of the cross-pollination required for setting fruits was accomplished. Better luck next year.

Hosta: Of the six varieties of hostas that thrive in my garden year in and year out, none was ever so spectacular and fragrant as a new variety called Royal Standard. It is a vigorous, large-leaved variety developed from the old August lily (*Subcordata grandiflora*), and it is in every respect a champion. This August the pure white bloom stalks reached heights of more than three feet and the early evenings were haunted by their perfume. The height of the blooms will make a fine addition to the all-green summer dress of the azalea plantings, and I expect to divide my hosta clumps in late fall or early spring and to place the divisions between dwarf azaleas in the shadier sections of the garden.

Iris: My bearded iris, divided and replanted two years ago, produced an excellent showing this year. Above everything, bearded iris must have sunshine, dry soil, and preferably a soil that is not too rich. They occupy quite happily the most exposed and arid areas in my beds. The clumps were so large this year that I thinned them during August by cutting or breaking off a few rhizomes from each one. Next August they must be dug in their entirety and divided as follows:

1. Dig and wash away all soil from the fleshy roots or rhizomes.

2. Cut and discard any soft or worm-eaten portions of the roots and soak for two hours in a solution of water and Phaltan or Captan (fungicides). Let dry a few hours in the sun before replanting.

3. Cut the clump into small sections, each section having leaves and a portion of roots. Discard the old center of the plant.

4. Cut off half the height of the leaves in the shape of a fan and remove half the length of the longest roots.

5. Plant in freshly prepared soil with very little fertilizer added. The planting depth should be as shallow as possible for anchorage.

6. Place several divisions of each color together and face all the "fans" in the same direction.

7. Water but do *not* mulch.

Looking Back at the Vegetable and Fruit Harvests

Broccoli: Counting both the early and late March plantings, I had a total of sixteen broccoli plants in my summer garden. By cutting the edible stalks regularly, and providing food and water during the periods of dry weather, both plantings produced well into the month of July. In addition to having as much as we wanted for table use, I had eleven pints for the freezer. Broccoli is so simple to grow, and a well-prepared bed of six to eight plants will produce table supplies for the small family. The seeds can be planted directly to the beds, small plants can be started in containers, or the plants can be purchased from your favorite gardening store.

String Bean and Pole Lima: Although my first plantings were rendered unproductive by the heat and drought of July, later plantings yielded sufficient quantities for eating and freezing. With weather as dependably uncertain as ours, the best insurance for all crops is a second planting wherever possible.

Tomato: Heavy mulches and regular watering brought my tomato crop through with plenty to eat, share, and can. With many quarts still in the freezer from last year, this year's crop went into making fifty pints of a favorite tomato-juice cocktail.

Eggplant: My two eggplants produced some prodigious fruits, but I suppose I shall not plant those purple satin beauties again. My family will not eat it. I stretched my culinary abilities to the utmost trying to prove its delectability. I served it under such exotic names as Eggplant Creole, Eggplant Parmesan, Eggplant Casserole, and plain old Eggplant Fritters, but eggplant by any name was a nothing. Pity, too—they are so pretty.

Swiss Chard: A six-foot row of Swiss chard amply supplied us with this very versatile vegetable. Unfortunately, Swiss chard is seldom planted in southern vegetable gardens. Heat-tolerant and vigorous, it served us in a number of ways from June to frost, being available when it was too hot to grow lettuce and such salad greens as turnips, mustard, and kale. The leaves of the chard are excellent both as a fresh green salad ingredient and cooked as one would cook spinach or turnip greens. The thick white stalks can be used in place of celery or cooked as an excellent substitute for the very expensive asparagus. The seeds can be sown directly to the beds in the spring and the leaves harvested a few at a time as needed. Chard is also an exceptionally ornamental vegetable and is as much of an asset to the flower garden as it is to the menu.

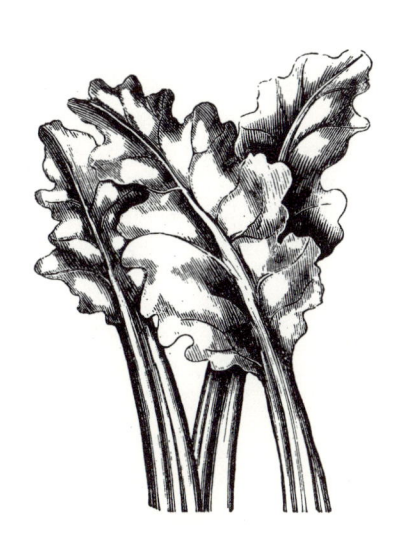

Muscadine Grape (Vitis rotundifolia): I confess to a bit of disappointment in my fellow Tarheels for their lack of knowledge and appreciation of one of our really great natural resources, the muscadine grape. These grapes, which flourished in the wilds, were noted and appreciated fully by both the Indians and the early settlers from England.

One of the members of Sir Walter Raleigh's Colony wrote the following words to show his opinion of this woodland bounty: "In 1584 we departed from England with two boats and found Roanoke Island on the fourth of July, and the smell was as sweet as if we had been in the midst of some delicate garden, and grapes grew abundantly, every shrub was covered, climbing toward the tops of high cedars and we think the like is not to be found."

Methinks to this day, nearly four hundred years later, their like has not been found, and now, thanks to the work of our agricultural research scientists, muscadine grapes, of which the scuppernong is only one of many varieties, are bigger and sweeter than ever.

The production of muscadines today is one of the fastest-growing horticultural industries in the state, with a major portion being grown in the southeastern counties. Most of those grown commercially are used for the production of superb wines that are most suitable for serving as dinner appetizers. Certain hardy varieties can be grown as far north as the Virginia line and westward to the foothills of the Blue Ridge. In addition to the wines, certain varieties are well suited for such home uses as jelly, jam, and juice making.

The most popular variety is Magnolia, a light bronze sweet grape that ripens over a long period. Other excellent varieties are Albemarle, Carlos, Chowan, Roanoke, Tarheel, Scuppernong, and Hunt. In my garden a Magnolia and a variety called Nevermiss Scuppernong are working agreeably on the same arbor. Both vines began to bear fruit the second season following planting, and this year, the third season since planting, they covered two-thirds of the arbor and were loaded with fruit.

Since some varieties require a second variety for pollination it is advisable to get some assistance with your selection. An excellent booklet called *Muscadine Grapes Production Guide for North Carolina*, Circular 535, is available from your county farm agent. There is no charge for this information, and it supplies all you need to know for starting your own home vineyard.

*Concord Grape:** The Concord, which ripened in July, also gave a good account of itself this year with the production of twenty pounds of the most perfect purple clusters I have ever grown. As always, eating the fresh fruits received first priority at our house, but there were plenty left over for jelly and a few pints for the freezer. (If you haven't eaten frozen grapes, try it for a winter treat. Cover fresh grapes in a medium syrup made of one cup of water to one cup of sugar. Freeze in plastic containers.)

*Both the Concord and Niagara grapes, easily grown and popular in the Carolinas, belong to the *Vitis labruscana* species.

A Year in My Garden

Strawberry: For me the growing of strawberries within the confines of the flower garden has not been as successful as my efforts with the grapes. I have concluded that their proper culture requires more space and better cultivation methods than I can supply. My experimentation with this fruit covers a span of many years. I have tried several recommended everbearing and standard varieties with lackadaisical results, but if I can judge by the crops I see in some gardens, I know that it can be done where growing conditions are good and space is ample.

The one notable exception to my list of strawberry failures is a little-known Alpine variety called Baron Solemacher. However, if you are more interested in size than in flavor, forget about the Baron. In my small area, which can accommodate only a couple of dozen plants, the neat, compact, nonrunning Baron does a good job. The smallness of the fruit is more than compensated for by the rare and delicate flavor of the berries, plus the fact that it begins to show ripened fruits by midsummer and continues until hard frost. For some unaccountable reason the birds bother them very little, whereas I have always had to keep a net over other strawberry varieties. Perhaps, like some gardeners, the birds find them too small for their efforts.

Summary of Garden Work for August

Lest you think that there is nothing to do in August except to evaluate the year's work and eat, take note, please, of the following August garden activities:

1. Among the flowers, shrubs, and roses, the watering, weeding, spraying, tip-pruning, and removal of faded flowers continued as usual

2. Ditto among the vegetables; just as the removal of faded flowers is necessary for continuous blooming, so is the regular harvesting of vegetables vital for their continuous production; during August, I harvested such foods as field peas, limas, snaps, okra, and tomatoes almost daily

3. In mid-August, I checked seed supplies on hand to be sure I had ample supplies of such cool-season vegetables as lettuce, Chinese cabbage, endive, turnips, etc.

4. I ordered pansy seeds and onion sets for September planting

5. Seeds of turnip, cabbage, broccoli, and collard were planted

6. The final application of iron chelate was given the azaleas

7. Plentiful amounts of potting soil were mixed and stored under cover to be ready for seed sowing, cutting making, and the potting of begonia, fern, geranium, and other tender summer plants for wintering under cover

8. "Laying-by" time was over for another year

Flowers of August

Ageratum (perennial), althea, begonia, black-eyed Susan, Boston daisy, canna, chrysanthemum, clematis, cleome, crape myrtle, dahlia, dianthus (Persian Rug), geranium, gladiolus, Hall's amaryllis, hibiscus, hosta, impatiens, liriope, lycoris, marigold, morning glory, nasturtium, ornamental pepper, phlox (summer), plumbago, rose, sedums in variety, sweet alyssum, vinca, zephyranthes

September

September and October may very well be a busier gardening season than the spring months of April and May. Many major changes and additions are made in the cool weather of fall, and foremost among them are the making and repair of cool-season lawns, bulb planting, making additions or changes in the tree and shrub portions of the garden, and planting fall bedding plants and cool-weather vegetables.

Fall Lawn Making*

Fescue and bluegrass are the evergreen perennial grasses favored by most piedmont gardeners, and fall is the time when such lawns should be made or renewed. For established lawns, fertilizing is done in September and October, preferably in September.

If an old lawn needs patching, scratch the areas, adding a bit of enriched soil, and sow with fresh seeds. Cover with a thin layer of pine or wheat straw that can be left to shade and protect the seedlings until the fresh grass covers all signs of the straw. In other words, leave the straw mulch in place. If the fall weather turns out to be dry, water the newly seeded areas regularly; water is less costly than a second seeding.

Winter produces a drab brown-out of a sunny hot lawn where Bermuda or zoysia grass (*Zoysia matrella*) is used. If you desire a green winter lawn, sow the annual Italian ryegrass (*Lolium multiflorum*) in the fall. Many lawn experts frown on the idea of overplanting summer lawns with ryegrass, feeling that the extra cover is detrimental to the permanent grasses. For many years we overplanted a Bermuda lawn successfully with a light seeding of Italian ryegrass, and as long as the amounts seeded are light in character, this can be done for other types of warm-season perennial grasses.

*For help with lawn making and maintenance, request a copy of John Harris and W. B. Gilbert, *Carolina Lawns*, Agricultural Extension Service Publication no. 292 (Raleigh, N.C.: Agricultural Extension Service, 1968).

Fall Bulb Planting

All the spring-flowering bulbs, both the large types, such as tulip (*Tulipa* spp.), daffodil, and hyacinth, and the smaller as well, are planted in the fall, preferably in the time interval between Labor Day and Thanksgiving.

Try Some of the Smaller Bulbs

Some of the loveliest flowers in the spring garden come from the small bulbs that cost little compared to the daffodil, tulip, and hyacinth. In addition, they usually multiply and bloom for many years with only a modicum of care. In this group of lesser bulbs are the crocus, glory-of-the-snow, winter aconite (*Eranthis hyemalis*), snowdrop, snowflake, grape hyacinth (*Muscari botryoides*), and the squills or scillas (*Scilla hispanica*).

It is difficult to understand why these small bulbs are so neglected. A dozen crocus bulbs planted by the doorstep, or a like number of winter aconite or the sky-blue glory-of-the-snow, will provide the garden's earliest blooms and multiply in time to produce large showy colonies of vivid color. Glory-of-the-snow has the added advantage of self-seeding prolifically and is therefore excellent for naturalizing along woodland paths where its diminutive beauty cannot be overlooked.

Elsewhere in this book I have spoken rather negatively of the tulip. In recognition of the gardeners who consider them a successful garden subject, let me say that, like any other plant, they should be tried and judged on their performance in the individual garden. Tulips are also planted in the fall.

My experience with daffodils has been much more satisfying. Where drainage is not too great a problem, daffodils will grow and multiply. In fact, I have been pleasantly surprised to see how well they can manage with the rather poor drainage that characterizes most of my garden. Good drainage, of course, is preferred for their culture, and large clumps that have ceased to bloom will usually resume flowering when the clumps are divided and replanted in well-prepared soil. These old clumps may be divided in the fall, if you know where they are growing. If you failed to mark their location before the tops disappeared in the summer, wait and divide them just when they are coming through the ground in January or February, or you may wait until later when the flowering is over.

How Deep to Plant Bulbs

Depth of planting for most bulbs, large or small, is about three to four times the length of the bulb. For example, a bulb two inches long should be planted six to seven inches deep. The soil should be prepared with humus and a little balanced-formula chemical fertilizer (8-8-8 or 5-10-10) to a depth of at least three inches below the bulb, since that is where the root growth occurs. Thus, for planting a daffodil six inches deep, the prepared bed should be nine or ten inches deep.

A Year in My Garden

Generally speaking, it is better to plant bulbs too deep than too shallow. There is not much danger of planting too deep. I recall a load of topsoil being inadvertently unloaded on a bed of naturalized daffodils in my old garden. The bulbs grew up through three feet of soil and bloomed profusely. A depth of seven or eight inches is better, however. Since I usually over-plant daffodils and Dutch iris with pansies in the fall and other low bedding plants such as begonias in the late spring, I usually plant all bulbs deep enough to escape damage from the shallow cultivation needed for planting these small biennials and annuals above them.

Selecting Daffodils and Other Bulbs

There are ten big divisions of daffodils based on the form of the flower, and within the ten divisions are hundreds of named varieties. King Alfred is certainly the best known of any named variety of yellow trumpet. However, it has not been outstanding in my gardens. I prefer Unsurpassable or Dutch Master. Other old daffodil favorites of mine are the white Thalia, John Evelyn, Actea, and the bunch-flowered bicolors, Laurens Koster and Geranium. Bulb catalogs are filled with newer and bigger ones each year, and it is fun to try a few that have special appeal, but tried-and-true ones, such as those named above, seldom fail to bloom each year.

I must also make my manners to the champion old-timer of the daffodil family. Each spring in the yards of deserted old farmhouses and along banks and ditches where they have strayed unaided are stands of a short-stemmed yellow daffodil called February Gold. For several years this great old-timer, which belongs in the *Cyclamineus* hybrid group, was omitted from most bulb catalog offerings. I am happy to see that it is once more available. Be sure to add a few to your garden. It is like planting a bit of garden history.

Hyacinth*

Hyacinths have always survived well for several seasons of consecutive bloom in my gardens when I have selected the best-drained sites for their planting. I recommend the small size (about two inches in diameter) for bedding purposes. Larger bulbs produce massive, top-heavy blooms that are highly susceptible to wind, snow, and ice damage. The smaller sizes are quite capable of producing fine mass-bedding effects, which is about the only effective way to use this rather stiff bulbous flower. In addition, smaller sizes are less costly.

Buy All Bulbs Early

It is a good idea to select and buy bulbs for fall planting as soon in the fall as they are available. Early purchase assures a better selection and

*I would be remiss if I failed to mention one of the Carolinas' rare plant treasures, the Roman hyacinth (*Hyacinthus orientalis albulus*). This fragrant and graceful small hyacinth, seen ever more rarely, exists in both single- and double-flowered forms in pink, white, and blue. One of my lifetime wishes has been to have a few of each in my garden. It is as unlikely an ambition as finding an emerald in the gem-stone mountains at Spruce Pine.

quality, since a few weeks of storage in the warm environment of the average gardening store can damage the growth and flowering vitality of perishable bulbs. Buy and store in a cool, dry, frost-free place on your own premises until they can be planted. Early or late bulb purchases in gardening stores should be carefully and individually checked to detect soft spots, overly dry conditions, or mechanical damage. Keep in mind that ornamental bulbs are like onions—which are also bulbs—and apply the same standards to the choice of daffodils, hyacinths, and other flowering bulbs that you would to onions for the table.

Flower Seed Sowing in September

Commercial growers of pansy plants, faced with the necessity of getting pansies large enough to sell in September, must plant their seeds in July and August. If this appears to be a simple matter that is easily handled by the professional nurseryman, consider the fact that pansy seeds germinate poorly in temperatures higher than seventy-five degrees. In July and August we have very little weather within that range. The result is a poor percentage of germination from these very costly seeds. By the time the cost of labor to transplant and market pansies is added, it is no wonder that pansies are now twenty cents each in garden stores. (I remember quite well that the first pansies I grew and sold in the old days were three cents each, and the customers complained of the high prices in those days, too!)

Growing My Own Pansies

Considering the four or five hundred pansies I need for planting my own fall garden, there is no answer except to grow my own. The seeds cost approximately five dollars, and an equal amount is needed for the potting-soil seeding mixture.

I prefer solid colors in pansies for mass bedding effects. Solid-color groupings are excellent design components, and to put my art on a practical basis, the solid-color seeds are considerably less costly than those of the fancy, ruffled color mixtures of hybrid varieties. My favorite colors are a clear yellow, pure white, and a light, sky blue. Other colors available in separate packets are purple, scarlet, apricot, lilac, and dark blue. Many seed catalogs classify the solid-color pansies as violas. (Botanically speaking, all pansies are violas.) Solid-color violas or pansies are smaller as a class than the more hybridized mixed-color pansies. Violas average two to two and a half inches in size and may be depended upon to produce myriads of blossoms on compact, dark green plants from January until May or June. My favorite strain of seeds is sold under the name of Clear Crystals by Stokes Seed, Inc., of Buffalo, N.Y.

If the temperatures in early September are cool, my seeds are planted around Labor Day. If not, I delay the planting until the middle of September, the latest planting date I have found to be successful. Using three standard seed flats (15' × 21'), I sow to each flat a single color—the clear blue, white, and yellow that I use in my spring garden. The seeds are covered just enough to hide them; the flats are carefully watered and put in a shaded and protected place for germination, a process that usually requires from ten days to two weeks. When a good stand has germinated, the seed flats are exposed to direct sunlight in gradual doses of exposure, particularly if the sun is hot as it often is in September.

By late October or early November, the pansy seedlings are usually large enough (three or four leaves) to transplant to peat pots for additional growth before the final planting. A short-cut may be taken at this stage: if the garden soil is well prepared, the tiny pansies may be planted directly to the garden, skipping the interim step of transplanting to peat pots. Additional watering will be required for this direct outdoor planting, but watering is less trouble than transplanting to pots and less costly.

In an average fall's pansy planting, my three seed flats of blue, white, and yellow pansies produce from a thousand to twelve hundred plants. This gives me more plants than my garden can accommodate, and the surplus makes fine gifts for family and gardening friends. It is a very satisfactory return for my investment.

Vegetable Seed Planting in September

The cool-season vegetables of fall should also be planted in September. These include radish, lettuce, endive, Chinese cabbage, onion (sets), and the salad greens mixture of mustard, turnip, and kale. The small plants of broccoli, cabbage, and collard started in August in peat pots were large enough to be planted to their final beds in September. These fall-planted vegetables require as much watering as the summer garden.

Some Fall-Planting Problems

The late summer insects create the fall-planted vegetables' worst problem. They seem to sense the approaching end of their feeding days, and their appetites fully reflect this instinct. The green cabbage worm is equally fond of the related broccoli and collards, and diligent dusting and hand-picking are in order during September to get these plants by. Fortunately, the number of cabbage worms and other insects decreases sharply after the first freeze.

A Culinary Suggestion

Chinese cabbage is a loose-leaved vegetable that is useful as a raw salad ingredient or combined with collard greens. Its delicate flavor and light green color improve the taste as well as the appearance of that rather pungent southern vegetable, the collard.

Summary of Garden Activities for September

1. Fed fescue (Kentucky 31) lawn and reseeded a few bare spots; mowed regularly to a height of two and a half inches; removed all clippings

2. Selected and purchased a few new daffodils, Dutch iris, and crocus to be planted in October when the summer annuals have been removed

3. Made tentative plans for shifting some shrubbery, discarding two or three plants and buying a couple of new ones; actual changes to be made in October or November when the weather is cooler

4. Sowed pansy seeds and seeds of radish, lettuce, endive, Chinese cabbage, turnip, and mixed greens

5. Transplanted small peat-pot-grown seedlings of broccoli, cabbage, and collard to well-prepared garden beds

6. Planted onion sets for winter and spring use

7. Battled the fall-feeding insects

8. Continued regular rose sprayings

9. Following a five-inch rainfall on 1 September, fed all summer annuals to maintain green color until frost

10. Relished daily ambrosia-and-nectar of ripening scuppernong grapes; ah, the good land!

11. Gave away eggplants

Flowers of September

Agapanthus, ageratum (perennial), althea, begonia, black-eyed Susan, camellia sasanqua, Christmas cherry or pepper, chrysanthemum, clematis, colchicum, cleome, dianthus (Persian Carpet), geranium, ginger lily, hibiscus, hosta, liriope, lycoris, marigold, plumbago, rose, vinca

October

One of the disadvantages of life in the tropics, according to E. H. "Chinese" Wilson, was the monotony of flowers always in bloom and leaves forever green. Wilson, a plant explorer and horticulturist for Arnold Arboretum in Massachusetts during the first quarter of this century, spent much of his working life in the tropics, and he sorely missed the autumnal brilliance and the snowy winters of New England.

By October, like "Chinese" Wilson, I, too, am ready for a change of season, and this year the change came earlier than expected. Although the average date for the first frost of fall is around the middle of October, this year we had three heavy frosts the first week of the month. Fortunately, the ground temperatures were still warm enough to prevent severe damage, and there were roses, chrysanthemums, and perennial ageratum left in plentiful supply.

Getting the Garden Ready for Winter

Even in years when frost is not so premature, I begin by the end of September and work intermittently throughout October to complete the preparations for the protection and winter storage of tender summer flowers, potted plants, rooted cuttings and the cultivation of beds for planting the spring flowers.

Preparing tender plants for wintering indoors or under cover involves several small details. Begonias, geraniums, coleus, wandering Jew, Boston ferns, Boston daisies, impatiens, lantana, and fuchsias that have grown outdoors in beds or containers should be lifted, cut back severely, potted in containers of fresh soil, and made ready for temporary shelter from frost on short notice.

Christmas cherries or peppers and chrysanthemums are often at the peak of their beauty in early October. A few of these should be lifted, potted, kept in a cool, shady spot for a few days of adjustment, and then taken indoors later in the month to be enjoyed for several weeks.

House plants that have summered outside require some attention too before returning indoors to spend the winter. Pots need scrubbing, and plants should be carefully inspected and sprayed for slugs, scale, white flies, pill bugs, and other insects that would like to spend the winter in the house. Foliage should be cleaned by syringing or washing with a mild soapy water. Remove weak and dead portions, and collect and clean drip saucers for use on short notice.

With everything ready for the final move indoors, delay the actual transfer as long as you can. An unheated building or shelter of any kind where light and air can circulate is a better environment than the average modern house. So keep the tender plants outside as long as possible.

Fall Care of Tender Bulbs

Gladiolus: Greensboro, N.C., is on the borderline of winter hardiness for gladioli. Their survival depends a good deal on the quality of the drainage, and I have had these bulbs survive several years without taking them up in the fall for winter storage. For choice varieties, however, I recommend that they be dug and stored in the following manner: as soon as the tops have turned brown, dig (leaving the tops on), shake off the dirt, and spread on newspapers or in an open box to complete the ripening of the tops. Ripening is complete when the tops separate easily from the bulbs or corms. Remove any remaining dried dirt, and store bulbs in dry peat moss in an open box or bag in a cool basement or storeroom.

Dahlias: Allow dahlias to stand for four or five days after frost has blackened the foliage to give the roots the last bit of sustenance remaining in the stalks. On a dry clear day, if possible, cut off the stalks to a length of eight or ten inches. Dig carefully to prevent breakage or damage to the potato-like roots. Shake off as much of the dirt as you can and lay the plant on its side to prevent water from collecting in the hollow, tubelike stems. Put in the sun to dry for a few hours, and store temporarily in a cool and dark moist place for a few days of additional drying. Store finally in baskets or boxes, packed lightly in dry peat moss, sphagnum, or leaves. Store for winter at a temperature of thirty-five to forty-five degrees.

Caladium (*Caladium bicolor*) *and Tuberous Begonias*: By early September water should be applied more and more sparingly as these bulbs approach their dormant period. When frost is imminent, dig with the tops left on and spread bulbs, tops and all, on newspapers in a cool dry place for additional curing or drying. When the tops can be removed without tugging, store cleaned bulbs in dry peat moss or sphagnum in a temperature of about fifty degrees.

Some gardeners report that they have stored both caladiums and tuberous begonias quite satisfactorily by leaving them in the pots of soil in which they had been growing in the summer. The pots are allowed to dry out in September and no water is supplied through the winter. Storage temperatures should be the same whether storage is in pots of soil or in boxes or bags of peat moss. The potted bulbs will require fresh potting soil and watering to resume growth the following spring.

Winterizing Tender and Hardy Rooted Cuttings

Provident gardeners make a practice of rooting cuttings of such tender plants as geranium, wandering Jew, begonia, fuchsia, coleus, impatiens, and the like off and on throughout the mid and late summer. When winter comes, protection must be provided for these small tender plants, as well as for their larger parents.

Although my winter storage facilities are limited to a sunny kitchen and the small window greenhouse, I use approximately half of the total space for the young rooted plants. In many instances, these young plants are more vigorous the following summer than their parents, who may have become less vigorous in their old age.

Rooted cuttings of hardy outdoor plants (rose, azalea, camellia, boxwood, holly, dianthus, candytuft, clematis, Carolina jessamine, etc.) made throughout the summer do not require the high level of indoor protection necessary for the survival of the tender rooted cuttings listed above, but they do need some protection, at least for their first year.

A Year in My Garden [107]

A simple cold frame adjoining a house or wall on the southern or western exposure would be ideal for the storage of these hardy plants through their first winter. Such a frame could be made of cinder blocks or heavy boards with a hinged lid of glass or clear plastic. Only during freezing weather would the lid need to be closed.

An unheated building with a sunny window will do also, and I use shelves across a west window in the workshop for keeping my rooted hardy cuttings alive during the winter. Water is supplied very sparingly throughout the winter months, but in late February both watering and fertilizing are resumed to promote new growth before planting in the open beds when the spring weather becomes settled.

(Incidentally, the May-rooted rose cuttings that grew and were planted in an open bed in midsummer continued to grow and produced several blossoms before frost. However, I did not consider them well enough established to risk going through the winter without some protection. In late November when all the leaves had shed from the small bushes, I encircled them with a ring of poultry wire and carefully covered them with small tip-end boughs of pine.)

A Special October Reminder

There are no figures to prove it, but I firmly believe that more trees and shrubbery die from lack of water in the fall than at any other season. Gardeners are lulled into forgetfulness by the cooler weather and forget that we frequently have prolonged periods of drought at summer's end.

Dogwoods are especially susceptible to such periods of dry weather, even three or four years after planting. Azaleas, camellias, boxwoods, and other surface-rooted shrubs suffer more in dry spells than deeper-rooted plants, so these too should have extra water. As a matter of fact, all evergreens should have plenty of water in their systems before the first hard freeze of the winter. This extra moisture helps to minimize the foliage burns at such periods.

Preparing Fall Garden Beds for Spring Flowers

Beginning gardeners, as well as newcomers from colder sections of the country, are usually surprised to learn that the spring gardens of the Carolinas must be planted in the fall to make their best showing the following spring. Spring-flowering bulbs (daffodil, tulip, hyacinth, etc.) are available only in the fall, and bedding biennials such as pansy, sweet william, and forget-me-not, as well as the bedding perennials, also need to be planted in the fall to develop good root systems.

As soon as I had rid my garden of the frost-killed summer annuals in early October, the spaces they occupied were covered with a two-to-three-inch layer of leaf compost (or peat moss) and a moderate sprinkling of 8-8-8 fertilizer. The compost and fertilizer were thoroughly mixed with the rotary cultivator. In more limited spaces, the mixing was done with the potato digger. The garden was then ready for planting the bulbs, already on hand in the cool workshop, and the pansy transplants that were still growing in their seed flats until large enough to plant in their bedding sites in mid-November. When the bulbs and pansies are planted, any additional biennials and perennials can be added, as late as December or in early spring if desired.

The End of the Summer Vegetables

Although the three early October frosts blackened the tops of the lima beans, okra, tomatoes, and bell peppers, the nearly matured vegetables growing on these plants continued to ripen and furnished adequate table supplies until late October when a temperature in the upper twenties delivered the coup de grace.

On the afternoon of 21 October, the weather bureau issued a warning of the impending drop, and I was able to gather all of the remaining edible beans, tomatoes, and peppers safely indoors for subsequent use. These included the large and medium-sized green tomatoes that were stored in the workshop for gradual ripening. On the following morning I lost no time getting the plant remains of the tender summer vegetables off the premises. Such haste is not mandatory, but frost-blackened plants are no asset to the garden nor to the spirits, and the sooner they are done away with, the less chance their insect and disease inhabitants have to attach themselves to other plants.

Cool-Weather Vegetables: Cool-season vegetables that were planted in August and September suffered no damages whatever from any of October's frosty weather. Collards, salad greens, onions, lettuce, radishes, broccoli, and Chinese cabbage, as well as the leftover summer crop of Swiss chard, continued to grow and be consumed in October. Weather permitting, they should produce for another two months.

Summary of Garden Activities for October

1. Prepared tender plants and rooted cuttings for wintering indoors

2. Stored hardy rooted cuttings in unheated, sunny workshop windows

3. Dug dahlias and gladioli and prepared for winter storage

4. Watered dogwoods and other shrubbery through dry weather regardless of the temperatures

5. Gathered the last of the summer vegetables

6. Cleared all frost-killed annuals and vegetables from premises

7. Prepared bedding sites for planting bulbs and pansies in November

8. Enjoyed cool-season vegetables and fall colors

9. On 28 October the snowbirds came home for the winter

Flowers of October

Ageratum, aster (perennial), begonia, black-eyed Susan, camellia sasanqua, clematis, cleome, Christmas pepper, chrysanthemum, dahlia, ginger lily, Japanese anemone, marigold, osmanthus, rose, sedum, vinca

November

Carolina Novembers belong in the never-never season between summer and winter. There are many "shirt-sleeve" days in which to complete the fall gardening work in a leisurely fashion and still allow plenty of time to enjoy cooler weather and the autumn colors—and to renew one's acquaintance with the less flamboyant charms of the winter garden.

With all of the deciduous leaves tucked away in their special niches of the life cycle, the cool-season lawns are lush and clean, the evergreenery is rain-washed and polished, and the glistening red berries of pyracantha, nandina, holly, dogwood, and hawthorn are happy reminders of the holiday season just around the corner.

The structural beauty of the deciduous members of the garden is at its best during this season and throughout the winter. The ironwood, crape myrtle, star magnolia, forsythia, flowering quince, crab apple, and maple reveal again the half-forgotten delicacy of their branches, buds, and barks. Only in the snowy tracery of deepest winter could they be more beautiful.

In a more practical vein November is the time to evaluate the quality of the garden design, to find the weak spots and to decide what can be done to improve the garden's winter appearance; in the South, the winter garden can and should be beautiful.

November Gardening Weather

This year, from early October through the month of November, we had our usual up-and-down weather. To recap briefly, we had a five-inch rainfall the first of September, but less than an inch for the ensuing two and a half months. Frost came about two weeks early (1 October), accompanied by record-breaking low temperatures. For the next three weeks the weather was warm, followed by another cold snap in late October.

In early November summer returned in earnest with daytime highs in the low and middle eighties. All of the tender summer annuals and vegetables were killed in October, but the hardier blossoms of the rose, chrysanthemum, and aster, as well as a sprinkling of clematis, canna, dianthus, and camellia, bloomed here and there until late November. Fall crops of broccoli, lettuce, collard, onion, radish, cabbage, salad greens, and Swiss chard grew and flourished throughout the month.

A Year in My Garden [109]

November Gardening Activities

My major gardening chores throughout November were the extra watering necessitated by the short rainfall, continued preparation for planting of the spring garden, and putting the entire garden to bed for the winter. Again I emphasize the need for water during our dry falls. Stands of deciduous trees and shrubs, as well as evergreens, are highly susceptible to dry-weather damage for as much as three to five years after planting. These plants, as well as the rose garden, should be given a thorough weekly soaking until the winter rainfall begins. Shallow-rooted bedding plants (pansies, vegetables, etc.) that make rapid growth this season should have two to three waterings per week.

Preparing Beds in Dry Weather

Planting areas that contain plentiful amounts of organic matter remain friable during dry weather and may be cultivated whenever desired. On the other hand, beds of heavy clay content must have moisture to be workable. In case of drought the hose can be used to moisten the soil. Water must be applied judiciously, however. If too much is used, the heavy clay will lie in clods to be sunbaked to adobe consistency. A simple test is to squeeze a handful of soil and drop it on the ground. If it falls apart readily, it is right for digging. Soil for fall beds is prepared in the usual way.

Planting in November

Although planting can be done in October or earlier, November is my favorite month to plant all types of spring bulbs and bedding plants for the spring and early summer garden. With the cooler weather at the end of the month, less watering is needed to get these plants established.

Among those bedding plants liking November planting are the pansy, sweet william, wallflower, daisy, columbine, foxglove, forget-me-not, canterbury bell, dianthus, candytuft, lupine, hollyhock, arabis, alyssum, spring phlox, and liriope. Planted in the fall they have a full winter to establish the strong rooting systems they need for spring's fullest flowering.

Balled and burlapped evergreens, as well as container-grown nursery stock, may be more successfully planted in November and later in the winter. I would call your attention, however, to the advisability of waiting until December or January to plant bare-rooted deciduous trees and shrubs. By waiting until this time of relative dormancy, trees as large as ten to twelve feet high may often be transplanted safely without a cumbersome dirt ball.

When transplanting bare-rooted trees or shrubs, take pains to lift as much of the root system as possible without damage. Dig a hole large enough to spread the roots in their natural position and at the same depth they were growing before being dug. Fill with improved dirt pressed around and under the roots, water, anchor, mulch, and care for in the same way required for balled and burlapped nursery-grown stock.

Clearing Away the Autumn Leaves

Clearing away the autumn leaves so that the lawn grasses can grow, replenishing the mulches for the garden's winter protection, and beginning a new compost pile for the next year are all overlapping operations. As I have noted previously, we have few trees of leafy consequence in our own yard and must rely on other sources for our leaf supplies.

This year we have tried a new arrangement that might be of interest. A friend, who has too many trees to permit him to grow the vegetables and flowers that require sun, saves his leaves for us, and we share our produce with him. The leaves are collected in disposable bags, which we help to supply, and we haul the leaves away when a batch is ready.

Regardless of leaf source, chopped, shredded, or composted leaves should be used in the preparation and maintenance of the fall and winter garden just as in the spring and summer garden.

The Birds Come Home in November

By late November many of the birds that had left in early summer for cooler regions had returned, and transients were stopping by for a quick lunch on their way to Florida and Central America. On an early morning in late November, I noted in a short span of time a cardinal, two towhees, juncos in droves, a red-headed woodpecker, three chickadees, and a pair of mourning doves. All I lacked was a partridge for my pear tree! By the end of November, practically everything had been done to make the garden safe and comfortable for winter and spectacular for spring. It was time for the turkey.

Summary of Garden Activities for November

1. Cut back 50 percent of the roses in mid-November to minimize wind damages; sprayed for the last time; replenished mulch

2. Planted pansies, bulbs, and other bedding plants

3. Began a new compost pile for next year's use

4. Hauled a lot of leaves; mulched the entire garden with same

5. Spaded chopped leaves into fallow vegetable beds to "mellow" for next year's crop

6. Completed clean-up of spent chrysanthemum, sedum, summer phlox, liriope seed pods, and Siberian iris tops

7. Brought all tender plants indoors; filled the window greenhouse with begonias, geraniums, ferns, wandering Jew, and all the makings for next year's hanging baskets

8. Watered regularly until late November when the dry spell finally came to an end

9. Planted container-grown pyracanthas for espaliering on fence

10. Continued to do battle with aphids (roses), cabbage worms, and white flies

11. Fertilized cool-season grass

Flowers of November

Aster, black-eyed Susan, Boston daisy, camellia sasanqua, chrysanthemum (late), clematis, dianthus, rose

December

Amid thunder, lightning, howling wind, and hail, Hecate and her three witches midwifed the birth of December. Through the stormy midnight hours I listened in wonder and worry for the safety of both friends and flowers, but when I awoke to the dawn of 1 December, friends were safe and the garden was serene. "Merely a cold front passing through on the heels of the late November warm spell," the weatherman described it. With the colder and more seasonal weather that followed this final fling of summer, it felt a lot more like Christmas and a lot less like gardening.

It is an excellent arrangement to have Christmas come in late December. By this date, garden work is at its lowest ebb and the mind can concentrate fully on the seasonal matters at hand. And, for the provident gardener who has kept abreast of the garden chores as the needs arose throughout the fall, the few things left to be done outside in December may be regarded as welcome breaks in the routine matters of shopping, cooking, and wrapping packages.

Some Transplanting in December

Although the frost came early this year (1 October), the leaves of some of the deciduous trees and shrubs hung on until late in December, thus delaying the moving of a weigela and a cherry tree to better sites in my garden. And, as it always seems to happen, a shipment of grapevines and fruit trees ordered in September arrived during Christmas week. Such stock is usually shipped bare-rooted after the leaves have shed and should be planted as soon as possible upon being received. After a few hours of soaking the bare roots in a tub of water, all were planted, watered, and mulched. (It is not necessary to guy or anchor small trees less than six feet tall.)

With this planting my home orchard is complete. It consists of six dwarf apple trees planted in a row twelve feet apart along the base of the tallest (six feet) section of the fence. The branches will be pruned in future years, attached to the fence, and trained as informal espaliers since my garden is too small to allow their full natural growth. In addition to the six apples, my orchard has three pears, one plum, one fig, Alpine strawberries, raspberries, blueberries, and muscadine, Concord, and Niagara grapes. All of the fruits, like the vegetables, are integrated and combined with the ornamental members of the garden.

Some Transplanting Must Wait for Late February or Early March

There remain to be transplanted several small boxwoods and azaleas. However, these surface-rooted evergreens, as well as the camellias, dogwoods, and magnolias, seem to have their survival chances increased by the delay of transplanting until after the severest winter weather of January and February is past.

Cleanup Continues

Cleanup chores are light in nature but continuous through December. By early December chickweed is showing strong, wayward intentions, and a little weeding done early will save a good deal later on. There were also a few remaining spent stalks of late-flowering chrysanthemum, canna, day lily, and liriope to remove from the premises. The small black seeds that have formed on the liriope stalks by December were gathered and broadcast for future seedlings of this valuable evergreen perennial.

Growth Continues in December

Although December was colder this year than last, there were ample signs of new growth throughout the month. The foliage of the Dutch iris bulbs, which first appeared in September from plantings of previous years, was eighteen inches tall by Christmas and the green leaves of the fall-flowering colchicum and spider lily added a fresh look to the foreground beds. (If you have not grown colchicums and spider lilies, it is characteristic of their behavior to have the flowers pop out almost overnight in September, with their leaves appearing much later in the fall.)

The leaves of the Italian arum, silver-dappled and dramatic, are a feature of the December garden as they are throughout the rest of winter. Scattered about the garden I noted the appearance of very small new plants of arum growing from the seeds that I scattered about last fall. The arum blooms with a spathelike greenish-white flower in early spring. The seeds from this flower, which ripen to a brilliant red, are much prized by the birds. If you want to save these seeds for scattering in the garden or sowing in pots for additional plants, protect them with a screen-wire cover or a meshed citrus-fruit bag salvaged from your shopping.

Seedlings of honesty scattered last summer continued to germinate throughout December, a process that began in the late summer. Those seedlings that germinated in the early fall boasted six to eight leaves by Christmas; these plants will be large enough to bloom this spring. The later-germinating seedlings will grow vegetatively throughout the entire year to make prodigious plants for the following spring.

The venturesome, early-flowering daffodils had also broken the ground surface by December. This is not unusual behavior, and if the weather remains on the cold side most of January and February, the daffodils will manage quite well.

The young pansies set out in November were retarded by the lower temperatures of December, but that is no problem either; extra fertilizer and the warm spring weather can produce flowering in a miraculously short time.

In spite of the uncertain performances I have had in the past with the spring anemones, I planted a couple of hundred this fall. The foliage, green and delicate, was five to six inches high and still growing in December. Coastal and more southerly gardens have better success with this beautiful bulb than we have around Greensboro, but with some extra sand in a well-drained planting location, I have managed to have some blooms to reward most of my attempts.

Some Old Growth Lingered

In spite of the early frosts, the leaves of the Callery pear lingered on into mid-December, almost without changing color. This fast-growing ornamental, disease-and-insect free, has been one of the most satisfactory small flowering trees I have grown in recent years.

The roses also held most of their leaves through December, a good omen for next summer's crop as well as proof that winter in earnest does not arrive here until after Christmas.

And a Few Vegetables Remain

December vegetable offerings are green—green collards, green onions, green lettuce, Chinese cabbage, Swiss chard, and salad greens. These leafy, vitamin-filled vegetables complement the tomatoes, peas, squash, broccoli, beans, and other foods that have been frozen and stored from the summer vegetable crops.

Time for Indoor Blooms

Thanks to my window greenhouse, I have some blooms continuously throughout the winter. Three young geraniums, small enough to put on the greenhouse upper shelf without drastic pruning, have been in bloom since October. One bright red specimen boasted seven blossoms on Christmas day and was honored by serving as centerpiece for the Christmas dinner table.

The potted bedding begonias, cut back severely for repotting last fall, have acquired five to six inches of new top growth since October and were also blooming for Christmas. These new sprouts will be just right for making cuttings in January.

Each season my window greenhouse executes some small project entirely on its own. A few days before Christmas, as I was watering, turning, and grooming the window greenhouse plants, I noted that dozens of begonia seedlings had sprouted at the base of one of the begonias that had been left in its original hanging basket. I hope to nurse these seedlings along until transplanting stage in late spring. I had no idea that the conditions in my tiny glass window box were right to germinate these powder-fine seeds. Perhaps next year I'll sow some begonia seeds of my own and see if I can get them through the winter. Their growing season is a long one, and most of the young plants that we buy in the gardening centers in the spring were sown in greenhouses in October. No wonder they are expensive.

December Is Amaryllis Month

The amaryllis (*Amaryllis belladonna*) is one of the easiest to grow of all the indoor forcing bulbs and provides a spectacular lift for the winter doldrums. Amaryllis bulbs market for prices from two to fifteen dollars, but if proper care is taken of them, they may be carried over to multiply and bloom for an indefinite number of years. A gift bulb of five or six years ago had bloomed each winter with increasing vigor (and offsets) with the following simple care.

Originally the bulb was potted in good soil in a clay pot only one inch larger than the bulb itself. The soil was tamped with a pencil firmly around the bulb, watered, and brought inside the house and placed where the light was good. Within a few days, new growth appeared. The pot was then moved to the direct light of a sunny east window, and water was applied approximately twice each week.

The blossom stalks grew rapidly and flowered satisfactorily. After they faded, the stalks were removed and the plant was left indoors in the sun to grow and remain green until late April or early May when it was sunk to the pot's rim in a shady spot in the open garden. Watering at this stage should be very scanty.

In the fall before frost, the pot was lifted, cleaned, and fresh dirt was spooned into the top to replace some of the original dirt. The plant was then brought indoors to repeat its growth cycle.

The amaryllis enjoys being potbound, so I repeated the routine described above until the bulb burst its pot. That took three years, and when it happened, I repotted the bulb, by then much larger than when I first got it, into another pot about an inch larger than the bulb.

This amaryllis produced a real surprise for me this year. Inadvertently it was put out to summer in a spot that received more water than a dormant amaryllis should have. One day in July I noted a brilliant red flower in a forgotten corner! It produced three blossom stalks throughout the summer, and I imagine that is all there will be this year. I really don't mind since I have grown a little weary of the blatant pomposity of my red amaryllis.

Caring for Christmas Plants

The poinsettia (*Euphorbia pulcherrima*), chrysanthemum, Christmas cherry, azalea, gloxinia (*Sinningia* spp.), and other plants are coaxed under carefully regulated greenhouse conditions into bloom for Christmas giving. Receivers enjoy such gifts but sometimes fret a good deal about them too.

Our over-heated, dry houses are totally unfit for plant longevity. Flowering time may be extended by careful attention to watering and storing the plant in a cooler room or unheated area during the hours when there are no viewers around.

Such plants should be protected from drafts, heat vents, and too much direct exposure to the sun through southern windows. Syringing the leaves with an atomizer (except for plants with woolly leaves such as the African violet or gloxinia) and placing the pot on a pebble-and-water-filled tray will increase the amount of humidity.

Outdoor plants such as the azalea or the chrysanthemum which have been forced for seasonal giving must be cared for after flowering with continued watering and proper light if they are to be transplanted later in the spring to the outdoor garden. Here again, unless you know that they are plants of a variety hardy for outdoor culture, this may be a waste of time. Unfortunately, even the florist who handled the plant sometimes cannot inform you on this point. My thoughts concerning a gift plant are that it should be cared for as well as you can, enjoyed, and discarded when it is no longer attractive.

A Little Time for the Birds

One of the quiet, serene joys of late December is bird watching, an activity that seems inextricably associated with gardening. Conservationists, gardeners, and ornithologists argue a bit about the advisability of feeding the birds throughout the winter. Where natural cover and food are as lacking as they are in some urban subdivisions, there is no other way to entice birds into the garden where they are both needed and enjoyed. Perhaps a compromise arrangement of merely supplementing their winter diet during spells of bad weather would be of benefit to all. It may well be that I am thinking more of my own pleasure than I am of insect control, but winter or summer, the chickadees, titmice, towhees, doves, and cardinals are as welcome in my garden as the flowers of spring.

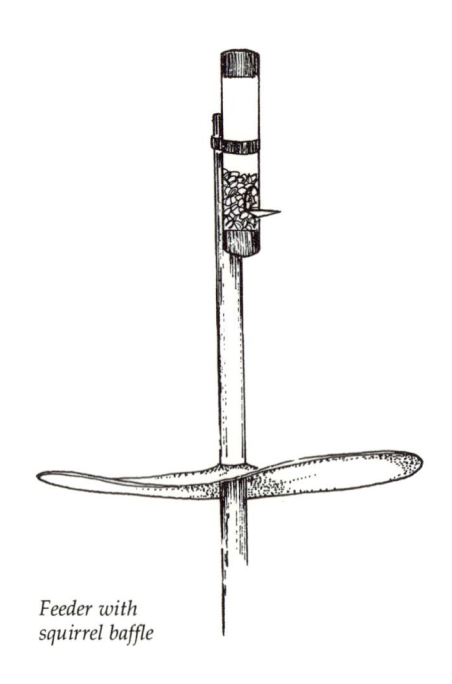

Feeder with squirrel baffle

This Year the Catalogs Came Early

It may be only a sign of the times, but more seed catalogs came early this year than I can ever remember—replete with new plant offerings and suggestions for gift giving. A seed catalog is a fine gift in itself, providing in its pages several hours of wishing material and quiet browsing. The new year's offerings of seeds and plants are as mouth-wateringly described as always, and the illustrators are surely undiscovered Redoutes or Prevosts.* Since it pleases me to believe, I am a happy pushover for their arts and guile. But, as I think back over my gardening years, more often than not I have been pleased with my purchases.

Now, at the beginning of another new year, I am preparing yet another seed and plant order. That same old routine? Never. It only seems that way to those who have never gardened. To those of us who have, no year is ever like its predecessor, and each one that passes—all too quickly—is better than the one before.

This year there will be asparagus grown from seeds, salsify to try for the first time, and some of those scarlet-flowered string beans that I once saw growing at the Wisley testing gardens near London. There will be some newcomers in the flower garden as well. A new strain of heat-resistant sweet pea to try, a few species tulips for the rockery, and the colorful gazania (*Gazania*) for the foreground garden. It looks like a great year coming up!

Summary of Garden Activities for December

1. Transplanted deciduous cherry tree, weigela shrub, and bare-rooted fruit trees and grapevines ordered in September

2. Continued light cleanup chores

3. Broadcast liriope seeds throughout garden for volunteer seedlings

4. Observed growing habits of plants in December

5. Continued to use and enjoy cool-season green vegetables

6. Tended flowers in window greenhouse

7. Fed and watched the birds

8. Made the new year's seed order

9. Enjoyed the holidays

Flowers of December

Camellia sasanqua, Christmas rose, pansy, snowdrop

(And a few off-season blooms of azalea, flowering quince, forsythia, pear, and crab apple. These blooms, either too late for last spring or dangerously early for the coming spring, look as strangely alien and out-of-step as a plastic daffodil "blooming" in a summer window box. This phenomenon is not too rare in the Carolinas, and little, if any, damage results from this behavior.)

---

*Pierre Joseph Redoute and Jean Louis Prevost were nineteenth-century lithographers famous for their prints of flowers and fruits.

Part Four
Sources of Gardening Information

County, State, and Federal Governmental Agencies

One of the most widely available and inexpensive sources for obtaining local and regional professional gardening information is our local Agricultural Extension Service, which is allied with our state land-grant colleges as well as with the United States Department of Agriculture. The services of these well-trained and experienced men and women are paid for from public funds and should be utilized as fully as possible. Staff members are known as agricultural extension agents or more familiarly as county agents. They are located in each county seat, and their telephone numbers are found under "County Government."

These trained horticulturists, agronomists, and home economists are eager to render as much help as they can. As their time allows, they are available for lectures, clinics, and special instruction; some maintain a library of slides, films, and special programs for garden study; they will answer as many personal questions as they can pertaining to individual problems of lawn management; the choice and culture of vegetables, fruits, and flowers; soil testing and improvement; and the diagnosis of plant problems and treatment.

A lode of helpful information is available from your county agent in the form of leaflets, circulars, and bulletins published by both the state and federal agencies. Many may be had without cost and need only be requested at your county agricultural office. The county agent may also furnish a list of federal publications, or you can request a list directly from the superintendent of documents, U.S. Government Printing Office, Washington, D.C. 20402.

State and National Garden Club Organizations

Garden Clubs

Throughout the Carolinas and surrounding states, there are hundreds of neighborhood garden clubs operating under the auspices of state garden club organizations, and these are, in turn, affiliated with a national organization known as The National Council of State Garden Clubs, Inc.

In North Carolina alone there are more than eight hundred local clubs, with a combined membership of over eighteen thousand. This large and influential organization deserves much of the credit for the progress made in the past years in home and neighborhood improvement, conservation and environmental legislation, gardening education, and related activities.

If there is no garden club in your community, why not organize one? For instructions write The Garden Club of North Carolina, Inc., Box 112585, Raleigh, N.C. 27605. Residents of other states can obtain the address of the local state office by writing The National Council of State Garden Clubs, Inc., St. Louis, Mo. 63110.

Gardening Centers

Gardening centers are an outgrowth of the garden club movement. They are community clearing houses for information about local garden activities and gardening information in general. At this writing there are twenty-nine such centers in North Carolina. Most of them are located in the larger towns in space provided by stores, office buildings, libraries, or museums. Each houses a lending library of garden books, seed catalogs, garden magazines, and other gardening information; sponsors exhibits of various types; and provides a meeting place for small garden groups. Help with the organization of such community gardening centers is also available through the state garden club office.

Local and Regional Flower Shows

Flower shows for all seasons are a regular feature of garden club activities in the Carolinas. Everyone can attend, and people go by the thousands. In these shows are exhibited the best of new varieties of flowers, vegetables, and fruits grown by amateurs as well as commercial producers. In addition to horticulture, an artistic division for the purpose of displaying the art of flower arranging is usually included.

Commercial exhibits, especially those shown at the large regional flower shows, present the newest in machinery, tools, fertilizers, insecticides, containers of all kinds, garden furnishings, fountains, and the like.

A flower show offers a fine opportunity to learn a good deal in a hurry, and the serious gardener should take along a notebook for recording pertinent observations. Watch the news media for dates and places of regional and local flower shows.

Garden Classes

Short courses on home gardening are becoming more numerous. Watch your news media for announcements of such classes and clinics offered through the National Educational Television Network, commercial radio and television stations, YWCAs, community colleges, garden clubs, and arts councils.

Correspondence Courses

The College of Agriculture of the Pennsylvania State University offers a variety of home correspondence courses for gardeners at a very nominal cost; in fact, the charges are designed to cover only the cost of paper and mailing. Courses cover a variety of topics including propagation of plants, home floriculture, landscape planning for small properties, rose gardening, home vegetable gardening, small fruits, the home greenhouse, and more than a dozen others.

In my early years of gardening I took a number of these courses, and I have never found a more pleasant and well-organized way in which to learn how to garden.

For information and a list of courses and costs, write The Pennsylvania State University, College of Agriculture, Extension Service, University Park, Pennsylvania.

Public Gardens and Arboreta

North Carolina

Airlie Gardens
Wilmington, N.C.

Biltmore Gardens
Asheville, N.C.

Daniel Boone Wild Flower Garden
Boone, N.C.

Elizabethan Garden
Manteo, N.C.

North Carolina Botanical Garden
Chapel Hill, N.C.

Orton Plantation
Wilmington, N.C.

Reynolda Gardens
Winston-Salem, N.C.

Sarah P. Duke Memorial Garden
Durham, N.C.

Tryon Palace Gardens
New Bern, N.C.

For a complete list of North Carolina gardens, descriptions, fees (if any), dates when open, and travel directions, request a copy of "North Carolina Garden Guide," N.C. Department of Conservation and Development, Raleigh, N.C. 27611.

South Carolina

Brookgreen Gardens
Murrell's Inlet, S.C.

Cypress Gardens
Oakley, S.C.

Edisto Gardens
Orangeburg, S.C.

Magnolia Gardens
Charleston, S.C.

Middleton Gardens
Charleston, S.C.

Regional Gardens

Arnold Arboretum
Jamaica Plain, Mass.

Bellingrath Gardens
Mobile, Ala.

Bishop's Garden
Washington Cathedral, Washington, D.C.

Boston Public Garden
Boston, Mass.

Brooklyn Botanic Garden
Brooklyn, N.Y.

Cypress Gardens
Cypress Gardens, Fla.

Dumbarton Oaks
Washington, D.C.

Fairchild Tropical Garden
Cocoanut Grove, Fla.

Founder's Memorial Gardens
Athens, Ga.

Gardens of Colonial Williamsburg
Williamsburg, Va.

Hershey Gardens
Hershey, Pa.

Ida Cason Calloway Gardens
Pine Mountain, Ga.

Japanese House and Garden
West Fairmont Park, Pa.

Kitchen Garden of Mount Vernon
Mount Vernon, Va.

Longwood Gardens
Kennett Square, Pa.

Missouri Botanical Gardens
St. Louis, Mo.

Mountain Lake Sanctuary
Lake Wales, Fla.

National Arboretum
Washington, D.C.

New York Botanical Garden
Bronx, N.Y.

Sherwood Gardens
Baltimore, Md.

Winterthur
Wilmington, Del.

There are a number of fine private gardens and estates in the Carolinas, Virginia, and Georgia open at special seasons of the year. Watch your newspapers for the places and dates.

Plant Societies

For gardeners interested in a particular plant, there are several societies that exist for the promotion of individual flowers and shrubs. Membership is open to all, and joining fees are usually reasonable. Official publications in the form of leaflets, bulletins, or magazines containing information on new varieties, culture, and sources are a part of the privileges of membership. Many societies also operate a lending library and sponsor seed exchanges among members. For additional information write to the plant society of your choice:

African Violet:
African Violet Society of America, Inc.
Box 1326, Knoxville, Tenn. 37901

Begonia:
American Begonia Society, Inc.
1431 Coronada Terrace, Los Angeles, Calif. 90026

Boxwood:
The American Boxwood Society
Box 85, Boyce, Va. 22620

Cacti and Succulents:
Cactus and Succulent Society of America, Inc.
Box 167, Reseda, Calif. 91335

Camellia:
The American Camellia Society
Box 212, Fort Valley, Ga. 31030

Chrysanthemum:
National Chrysanthemum Society, Inc.
8504 LaVerne Drive, Adelphi, Md. 20763

Daffodil:
The American Daffodil Society
89 Chichester Rd., New Canaan, Conn. 06840

Dahlia:
The American Dahlia Society, Inc.
92–21 W. Delaware Dr., Mystic Islands, Tuckerton, N.J. 08087

Fern:
American Fern Society
Department of Botany, University of Tennessee, Knoxville, Tenn. 37916

Fuchsia:
The American Fuchsia Society
738 22nd Ave., San Francisco, Calif. 94121

Geranium:
International Geranium Society
1413 Shoreline Dr., Santa Barbara, Calif. 93105

Gladiolus:
North American Gladiolus Council
234 South St., South Elgin, Ill. 60177

Hemerocallis (day lily):
The American Hemerocallis Society
Box 586, Woodstock, Ill. 60098

Holly:
The Holly Society of America, Inc.
Box 8445, Baltimore, Md. 21234

Indoor Gardens:
The Indoor Light Gardening Society of America, Inc.
1316 Warren Rd., Lakewood, Ohio 44107

Iris:
The American Iris Society
2315 Tower Grove Ave., St. Louis, Mo. 63110

Lily:
North American Lily Society
North Ferrisburg, Vt. 05473

Peony:
American Peony Society
107½ W. Main St., Van Wert, Ohio 45981

Rhododendron:
American Rhododendron Society
24450 S.W. Graham's Ferry Rd., Sherwood, Oregon 97140

Rose:
American Rose Society
Box 30,000, Shreveport, La. 71130

Wild Flowers:
North Carolina Wild Flower Preservation Society, Inc.
2111 Braxton Lane, Greensboro, N.C. 27408

All-America Selections

Trial testings of new plants are made each year by a group of competent growers supported by commercial nurserymen and seedmen. This group is known as All-America Selections. The testing is done in a variety of climates and soils in the United States, and the results are carefully evaluated. The recommendations made by this group and the information concerning seed and plant introductions are helpful for the beginner as well as the experienced gardener. Check the news media for All-America evaluations.

Where to Buy Seeds, Plants, and Garden Supplies

Gardening catalogs are fine reference materials as well as sources for the raw materials of gardening. Many seed firms distribute their catalogs without charge, and a supply of these publications should be on the shelves of every gardener. The following is a list of some of the old and well-established mail-order garden-supply firms:

A.M. Grootendorst
Box 123, Benton Harbor, Mich. 49022
(bulbs, perennials)

Bountiful Ridge Nurseries, Inc.
Princess Anne, Md. 21853
(fruits, nuts, berries)

Burgess Seed and Plant Co.
Galesburg, Mich. 49053
(seeds, perennials)

Burpee Seed Co.
Box 6929, Philadelphia, Pa. 19132
(seeds, plants)

Carroll Gardens
Westminster, Md. 21157
(perennials, herbs, shrubs, bulbs)

Conard and Pyle Co.
West Grove, Pa.
(roses)

Di Giorgi Co.
Council Bluffs, Iowa 51504
(seeds)

Dirk Visser and Co.
Box 295, Ipswich, Mass. 01938
(bulbs)

Fruitland Nurseries
2505 Washington Rd., Augusta, Ga. 30904
(shrubs, trees)

Gardens of the Blue Ridge
Ashford, N.C. 28603
(native plants)

George W. Park Seed Co.
Greenwood, S.C. 29646
(seeds, plants, bulbs)

Greene Herb Gardens
Greene, R.I.
(herbs)

Sources of Gardening Information [121]

H. G. Hastings Co.
Box 4088, Atlanta, Ga. 30302
(seeds, plants, bulbs, trees)

Inter-State Nurseries
522 E. St., Hamburg, Iowa 51640
(trees, shrubs, bulbs)

Jackson and Perkins
Medford, Oregon 97501
(roses)

Laurel Hill Herb Farm
Falls Village, Conn.
(herbs)

Melvin E. Wyant
Mentor, Ohio 44060
(roses)

Michigan Bulb Co.
Dept. RG, Box 1457, Grand Rapids, Mich. 49550
(bulbs)

Nicholas Garden Nursery
1190 North Pacific Highway,
Albany, Oregon 97321
(herbs, rare seeds)

Rex D. Pearce
Moorestown, N.J.
(rare seeds)

Spring Hill Nurseries
Tipp City, Ohio 45366
(trees, shrubs, perennials)

Stark Brothers
Louisiana, Mo. 63353
(fruits, nuts)

Stern's Nurseries
Geneva, N.Y. 14456
(trees, shrubs, perennials)

Stokes Seeds, Inc.
Box 548, Buffalo, N.Y. 14240
(seeds)

Tingle Nursery Co.
Pittsville, Md. 21850
(trees, shrubs)

Van Bourgondien's
Box A, Babylon, N.Y. 11702
(bulbs)

Wayside Gardens Co.
Hodges, S.C. 29653
(perennials, bulbs, trees, shrubs)

White Flower Farm
Litchfield, Conn. 06759
(perennials, bulbs)

In addition, native and cultivated plants and seeds of North Carolina which are for sale are listed bimonthly in the pages of *Agricultural Review*, a publication of the Department of Agriculture, Raleigh, N.C. There is no charge for a subscription to this paper. For a list of firms selling trees and shrubs, request a copy of "Plant Buyer's Guide," issued by the Brooklyn Botanic Garden, 1000 Washington Ave., Brooklyn N.Y. 11225 ($1.50).

Gardening Books and Periodicals

How to select suitable plants, grow them successfully, and combine them in a garden of satisfying design cannot be mastered in a season or two. Judging from the ever-growing number of participants, however, one must conclude that gardening is one of those happy activities that generates enough seasonal success to support continuing efforts. To speed the pace of achievement, there is no form of information so generally available as the written experience of other gardeners which has been recorded in the thousands of books about gardening in circulation today.

In my early learning years I found much help in the pages of a one-volume gardening encyclopedia and a basic gardening book that answered many of my questions about how to prepare the soil, propagate plants, and take care of them. I would recommend two such books as the nucleus of the beginner's gardening library. From this modest beginning, books may be added on gardening history, design, plant care, and any special plant interests that time and experience might bring forth.

General Gardening

Bailey, Liberty Hyde. *Manual of Cultivated Plants*. New York: Macmillan Co., 1949. Guide to plant identification suitable for home gardener.

Bailey, Ralph. *Gardener's Daybook*. New York: M. Evans and Co., Inc., 1965. Home garden activities for each day of the year.

Bush-Brown, James, and Bush-Brown, Louise. *America's Garden Book*. New York: Charles Scribner's Sons, 1939. One-volume reference for beginners.

Everett, Thomas H., ed. *New Illustrated Encyclopedia of Gardening*. New York: Greystone Press, 1966. 13 vols. Illustrated reference on a wide variety of horticultural subjects written for the amateur gardener.

Hastings, Louise, and Hastings, Donald. *The Southern Garden Book*. Garden City, N.Y.: Doubleday and Co., 1948. Contains regional gardening information written for beginners.

Hudson, Charles J., Jr. *Hudson's Southern Gardening*. Atlanta, Ga.: Tupper and Love, 1953. Practical handbook of gardening in the South.

Lawrence, Elizabeth. *A Southern Garden*. Chapel Hill: University of North Carolina Press, 1967. Woody plants, perennials, bulbs, and vines for southern gardens.

Manning, Laurence. *The How and Why of Better Gardening*. New York: D. Van Nostrand Co., Inc., 1953. Gardening and its relationship to soil, climate, and geography.

Taylor, Norman. *Encyclopedia of Gardening*. Boston: Houghton Mifflin Co., 1956. Introductory material to horticulture and landscape design.

Wister, John C. *Woman's Home Companion Garden Book*. New York: Greystone Press, 1960. General reference book for amateurs.

Garden Design

Church, Thomas D. *Gardens Are for People*. New York: Rheinhold Publishing Co., 1955. Well-illustrated introduction to home garden design with emphasis on the informal garden.

Crowe, Sylvia. *Garden Design*. New York: Hearthside Press, Inc., 1959. History and theory of garden design; materials and styles of gardening.

Dietz, Marjorie J. *Landscaping and the Small Garden*. New York: Doubleday and Co., 1973. Answers many questions about home garden design; includes comprehensive plant lists.

Grant, John A., and Grant, Carol L. *Garden Design*. Seattle: University of Washington Press, 1954. Description of plant groups, their character, and how to assemble them in the landscape.

Grasby, Nancy. *Imaginative Small Gardens*. New York: Hearthside Press, 1963. Planning new small gardens and renovating old ones.

Korbobo, Raymond P. *Complete Home Landscaping and Garden Guide*. New York: Wm. H. Wise and Co., 1954. Practical instructions for making and executing your own landscape plan.

Lamson, Mary Deputy. *Landscape with Shrubs and Flowering Trees*. New York: M. Barrows and Co., 1952. Practical guide to easy-maintenance plantings of trees and shrubs.

Ortloff, H. Stuart, and Raymore, Henry B. *The Book of Landscape Design*. New York: M. Barrows and Co., 1959. How to design and plant the home grounds.

———. *Color and Design for Every Garden*. New York: M. Barrows and Co., 1952. Introduction to garden design; plans for perennial borders.

Smith, Alice Upham. *Patios, Terraces, Decks, and Roof Gardens*. New York: Hawthorn Books, Inc., 1969. How to design, build, and decorate outdoor living areas.

Miscellaneous

Ballard, Ernesta Drinker. *Garden in Your House*. New York: Harper and Brothers, 1958. Advanced, illustrated book on culture and use of house plants.

Baumgardt, John Philip. *Hanging Plants for Home, Terrace, and Garden*. New York: Simon and Schuster, 1972. Cultural instructions and suggestions for displaying a variety of container plant materials.

Behme, Robert Lee. *The Outdoor How-to-Build-It Book*. New York: Hawthorn Books, Inc., 1971. 425 photos and 50 drawings for building many types of outdoor garden structures.

Berrall, Julia S. *The Garden*. New York: Viking Press, 1966. An illustrated history of gardening from the Pharaohs to today.

Brimer, John Burton. *Homeowner's Complete Outdoor Building Book*. New York: Popular Science Publishing Co., 1971. Complete plans and instructions for building shelters, fences, gates, birdhouses, and other outdoor structures.

Foley, Daniel J. *The Flowering World of "Chinese" Wilson*. New York: Macmillan Co., 1969. Selections and editorial comments from the writings of plant explorer E. H. "Chinese" Wilson.

———. *Garden Ornaments, Complements, and Accessories*. New York: Crown Publishers, 1972. Illustrated ways to use a variety of garden ornaments and a list of sources.

Green, Charlotte Hilton. *Trees of the South*. Chapel Hill: University of North Carolina Press, 1939. Nontechnical descriptions of native Carolina trees with pictures of barks, leaves, and fruits.

Greene, Wilhelmina F., and Blomquist, Hugo L. *Flowers of the South*. Chapel Hill: University of North Carolina Press, 1953. Descriptions and sketches of 500 southern wild flowers.

Halfacre, R. Gordon. *Carolina Landscape Plants*. Raleigh, N.C.: Sparks Press, 1971. Heights, spreads, special features, and uses of evergreen and deciduous shrubs and trees for Carolina gardeners.

Hull, George Frederick. *The Know-Nothing Gardener's Guide to Success*. New York: Hawthorn Books, 1969. Information about a variety of garden problems common to the beginner.

Hylander, Clarence J. *Wild-Flower Book*. New York: Macmillan Co., 1954. Descriptions and pictures of more than 500 wild flowers.

Justice, William J., and Bell, C. Ritchie. *Wild Flowers of North Carolina*. Chapel Hill: University of North Carolina Press, 1968. Pictures and descriptions of North Carolina wild flowers.

Lawrence, Elizabeth. *Gardens in Winter*. New York: Harper and Brothers, 1961. On the particular beauty of the Carolina winter garden and winter gardens in general.

Steffek, Edwin F. *Wild Flowers and How to Grow Them*. New York: Crown Publishers, Inc., 1954. Descriptions and cultural requirements of wild flowers.

Stout, Ruth. *No-Work Garden Book*. Emmaus, Pa.: Rodale Press, 1971. How the author uses mulch to decrease maintenance and improve soil.

Taloumis, George. *Container Gardening Outdoors*. New York: Simon and Schuster, 1972. Creative approach to outdoor container gardening for the apartment or city dweller.

Wells, Bertram Whittier. *The Natural Gardens of North Carolina*. Chapel Hill: University of North Carolina Press, 1967. Keys and descriptions of the herbaceous native North Carolina plants.

West, Victoria Mary Sackville. *A Joy of Gardening*. New York: Harper and Brothers, 1958. A famous English gardener shares knowledge and experience with American gardeners.

Westcott, Cynthia. *Are You Your Garden's Worst Pest?* Garden City, N.Y.: Doubleday and Co., 1961. Guide to pest and disease control for the home gardener.

Wheeler, Esther, and Lasker, Annabel Combs. *The Complete Book of Flowers and Plants for Interior Decoration*. New York: Hearthside Press, 1969. Pictures, step-by-step directions for use of commonplace and exotic materials for decorating the home interior.

Books about Special Plants

Abraham, George "Doc," and Abraham, Katy. *Raise Vegetables without a Garden*. Barrington, Ill.: A.B. Morse Co., 1974. How to grow recommended varieties of vegetables, herbs, and fruits in containers.

Baker, Jerry. *Make Friends with Your Fruit Trees*. New York: Simon and Schuster, 1973. An introduction to the growing requirements of orchard fruits, nuts, and berries.

———. *Make Friends with Your Perennials and Biennials*. New York: Simon and Schuster, 1973. Bedding plants for sun and shade and how to grow them.

———. *Make Friends with Your Roses*. New York: Simon and Schuster, 1973. Illustrated introduction to the cultural requirements of roses for beginners.

———. *Make Friends with Your Vegetable Garden*. New York: Simon and Schuster, 1973. How to prepare soil, plant, grow, and harvest several of our most popular table vegetables; written for the beginner.

Bassity, Matthew A.R. *The Magic World of Roses*. New York: Hearthside Press, 1966. History and legends of roses; planting guide by states; well illustrated.

Boer, Arie F. den. *Ornamental Crab Apples*. American Association of Nurserymen, 1959. Excellent guide for selecting and caring for ornamental crab apples; sketches show leaf, blossom, fruit, and tree-form habits of the most popular crab apples grown today.

Bush-Brown, James. *Shrubs and Trees for the Home Landscape*. Philadelphia, Pa.: Chilton Co., 1963. Illustrated alphabetical descriptions of several hundred trees and shrubs suitable for the home landscape.

Campbell, Mary Mason. *Betty Crocker's Kitchen Gardens*. New York: Universal Publishing Co., 1971. A year-around guide for growing and using herbs.

Carleton, R. Milton. *Vegetables for Today's Gardens*. Hollywood, Calif.: Wilshire Book Co., 1972. Excellent starter book for inexperienced gardeners; covers site selection, soil preparation, tools, and vegetables for all seasons.

Coffin, Marian Cruger. *Trees and Shrubs for Landscape Effects*. New York: Charles Scribner's Sons, 1953. The use of trees in garden design is stressed in this book.

Davis, Ben Arthur. *Day Lilies and How to Grow Them*. Atlanta, Ga.: Tupper and Love, 1954. Selecting day lilies for southern gardens; how to grow and use them.

Foley, Daniel J. *Ground Covers for Easier Gardening*. Philadelphia, Pa.: Chilton Co., 1961. Broad, comprehensive treatment of ground covers from vines to shrubs and some new, creative ways of using them.

Hottes, Alfred Carl. *The Book of Shrubs*. New York: A.T. DeLaMare Co., 1952. Descriptions and suggested uses of several hundred shrubs; plantings to attract birds, those for difficult sites, shade, etc.

———. *Climbers and Ground Covers*. New York: A.T. DeLaMare Co., 1947. Hardy and subtropical vines and ground covers for all purposes.

Hume, H. Harold. *Azaleas: Kinds and Culture*. New York: Macmillan Co., 1949. Classes and varieties of azaleas; hardiness information; cultural needs.

———. *Camellias*. New York: Macmillan Co., 1951. Camellia history, geography, types, and varieties; how to propagate and grow.

———. *Hollies*. New York: Macmillan Co., 1960. Types of holly with common and scientific names; cultural methods and landscape uses; illustrations.

Ishimoto, Tatsuo, and Ishimoto, Kiyoko. *The Art of Shaping Shrubs, Trees, and Other Plants*. New York: Crown Publishers, Inc., 1966. A profusely illustrated comparison of the European topiary style of pruning and the informal, creative style of pruning done in the Orient.

Miles, Bebe. *The Wonderful World of Bulbs*. Princeton, N.J.: D. Van Nostrand Co., 1963. Classification, culture, and landscape uses of bulbs for beginners.

Parcher, Emily Seaber. *Shady Gardens*. New York: Prentice-Hall, Inc., 1955. Helpful reference for growing small plants in shady areas; lists of shade-tolerant wild flowers, perennials, annuals, and biennials.

Perkins, Harold O. *Espaliers and Vines for the Home Gardener*. Princeton, N.J.: D. Van Nostrand Co., 1964. Home gardener's guide for selecting and training formal and informal espaliers.

———. *Ornamental Trees for Home Grounds*. New York: E.P. Dutton and Co., 1965. Advice on the selection of the best trees for specific properties; their variety of form, planting, and care.

Pond, Barbara. *A Sampler of Wayside Herbs*. Riverside, Conn.: Chatham Press Inc., 1973. Old and new ways of using many familiar roadside plants.

Rockwell, Frederick Frye, and Grayson, Esther C. *The Complete Book of Bulbs*. Garden City, N.Y.: The American Garden Guild and Doubleday and Co., 1953. A practical manual of the uses, cultivation, and propagation of more than 100 species of hardy and tender bulbs.

Taylor, Norman. *The Guide to Garden Shrubs and Trees*. Boston: Houghton Mifflin Co., 1965. Identity and culture of 500 trees, shrubs, and vines for home gardens; illustrated.

Van Ness, Martha. *Cacti and Succulents Indoors and Outdoors*. New York: Van Nostrand Rheinhold Co., 1971. Index of plants, sources, and culture for cacti and succulents for all parts of North America; recommended for apartment and city gardeners.

Walker, Marian C. *Dahlias for Every Garden*. New York: M. Barrows and Co., 1954. Useful for both gardener and exhibitor; dahlia divisions and descriptions of this large plant group.

Whitehead, Stanley B. *Garden Clematis*. London, Eng.: John Gifford, Ltd., 1959. Introduction to the many forms, culture, uses, and propagation of the large clematis family.

Wilson, Helen Van Pelt. *Geraniums Pelargoniums*. New York: M. Barrows and Co., 1957. Guide to the types, uses, and culture of the many classes of geraniums.

———. *Perennials for Every Garden*. New York: M. Barrows and Co., 1953. Lists of best varieties, colors, suggested uses, and cultures for such standard perennials as phlox, peony, iris, and day lily.

Periodical Gardening Literature

American Horticultural Magazine
American Horticultural Society
901 N. Washington St., Suite 704
Alexandria, Va. 22314

The American Rose
American Rose Society
Box 30,000, Shreveport, La. 71130

Avant Gardener
Horticultural Data Processors
Box 489, New York, N.Y. 10028

The Floral Magazine
George W. Park Seed Co.
Box 31, Greenwood, S.C. 29646

Flower and Garden
4251 Pennsylvania Ave., Kansas City, Mo. 64111

The Gardener
Men's Garden Club of America
5560 Merle Hay Rd., Des Moines, Iowa 50323

Garden Journal
The New York Botanical Garden
Bronx, N.Y. 10458

Home Garden
Flower Grower Publishing, Inc.
1 Park Ave., New York, N.Y. 10016

Horticulture
Massachusetts Horticultural Society
300 Massachusetts Ave., Boston, Mass. 02115

House and Garden Guide
Conde Nast Publications, Inc.
420 Lexington Ave., New York, N.Y. 10017

Plants and Gardens
Brooklyn Botanic Garden
1000 Washington Ave., Brooklyn, N.Y. 11225

Southern Gardens
Wing Publications, Inc.
Box 3, Columbia, S.C. 29202

Southern Living
Box 523, Birmingham, Ala. 35201

Under Glass
Lord and Burnham
Box 114, Irvington, N.Y. 10533

Glossaries and Index

Glossary of Scientific Plant Names

The following list is based on the nomenclature found in *The Manual of Cultivated Plants* by Liberty Hyde Bailey; *The Standard Cyclopedia of Horticulture*, vols. I, II, and III, by Liberty Hyde Bailey; and *The Catalog of the American Joint Committee on Horticultural Nomenclature*.

Scientific Name / Common Name

Abelia grandiflora / Abelia
Acer / Maple
Acer palmatum / Japanese maple
Acer platanoides / Norway maple
Acer rubrum / Red maple
Acer saccharinum / Silver maple
Acer saccharum / Sugar maple
Adiantum pedatum / Maidenhair fern, American maidenhair fern
Aesculus / Buckeye
Agapanthus umbellatus / Agapanthus, lily-of-the-Nile
Ageratum Houstonianum / Ageratum
Ajuga reptans / Ajuga
Allium spp. / Onion
Althaea rosea / Hollyhock
Amaranthus bicolor / Amaranthus, Joseph's-coat
Amaryllis belladonna / Amaryllis
Amelanchier laevis / Serviceberry, Juneberry, shadblow
Anemone coronaria / Poppy anemone, spring anemone
Anemone hupehensis / Japanese anemone, fall anemone
Antirrhinum majus / Snapdragon
Aquilegia canadensis / Columbine
Arabis albida / Arabis, rock-cress
Armeria splendens / Armeria
Arum italicum / Italian arum

Scientific Name / Common Name

Asarum arifolium / Mottled wild ginger
Asarum canadense / Canada wild ginger
Asclepias tuberosa / Butterfly weed
Aspidistra lurida / Aspidistra, cast-iron plant
Asplenium platyneuron / Ebony spleenwort
Aster / Aster, Michaelmas daisy (perennial)
Astilbe / Astilbe
Aubrietia deltoidea / Aubrietia
Aucuba japonica / Aucuba
Azalea spp. / *See* Rhododendron

Baptisia australis / Baptisia, wild indigo
Begonia spp. / Begonia
Begonia Evansiana / Hardy begonia
Begonia semperflorens / Bedding begonia
Bellis perennis / English daisy
Berberis vulgaris / Barberry
Bergenia cordifolia / Bergenia
Betula / Birch
Betula nigra / River birch
Boltonia asteroides / Boltonia
Bougainvillea / Bougainvillea, bougainville
Browallia americana / Browallia
Buddleia Davidii / Butterfly bush
Buxus sempervirens / Boxwood
Buxus sempervirens var. *arborescens* / American boxwood
Buxus sempervirens var. *suffruticosa* / English boxwood, dwarf boxwood

Caladium bicolor / Caladium
Calendula officinalis / Calendula, pot-marigold
Callicarpa americana / Beautyberry, French mulberry
Callistephus chinensis / Aster (annual)
Calycanthus floridus / Sweet shrub, sweet-betsy
Camellia japonica / Camellia, japonica (fall and winter flowering)
Camellia sasanqua / Camellia, sasanqua (fall flowering)
Campanula / Campanula, bellflower

Scientific Name / Common Name

Campanula medium / Canterbury bells
Campsis radicans / Trumpet vine, trumpet creeper
Canna generalis / Canna
Capsicum frutescens / Bell pepper
Carpinus / Hornbeam
Carpinus caroliniana / Ironwood, American hornbeam
Carya ovata / Hickory, shag-bark hickory
Catalpa / Catalpa
Celastrus scandens / Bittersweet, American bittersweet
Celosia argentea / Celosia, cockscomb
Celtis / Hackberry
Centaurea cyanus / Cornflower, bachelor's-button
Cercis canadensis / Redbud
Chaenomeles japonica / Japanese quince, cydonia, japonica
Cheiranthus cheiri / Wallflower
Chimaphila maculata / Pipsissewa
Chionanthus virginica / Fringe tree, granddaddy-greybeard
Chionodoxa Luciliae / Glory-of-the-snow
Chrysanthemum / Chrysanthemum, mums
Chrysanthemum maximum / Shasta daisy
Chrysogonum virginianum / Green-in-gold, golden star
Citrus taitensis / Dwarf orange
Cladrastis lutea / Yellowwood
Clematis Jackmanii / Large-flowered clematis
Cleome spinosa / Cleome, spiderflower
Clerodendrum trichotomum / Clerodendrum
Cleyera japonica / Cleyera
Colchicum autumnale / Colchicum, fall crocus
Coleus Blumei / Coleus
Colocasia antiquorum / Elephant's-ear
Coreopsis lanceolata / Coreopsis
Cornus florida / Dogwood
Cornus stolonifera / Red-stemmed dogwood
Cosmos bipinnatus / Cosmos
Cotinus / Smoke tree

[128] *Carolina Home Gardener*

Scientific Name / Common Name

Cotoneaster horizontalis / Cotoneaster
Crataegus / Hawthorn
Crataegus apiifolia / Parsley-haw, hawthorn
Crataegus Crus-galli / Cockspur thorn, hawthorn
Crataegus oxyacantha / English hawthorn
Crinum / Crinum, milk-and-wine lily
Crocus biflorus / Crocus
Cucurbita pepo / Gourd
Cynodon dactylon / Bermuda grass, wire grass
Cytisus scoparius / Scotch broom

Dahlia pinnata / Dahlia
Danae racemosa / Poet's laurel, Alexandrian laurel
Daphne cneorum / Daphne
Delphinium cultorum / Larkspur (biennial)
Delphinium grandiflorum / Delphinium (perennial)
Deutzia gracilis / Deutzia
Dianthus / Dianthus
Dianthus barbatus / Sweet william
Dianthus deltoides / Maiden pink
Dianthus plumarius / Garden pink
Dicentra cucullaria / Dutchman's-breeches
Dicentra eximia / Bleeding heart
Digitalis purpurea / Foxglove
Dionaea muscipula / Venus's flytrap
Doronicum caucasicum / Doronicum, leopard's-bane

Echinops exaltatus / Globe thistle
Elaeagnus / Elaeagnus
Elaeagnus pungens / Evergreen elaeagnus
Elaeagnus umbellata / Russian olive
Epigaea repens / Trailing arbutus
Eranthis hyemalis / Winter aconite
Eriobotrya japonica / Loquat
Erythronium americanum / Trout-lily
Escallonia / Escallonia
Eschscholtzia californica / California poppy
Euonymus / Euonymus

Scientific Name / Common Name

Euonymus alatus / Winged euonymus
Euonymus Fortunei / Winter creeper
Euphorbia marginata / Snow-on-the-mountain, spurge
Euphorbia pulcherrima / Poinsettia
Exochorda racemosa / Pearlbush

Fagus grandifolia / American beech
Fatshedera lizei / Tree ivy
Festuca / Fescue
Forsythia intermedia / Forsythia
Fraxinus americana / American ash, white ash
Fuchsia procumbens / Fuchsia

Gaillardia aristata / Gaillardia
Galanthus nivalis / Snowdrop
Galax aphylla / Galax
Gardenia jasminoides / Cape jasmine, gardenia
Gazania / Gazania
Gelsemium sempervirens / Carolina yellow jessamine
Geranium maculatum / Wild geranium
Gerbera Jamesonii / Gerbera, Transvaal daisy
Ginkgo biloba / Ginkgo
Gladiolus / Gladiolus
Gleditsia triacanthos / Thornless honey locust

Halesia carolina / Carolina silverbell
Hedera helix / English ivy
Hedychium coronarium / Ginger lily
Helichrysum bracteatum / Strawflower, everlasting
Helleborus niger / Christmas rose
Helleborus orientalis / Lenten rose
Hemerocallis / Day lily
Hepatica acutiloba / Sharp-lobed hepatica
Hepatica triloba / Round-lobed hepatica
Hesperis matronalis / Sweet rocket
Heuchera americana / Alum root
Heuchera sanguinea / Coral-bell
Hibiscus coccineus / Rose-mallow, hibiscus
Hibiscus syriacus / Althea, rose of Sharon

Scientific Name / Common Name

Hosta / Hosta, plantain lily, funkia
Houstonia caerulea / Bluet
Hoya carnosa / Hoya, wax-vine
Hyacinthus / Hyacinth
Hyacinthus orientalis / Dutch hyacinth, hyacinth
Hyacinthus orientalis albulus / Roman hyacinth
Hydrangea hortensia / Florists' hydrangea
Hydrangea paniculata var. *grandiflora* / Peegee hydrangea
Hydrangea petiolaris / Climbing hydrangea
Hydrangea quercifolia / Oak-leaf hydrangea
Hypericum calycinum / Hyperion, St.-John's-wort

Iberis sempervirens / Hardy candytuft
Ilex / Holly
Ilex cassine / Cassine holly, Dahoon holly
Ilex cornuta / Chinese holly
Ilex cornuta var. *Burfordi* / Burford holly
Ilex cornuta var. *rotundifolia* / Dwarf Chinese holly
Ilex crenata / Japanese holly
Ilex crenata var. *convexa* / Convexa holly
Ilex crenata var. *Helleri* / Heller holly
Ilex crenata var. *Hetzi* / Hetz holly
Ilex decidua / Possum-haw holly
Ilex opaca / American holly
Ilex opaca var. *Croonenburg* / Croonenburg holly
Ilex opaca var. *Fosteri* / Foster's holly
Ilex verticillata / Winterberry
Ilex vomitoria / Yaupon
Ilex vomitoria compacta / Dwarf yaupon
Impatiens balsamina / Impatiens, patience plant
Ipomoea purpurea / Morning glory
Iris germanica / Bearded iris, pogoniris
Iris sibirica / Siberian iris
Iris xiphium / Dutch iris

Jasminum nudiflorum / Winter jasmine
Juniperus chinensis / Pfitzer juniper

Glossary of Scientific Plant Names [129]

Scientific Name / Common Name

Juniperus horizontalis conferta / Shore juniper
Juniperus virginiana / Cedar, red cedar

Kerria japonica / Kerria, globeflower
Kniphofia uvaria / Redhot poker, torchflower
Kochia scoparia / Kochia, summer cypress
Koelreuteria paniculata / Goldenrain tree
Kolkwitzia amabilis / Beauty bush

Laburnum alpinum / Goldenchain tree
Lagerstroemia indica / Crape myrtle
Lamium maculatum / Henbit
Lantana camara / Lantana
Lathyrus odoratus / Sweet pea (annual)
Leucojum aestivum / Summer snowflake
Leucojum vernum / Spring snowflake
Leucothoe Catesbaei / Leucothoe
Ligustrum spp. / Ligustrum
Ligustrum lucidum / Waxleaf ligustrum
Ligustrum vulgare / Privet
Lilium candidum / Easter lily, Madonna lily
Lilium superbum / Turk's-cap lily, American turk's-cap lily
Liquidambar styraciflua / Sweet gum
Liriodendron tulipifera / Tulip poplar
Liriope muscari / Liriope, lily-turf
Lobelia cardinalis / Cardinal flower
Lobelia erinus / Lobelia (annual)
Lobularia maritima / Sweet alyssum
Lolium multiflorum / Italian ryegrass
Lonicera fragrantissima / Winter honeysuckle, Sweet-Breath-of-Spring
Lonicera sempervirens / Coral honeysuckle, trumpet honeysuckle
Lunaria annua / Honesty, money plant
Lupinus diffusus / Sandhill lupine
Lupinus polyphyllus / Lupine
Lycoris radiata / Lycoris, red spider lily

Scientific Name / Common Name

Lycoris squamigera / Hall's amaryllis
Lysimachia punctata / Loosestrife

Magnolia / Magnolia
Magnolia acuminata / Cucumber magnolia
Magnolia grandiflora / Evergreen magnolia
Magnolia soulangeana / Saucer magnolia, tulip-tree
Magnolia stellata / Star magnolia
Mahonia Bealei / Mahonia, Oregon hollygrape
Malus spp. / Apple, crab apple
Matthiola incana / Stock
Mertensia virginica / Virginia bluebell
Mirabilis jalapa / Four o'clock
Monarda didyma / Beebalm, horsemint
Muscari botryoides / Grape hyacinth
Myosotis sylvatica / Forget-me-not

Nandina domestica / Nandina
Narcissus spp. / Daffodil
Narcissus bulbocodium / Hoop-petticoat daffodil
Nephrolepis exaltata / Boston fern
Nerium oleander / Oleander
Nicotiana alata / Flowering tobacco
Nigella damascena / Nigella, love-in-a-mist
Nyssa sylvatica / Black gum, sour gum

Oenothera perennis / Evening primrose
Opuntia / Prickly pear
Osmanthus aquifolium / Holly osmanthus
Osmanthus Fortunei / Osmanthus, tea-olive
Oxydendrum arboreum / Sourwood

Pachysandra terminalis / Pachysandra
Paeonia lactiflora / Peony
Papaver orientale / Oriental poppy
Papaver rhoeas / Shirley poppy
Pelargonium / Geranium
Pelargonium peltatum / Ivy-leaved geranium
Penstemon / Penstemon, beard-tongue

Scientific Name / Common Name

Petunia hybrida / Petunia
Philadelphus coronarius / Mock orange
Phlox divaricata / Spring phlox, blue spring phlox
Phlox Drummondii / Drummond phlox, annual phlox
Phlox nivalis / Moss pink
Phlox paniculata / Summer phlox, hardy phlox
Phlox subulata / Thrift, moss pink
Photinia glabra / Photinia
Photinia serrulata / Photinia
Picea rubra / Red spruce
Pieris floribunda / Andromeda, mountain pieris
Pieris japonica / Pieris, lily-of-the-valley shrub
Pinus spp. / Pine
Pinus strobus / White pine
Pittosporum tobira / Pittosporum
Platanus occidentalis / Sycamore
Platycodon grandiflorum / Balloon flower
Plumbago spp. / Plumbago, leadwort
Polemonium caeruleum / Polemonium, Jacob's ladder
Polygonatum biflorum / Small Solomon's seal
Polygonatum commutatum / Great Solomon's seal
Polystichum acrostichoides / Christmas fern
Populus tremuloides / Aspen, quaking aspen
Portulaca grandiflora / Portulaca, rose-moss
Primula vulgaris / Primrose
Prunus spp. / Cherry, peach, plum
Prunus glandulosa / Flowering almond
Prunus laurocerasus caroliniana / Carolina cherry laurel
Prunus laurocerasus officinalis / English laurel
Prunus laurocerasus schipkaensis / Schipka laurel, schip laurel
Prunus serrulata / Japanese flowering cherry
Punica granatum / Pomegranate
Pyracantha coccinea / Pyracantha, firethorn
Pyrethrum / Painted daisy
Pyrus / Pear
Pyrus Calleryana / Callery pear
Pyrus communis / Kieffer pear

Scientific Name	Common Name
Quercus	Oak
Quercus alba	White oak
Quercus palustris	Pin oak
Quercus phellos	Willow oak
Quercus stellata	Post oak
Quercus virginiana	Live oak
Rhododendron spp.	Rhododendron, azalea
Ricinus communis	Castor bean
Rosa spp.	Rose
Rudbeckia hirta	Gloriosa daisy
Rudbeckia serotina	Black-eyed Susan
Rumex patientia	Dock
Saintpaulia ionantha	African violet
Salix spp.	Willow
Salix discolor	Pussy willow
Salix matsudana var. *tortuosa*	Corkscrew willow
Salvia	Sage
Salvia splendens	Scarlet sage
Sanguinaria canadensis	Bloodroot
Saxifraga sarmentosa	Strawberry geranium, strawberry begonia
Scabiosa japonica	Scabiosa, pincushion flower
Scilla hispanica	Squill, Spanish bluebell, scilla
Sedum acre	Sedum, stonecrop
Sedum sieboldii	Siebold sedum
Sedum spectabile	Great sedum
Sempervivum tectorum	Hen-and-chicks
Senecio cruentus	Cineraria
Shortia galacifolia	Oconee bell
Sinningia	Gloxinia
Sisyrinchium angustifolium	Blue-eyed grass
Skimmia Reevesiana	Skimmia
Solanum pseudo-capsicum	Christmas cherry, Jerusalem cherry
Solidago odora	Goldenrod
Sorghum halepense	Johnson grass
Spathiphyllum patinii	Spathiphyllum
Spiraea bumalda var. Anthony Waterer	Summer spirea
Spiraea Vanhouttei	Vanhoutte spirea
Stellaria	Chickweed
Stokesia laevis	Stokesia, Stokes' aster
Symphoricarpos albus	Snowberry
Syringa vulgaris	Lilac
Tagetes	Marigold
Tagetes erecta	African marigold
Tagetes patula	French marigold
Thermopsis caroliniana	Thermopsis
Thunbergia alata	Black-eyed Susan vine
Tiarella cordifolia	Foam flower
Tilia	Linden
Tilia cordata	Small-leaved linden
Trachelospermum jasminoides	Confederate jasmine, star jasmine
Tradescantia	Spiderwort
Trillium grandiflorum	Snow trillium
Trillium nervosum	Catesby's trillium
Trillium sessile	Toad trillium
Tropaeolum majus	Nasturtium
Tsuga canadensis	Canadian hemlock
Tsuga caroliniana	Carolina hemlock
Tulipa spp.	Tulip
Ulmus	Elm
Ulmus alata	Cork-bark elm
Ulmus americana	American elm
Ulmus chinensis	Chinese elm
Verbena hybrida	Garden verbena
Veronica incana	Veronica, speedwell
Viburnum spp.	Viburnum
Viburnum Carlesii	Fragrant viburnum
Viburnum rhytidophyllum	Leatherleaf viburnum
Viburnum tomentosum	Japanese snowball, snowball
Vinca	Periwinkle
Vinca major	Large-leaf periwinkle
Vinca minor	Small-leaf periwinkle
Vinca rosea	Annual periwinkle, vinca
Viola blanda	Sweet white violet
Viola cornuta	Bedding pansy
Viola papilionacea	Confederate violet
Viola pedata	Bird's-foot violet
Viola tricolor	Variegated pansy
Vitex agnus-castus	Vitex, chaste tree
Vitis spp.	Grape
Vitis labruscana	Concord and Niagara
Vitis rotundifolia	Muscadine, scuppernong
Weigela florida	Weigela
Yucca aloifolia	Yucca, Spanish bayonet
Zebrina pendula	Wandering Jew
Zephyranthes	Zephyr lily, Zephyranthes
Zephyranthes atamasco	Atamasco lily
Zephyranthes candida	Fairy lily
Zinnia elegans	Zinnia
Zoysia matrella	Zoysia, Manila grass

Glossary of Common Plant Names

Common Name / Scientific Name

Abelia / *Abelia grandiflora*
African marigold / *Tagetes erecta*
African violet / *Saintpaulia ionantha*
Agapanthus, lily-of-the-Nile / *Agapanthus umbellatus*
Ageratum / *Ageratum Houstonianum*
Ajuga / *Ajuga reptans*
Althea, rose of Sharon / *Hibiscus syriacus*
Alum root / *Heuchera americana*
Amaranthus, Joseph's-coat / *Amaranthus bicolor*
Amaryllis / *Amaryllis belladonna*
American ash, white ash / *Fraxinus americana*
American beech / *Fagus grandifolia*
American boxwood / *Buxus sempervirens arborescens*
American elm / *Ulmus americana*
American holly / *Ilex opaca*
Andromeda, mountain pieris / *Pieris floribunda*
Apple, crab apple / *Malus* spp.
Arabis, rock-cress / *Arabis albida*
Armeria / *Armeria splendens*
Ash / *Fraxinus americana*
Aspen, quaking aspen / *Populus tremuloides*
Aspidistra, cast-iron plant / *Aspidistra lurida*
Aster (annual) / *Callistephus chinensis*
Aster (perennial), Michaelmas daisy / *Aster*
Astilbe / *Astilbe*
Atamasco lily / *Zephyranthes atamasco*
Aubrietia / *Aubrietia deltoidea*
Aucuba / *Aucuba japonica*
Azalea / *Rhododendron* spp.

Balloon flower / *Platycodon grandiflorum*
Baptisia, wild indigo / *Baptisia australis*
Barberry / *Berberis vulgaris*

Bearded iris, pogoniris / *Iris germanica*
Beautyberry, French mulberry / *Callicarpa americana*
Beauty bush / *Kolkwitzia amabilis*
Bedding begonia / *Begonia semperflorens*
Beebalm, horsemint / *Monarda didyma*
Begonia / *Begonia* spp.
Bellflower / *Campanula* spp.
Bell pepper / *Capsicum frutescens*
Bergenia / *Bergenia cordifolia*
Bermuda grass, wire grass / *Cynodon dactylon*
Birch / *Betula*
Bird's-foot violet / *Viola pedata*
Bittersweet, American bittersweet / *Celastrus scandens*
Black-eyed Susan / *Rudbeckia serotina*
Black-eyed Susan vine / *Thunbergia alata*
Black gum, sour gum / *Nyssa sylvatica*
Bleeding heart / *Dicentra eximia*
Bloodroot / *Sanguinaria canadensis*
Blue-eyed grass / *Sisyrinchium angustifolium*
Bluet / *Houstonia caerulea*
Boltonia / *Boltonia asteroides*
Boston daisy / *Chrysanthemum*
Boston fern / *Nephrolepis exaltata*
Bougainvillea, bougainville / *Bougainvillea*
Boxwood / *Buxus sempervirens*
Browallia / *Browallia americana*
Buckeye / *Aesculus*
Burford holly / *Ilex cornuta* var. *Burfordi*
Butterfly bush / *Buddleia Davidii*
Butterfly weed / *Asclepias tuberosa*

Caladium / *Caladium bicolor*
Calendula, pot-marigold / *Calendula officinalis*
California poppy / *Eschscholtzia californica*
Callery pear / *Pyrus Calleryana*
Camellia, japonica / *Camellia japonica*
Camellia sasanqua, sasanqua / *Camellia sasanqua*
Campanula, bellflower / *Campanula*

Canada wild ginger / *Asarum canadense*
Canadian hemlock / *Tsuga canadensis*
Candytuft (perennial) / *Iberis sempervirens*
Canna / *Canna generalis*
Canterbury bell / *Campanula medium*
Cape jasmine, gardenia / *Gardenia jasminoides*
Cardinal flower / *Lobelia cardinalis*
Carolina cherry laurel / *Prunus laurocerasus* var. *caroliniana*
Carolina hemlock / *Tsuga caroliniana*
Carolina jessamine / *Gelsemium sempervirens*
Carolina silverbell / *Halesia carolina*
Cassine holly, Dahoon holly / *Ilex cassine*
Castor bean / *Ricinus communis*
Catalpa / *Catalpa*
Catesby's trillium / *Trillium nervosum*
Cedar, red cedar / *Juniperus virginiana*
Celosia, cockscomb / *Celosia argentea*
Cherry / *Prunus* spp.
Chickweed / *Stellaria*
Chinese elm / *Ulmus chinensis*
Chinese holly / *Ilex cornuta*
Christmas cherry, Jerusalem cherry / *Solanum pseudo-capsicum*
Christmas fern / *Polystichum acrostichoides*
Christmas rose / *Helleborus niger*
Chrysanthemum, mums / *Chrysanthemum* spp.
Cineraria / *Senecio cruentus*
Clematis / *Clematis Jackmanii*
Cleome, spiderflower / *Cleome spinosa*
Clerodendrum / *Clerodendrum trichotomum*
Cleyera / *Cleyera japonica*
Climbing hydrangea / *Hydrangea petiolaris*
Cockspur thorn, hawthorn / *Crataegus Crus-galli*
Colchicum, fall crocus / *Colchicum autumnale*
Coleus / *Coleus Blumei*
Columbine / *Aquilegia canadensis*

Common Name / Scientific Name

Concord and Niagara grape / *Vitis labruscana*
Confederate jasmine, star jasmine / *Trachelospermum jasminoides*
Confederate violet / *Viola papilionacea*
Convexa holly / *Ilex crenata convexa*
Coral-bell / *Heuchera sanguinea*
Coral honeysuckle, trumpet honeysuckle / *Lonicera sempervirens*
Coreopsis / *Coreopsis lanceolata*
Cork-bark elm / *Ulmus alata*
Corkscrew willow / *Salix matsudana* var. *tortuosa*
Cornflower, bachelor's-button / *Centaurea cyanus*
Cosmos / *Cosmos bipinnatus*
Cotoneaster / *Cotoneaster horizontalis*
Crab apple, apple / *Malus* spp.
Crape myrtle / *Lagerstroemia indica*
Crinum, milk-and-wine lily / *Crinum*
Crocus / *Crocus biflorus*
Croonenburg holly / *Ilex opaca* var. *Croonenburg*
Cucumber magnolia / *Magnolia acuminata*

Daffodil / *Narcissus* spp.
Dahlia / *Dahlia pinnata*
Daphne / *Daphne cneorum*
Day lily / *Hemerocallis*
Delphinium (perennial) / *Delphinium grandiflorum*
Deutzia / *Deutzia gracilis*
Dianthus / *Dianthus*
Dock / *Rumex patientia*
Dogwood / *Cornus florida*
Doronicum, leopard's-bane / *Doronicum caucasicum*
Drummond phlox, annual phlox / *Phlox Drummondii*
Dutch hyacinth, hyacinth / *Hyacinthus orientalis*
Dutch iris / *Iris xiphium*
Dutchman's-breeches / *Dicentra cucullaria*
Dwarf orange / *Citrus taitensis*
Dwarf yaupon / *Ilex vomitoria compacta*

Common Name / Scientific Name

Easter lily, Madonna lily / *Lilium candidum*
Ebony spleenwort / *Asplenium platyneuron*
Elaeagnus / *Elaeagnus pungens*
Elephant's-ear / *Colocasia antiquorum*
Elm / *Ulmus* spp.
English boxwood, dwarf boxwood / *Buxus sempervirens* var. *suffruticosa*
English daisy / *Bellis perennis*
English hawthorn / *Crataegus oxyacantha*
English laurel / *Prunus laurocerasus* var. *officinalis*
Escallonia / *Escallonia*
Euonymus / *Euonymus*
Evening primrose / *Oenothera perennis*

Fairy lily, zephyr lily / *Zephyranthes candida*
Fescue / *Festuca*
Flowering almond / *Prunus glandulosa*
Flowering tobacco / *Nicotiana alata*
Foam flower / *Tiarella cordifolia*
Forget-me-not / *Myosotis sylvatica*
Forsythia / *Forsythia intermedia*
Foster's holly / *Ilex opaca* var. *Fosterii*
Four o'clock / *Mirabilis jalapa*
Foxglove / *Digitalis purpurea*
Fragrant viburnum / *Viburnum Carlesii*
French marigold / *Tagetes patula*
Fringe tree, granddaddy-greybeard / *Chionanthus virginica*
Fuchsia / *Fuchsia procumbens*

Gaillardia / *Gaillardia aristata*
Galax / *Galax aphylla*
Gardenia, cape-jasmine / *Gardenia jasminoides*
Garden pink / *Dianthus plumarius*
Gazania / *Gazania*
Geranium / *Pelargonium*
Gerbera, Transvaal daisy / *Gerbera Jamesonii*
Ginger lily / *Hedychium coronarium*

Common Name / Scientific Name

Ginkgo / *Ginkgo biloba*
Gladiolus / *Gladiolus*
Globe thistle / *Echinops exaltatus*
Gloriosa daisy / *Rudbeckia hirta*
Glory-of-the-snow / *Chionodoxa Luciliae*
Gloxinia / *Sinningia*
Goldenchain tree / *Laburnum alpinum*
Goldenrain tree / *Koelreuteria paniculata*
Goldenrod / *Solidago odora*
Gourd / *Cucurbita pepo*
Grape / *Vitis* spp.
Grape hyacinth / *Muscari botryoides*
Great Solomon's seal / *Polygonatum commutatum*
Green-in-gold, golden star / *Chrysogonum virginianum*

Hackberry / *Celtis*
Hall's amaryllis / *Lycoris squamigera*
Hardy begonia / *Begonia Evansiana*
Hawthorn / *Crataegus* spp.
Heller holly / *Ilex crenata* var. *Helleri*
Hen-and-chicks / *Sempervivum tectorum*
Henbit / *Lamium maculatum*
Hepatica (round-lobed) / *Hepatica triloba*
Hepatica (sharp-lobed) / *Hepatica acutiloba*
Hetz holly / *Ilex crenata* var. *Hetzi*
Hibiscus, rose-mallow / *Hibiscus coccineus*
Hickory, shag-bark hickory / *Carya ovata*
Holly / *Ilex*
Holly osmanthus / *Osmanthus aquifolium*
Hollyhock / *Althaea rosea*
Honesty, money plant / *Lunaria annua*
Hoop-petticoat daffodil / *Narcissus bulbocodium*
Hornbeam / *Carpinus*
Hosta, plantain lily, funkia / *Hosta*
Hoya, wax-vine / *Hoya carnosa*
Hyacinth / *Hyacinthus*
Hydrangea (florists' hydrangea) / *Hydrangea hortensia*
Hypericum, St.-John's-wort / *Hypericum calycinum*

Glossary of Common Plant Names

Common Name	Scientific Name

Impatiens, patience plant / *Impatiens balsamina*
Ironwood, American hornbeam / *Carpinus caroliniana*
Italian arum / *Arum italicum*
Italian ryegrass / *Lolium multiflorum*
Ivy / *Hedera helix*
Ivy-leaved geranium / *Pelargonium peltatum*

Japanese anemone, fall anemone / *Anemone hupehensis*
Japanese flowering cherry / *Prunus serrulata*
Japanese holly / *Ilex crenata*
Japanese maple / *Acer palmatum*
Japanese quince, cydonia, japonica / *Chaenomeles japonica*
Japanese snowball, snowball / *Viburnum tomentosum*
Johnson grass / *Sorghum halepense*
Juniper / *Juniperus* spp.

Kerria, globeflower / *Kerria japonica*
Kieffer pear / *Pyrus communis*
Kochia, summer cypress / *Kochia scoparia*

Lantana / *Lantana camara*
Larkspur (biennial) / *Delphinium cultorum*
Leatherleaf viburnum / *Viburnum rhytidophyllum*
Lenten rose / *Helleborus orientalis*
Leucothoe / *Leucothoe Catesbaei*
Ligustrum / *Ligustrum* spp.
Lilac / *Syringa vulgaris*
Linden / *Tilia*
Liriope, lily-turf / *Liriope muscari*
Live oak / *Quercus virginiana*
Lobelia (annual) / *Lobelia erinus*
Loosestrife / *Lysimachia punctata*
Loquat / *Eriobotrya japonica*
Lupine / *Lupinus polyphyllus*
Lycoris, red spider lily / *Lycoris radiata*

Magnolia (evergreen) / *Magnolia grandiflora*
Mahonia, Oregon hollygrape / *Mahonia Bealei*

Common Name	Scientific Name

Maidenhair fern, American maidenhair fern / *Adiantum pedatum*
Maiden pink / *Dianthus deltoides*
Marigold / *Tagetes*
Michaelmas daisy, aster / *Aster*
Milk-and-wine lily / *Crinum*
Mock orange / *Philadelphus coronarius*
Morning glory / *Ipomoea purpurea*
Moss pink / *Phlox nivalis*
Mottled wild ginger / *Asarum ariofolium*
Mountain andromeda, mountain pieris / *Pieris floribunda*
Muscadine, scuppernong / *Vitis rotundifolia*

Nandina / *Nandina domestica*
Nasturtium / *Tropaeolum majus*
Nigella, love-in-a-mist / *Nigella damascena*
Norway maple / *Acer platanoides*

Oak-leaf hydrangea / *Hydrangea quercifolia*
Oconee bell / *Shortia galacifolia*
Oleander / *Nerium oleander*
Onion / *Allium*
Oriental poppy / *Papaver orientale*
Osmanthus, tea-olive / *Osmanthus Fortunei*

Pachysandra / *Pachysandra terminalis*
Painted daisy / *Pyrethrum*
Pansy / *Viola*
Parsley-haw, hawthorn / *Crataegus apiifolia*
Peach / *Prunus* spp.
Pear / *Pyrus* spp.
Pearlbush / *Exochorda racemosa*
Peegee hydrangea / *Hydrangea paniculata* var. *grandiflora*
Penstemon, beard-tongue / *Penstemon*
Peony / *Paeonia lactiflora*
Periwinkle (annual) / *Vinca rosea*
Periwinkle (perennial) / *Vinca major, Vinca minor*
Petunia / *Petunia hybrida*
Pfitzer juniper / *Juniperus chinensis*

Common Name	Scientific Name

Photinia / *Photinia glabra, P. serrulata*
Pieris, lily-of-the-valley shrub / *Pieris japonica*
Pin oak / *Quercus palustris*
Pine / *Pinus* spp.
Pipsissewa / *Chimaphila maculata*
Pittosporum / *Pittosporum tobira*
Plum / *Prunus* spp.
Plumbago, leadwort / *Plumbago capensis*
Poet's laurel, Alexandrian laurel / *Danae racemosa*
Poinsettia / *Euphorbia pulcherrima*
Polemonium, Jacob's ladder / *Polemonium caeruleum*
Pomegranate / *Punica granatum*
Poppy anemone, spring anemone / *Anemone coronaria*
Portulaca, rose-moss / *Portulaca grandiflora*
Possum-haw holly / *Ilex decidua*
Post oak / *Quercus stellata*
Prickly pear / *Opuntia* spp.
Primrose / *Primula vulgaris*
Privet / *Ligustrum vulgare*
Pussy willow / *Salix discolor*
Pyracantha, firethorn / *Pyracantha coccinea*

Redbud / *Cercis canadensis*
Red cedar / *Juniperus virginiana*
Redhot poker, torchflower / *Kniphofia uvaria*
Red maple / *Acer rubrum*
Red-stemmed dogwood / *Cornus stolonifera*
Rhododendron. See Azalea / *Rhododendron* spp.
River birch / *Betula nigra*
Roman hyacinth / *Hyacinthus orientalis albulus*
Rose / *Rosa* spp.
Rose-mallow, hibiscus / *Hibiscus coccineus*
Russian olive / *Elaeagnus umbellata*

Sage / *Salvia*
Sandhill lupine / *Lupinus diffusus*
Saucer magnolia, tulip tree / *Magnolia soulangeana*
Scabiosa, pincushion flower / *Scabiosa japonica*

Common Name	Scientific Name
Scarlet sage	*Salvia splendens*
Scilla, squill, Spanish bluebell	*Scilla hispanica*
Schipka laurel, schip laurel	*Prunus laurocerasus* var. *schipkaensis*
Scotch broom	*Cytisus scoparius*
Sedum	*Sedum* spp.
Serviceberry, Juneberry, shadblow	*Amelanchier laevis*
Shasta daisy	*Chrysanthemum maximum*
Shirley poppy	*Papaver rhoeas*
Shore juniper	*Juniperus horizontalis conferta*
Siberian iris	*Iris sibirica*
Silver maple	*Acer saccharinum*
Skimmia	*Skimmia Reevesiana*
Small-leaved linden	*Tilia cordata*
Small Solomon's seal	*Polygonatum biflorum*
Smoke tree	*Cotinus*
Snapdragon	*Antirrhinum majus*
Snowball, Japanese snowball	*Viburnum tomentosum*
Snowberry	*Symphoricarpos albus*
Snowdrop	*Galanthus nivalis*
Snowflake	*Leucojum vernum*
Snow-on-the-mountain, spurge	*Euphorbia marginata*
Snow trillium	*Trillium grandiflorum*
Sourwood	*Oxydendrum arboreum*
Spanish bayonet, yucca	*Yucca aloifolia*
Spathiphyllum	*Spathiphyllum patinii*
Spider lily, lycoris	*Lycoris radiata*
Spiderwort	*Tradescantia* spp.
Spirea	*Spiraea Vanhouttei*
Spring phlox, blue spring phlox	*Phlox divaricata*
Spruce, red spruce	*Picea rubra*
Squill, scilla, Spanish bluebell	*Scilla hispanica*
Star magnolia	*Magnolia stellata*
Stock	*Matthiola incana*
Stokesia, Stokes' aster	*Stokesia laevis*
Strawberry geranium, strawberry begonia	*Saxifraga sarmentosa*
Strawflower, everlasting	*Helichrysum bracteatum*
Sugar maple	*Acer saccharum*
Summer cypress	*Kochia*
Summer phlox, hardy phlox	*Phlox paniculata*
Summer spirea	*Spiraea bumalda* var. Anthony Waterer
Sweet alyssum	*Lobularia maritima*
Sweet gum	*Liquidambar styraciflua*
Sweet pea (annual)	*Lathyrus odoratus*
Sweet rocket	*Hesperis matronalis*
Sweet shrub, sweet-betsy	*Calycanthus floridus*
Sweet white violet	*Viola blanda*
Sweet william	*Dianthus barbatus*
Sycamore	*Platanus occidentalis*
Thermopsis	*Thermopsis caroliniana*
Thornless honey locust	*Gleditsia triacanthos*
Thrift, moss pink	*Phlox subulata*
Thunbergia, black-eyed Susan vine	*Thunbergia alata*
Toad trillium	*Trillium sessile*
Trailing arbutus	*Epigaea repens*
Tree ivy	*Fatshedera lizei*
Trout-lily	*Erythronium americanum*
Trumpet vine, trumpet creeper	*Campsis radicans*
Tulip	*Tulipa* spp.
Tulip poplar	*Liriodendron tulipifera*
Turk's-cap lily	*Lilium superbum*
Venus's flytrap	*Dionaea muscipula*
Verbena	*Verbena hybrida*
Veronica, speedwell	*Veronica incana*
Viburnum	*Viburnum* spp.
Vinca. *See* Periwinkle	*Vinca*
Violet	*Viola* spp.
Virginia bluebell	*Mertensia virginica*
Vitex, chaste tree	*Vitex agnus-castus*
Wallflower	*Cheiranthus cheiri*
Wandering Jew	*Zebrina pendula*
Waxleaf ligustrum	*Ligustrum lucidum*
Weigela	*Weigela florida*
White oak	*Quercus alba*
White pine	*Pinus strobus*
Wild geranium	*Geranium maculatum*
Willow	*Salix* spp.
Willow oak	*Quercus phellos*
Winged euonymus	*Euonymus alatus*
Winter aconite	*Eranthis hyemalis*
Winterberry	*Ilex verticillata*
Winter honeysuckle, Sweet-Breath-of-Spring	*Lonicera fragrantissima*
Winter jasmine	*Jasminum nudiflorum*
Yaupon	*Ilex vomitoria*
Yellowwood	*Cladrastis lutea*
Yucca, Spanish bayonet	*Yucca aloifolia*
Zephyr lily, Zephyranthes	*Zephyranthes*
Zinnia	*Zinnia elegans*
Zoysia, Manila grass	*Zoysia matrella*

Index

A

Abelia (*Abelia grandiflora*), 10, 21, 39
African marigold (*Tagetes erecta*), 64
African violet (*Saintpaulia ionantha*), 99, 114
Agapanthus, lily-of-the-Nile (*Agapanthus umbellatus*), 64
Ageratum (*Ageratum Houstonianum*), 52, 64, 66, 86, 106
Ajuga (*Ajuga reptans*), 12, 35, 76, 79, 81
Althea, rose of Sharon (*Hibiscus syriacus*), 21, 37, 45, 46, 64, 74, 92
Alum root (*Heuchera americana*), 54
Amaranthus, Joseph's-coat (*Amaranthus bicolor*), 86
Amaryllis (*Amaryllis belladonna*), 113–14
American ash, white ash (*Fraxinus americana*), 47, 48, 64
American beech (*Fagus grandiflora*), 47
American boxwood (*Buxus sempervirens arborescens*), 19, 77. *See also* Boxwood
American elm (*Ulmus americana*), 47
American holly (*Ilex opaca*), 47, 64, 100, 109; spraying, 24, 77; characteristics of, 40, 44, 48; in design, 54, 60–61. *See also* Foster's holly and Croonenburg holly
Andromeda, mountain pieris (*Pieris floribunda*), 42
Anemone, fall. *See* Japanese anemone
Anemone, spring. *See* Poppy anemone
Annuals: definition of, 52; use in gardens, 52, 71; herbs, 56; for test plantings, 71; lists of, 72, 80, 86; self-seeding, 72–73, 89, 91; for outdoor planting, 80; cuttings, 87, 97, 107–8; watering, 94, 95; fertilizing, 97
Apple, crab apple (*Malus* spp.), 22, 27; fruiting, 65, 67
Arabis, rock-cress (*Arabis albida*), 10, 110
Armeria (*Armeria splendens*), 50
Ash (*Fraxinus americana*), 48
Aspen, quaking (*Populus tremuloides*), 44
Aspidistra, cast-iron plant (*Aspidistra lurida*), 50, 64
Aster (annual) (*Callistephus chinensis*), 8, 80, 86, 97; (perennial) Michaelmas daisy (*Aster*), 50, 54, 109
Astilbe (*Astilbe*), 49
Atamasco lily (*Zephyranthes atamasco*), 54, 64
Aubrietia (*Aubrietia deltoidea*), 11
Aucuba (*Aucuba japonica*), 10, 11, 19, 21, 39, 44, 64, 94, 99
Azalea (*Rhododendron* spp.), 45, 47, 114; propagation of, 11, 93–94, 97, 107–8; planting, 12, 112; fertilizing, 15–16, 99; chlorosis of, 17, 88; pruning, 19, 21, 74; in design, 22, 35, 39, 41, 44, 54, 61, 62, 91, 100; winter care, 69; spraying, 92; Kurume, 15, 45, 46, 76, 78; macrantha, 15, 45, 46, 76, 78; Glen Dale hybrids, 15, 46, 76, 78; Gable hybrids, 15; Gumpo, 15, 46, 76, 87, 97; Satsuki hybrids, 15, 78; Exbury, 41; Mollis, 41, 42; Vaseyi, 41; Calendulaceum, 41; Indica, 43; Kaempferi, 46, 76, 78; Treasure, 48; Glamour, 48; Hershey red, 48; Snow, 78; Coral Bell, 78; Hinodegiri, 78; Hino-crimson, 78; Pink Pearl, 78; Fielder's white, 97

B

Balloon flower (*Platycodon grandiflorum*), 12
Baptisia, wild indigo (*Baptisia australis*), 54
Barberry (*Berberis vulgaris*), 21
Bearded iris, pogoniris (*Iris germanica*), 12, 24, 50, 61, 64, 68, 70, 77, 79, 87, 99, 100
Beautyberry, French mulberry (*Callicarpa americana*), 21, 42
Beautybush (*Kolkwitzia amabilis*), 11, 37, 45
Bedding begonia (*Begonia semperflorens*), 79, 80, 95; propagation of, 7, 8, 10, 65, 66, 67, 73, 86; in design, 52, 87, 92, 99, 104; pruning, 96, 113; winter care, 106–7
Beebalm, horsemint (*Monarda didyma*), 54
Begonia. *See* Bedding begonia
Bellflower (*Campanula* spp.), 64
Bell pepper (*Capsicum frutescens*), 8, 65, 70, 76, 84, 97
Bergenia (*Bergenia cordifolia*), 50
Bermuda grass, wire grass (*Cynodon dactylon*), 4, 17, 83, 103
Biennials: definition of, 51; plan for border, 51; list of, 51; herbs, 56; fertilizing, 76, 97; watering, 94, 95; fall planting, 102, 104–5, 110
Birch (*Betula*), 48
Bird's-foot violet (*Viola pedata*), 55
Bittersweet, American (*Celastrus scandens*), 37
Black-eyed Susan (*Rudbeckia serotina*), 64, 91, 92
Black-eyed Susan vine (*Thunbergia alata*), 86
Black gum (*Nyssa sylvatica*), 47
Bleeding heart (*Dicentra eximia*), 54
Bloodroot (*Sanguinaria canadensis*), 54
Blue-eyed grass (*Sisyrinchium angustifolium*), 54, 64
Bluet (*Houstonia caerulea*), 54
Boltonia (*Boltonia asteroides*), 50
Boston daisy (*Chrysanthemum*), 10, 66, 67, 106
Boston fern (*Nephrolepis exaltata*), 66, 67, 80, 86, 106
Bougainvillea, bougainville (*Bougainvillea*), 10
Boxwood (*Buxus sempervirens*), 11, 64; planting, 12, 112; fertilizing, 15–16; pruning, 19; spraying, 24, 77; in design, 35, 38, 44; winter care, 69, 73; propagation, 94, 107–8. *See also* American boxwood and English boxwood
Browallia (*Browallia americana*), 8, 64, 86
Buckeye, horse chestnut (*Aesculus*), 48
Bulbs, 102, 103, 104, 108; fertilizing, 15, 68; staking, 97; planting, 103–4, 110
Burford holly (*Ilex cornuta* var. *Burfordi*), 18, 19, 22, 40, 44, 47, 100, 109. *See also* Chinese holly
Butterfly bush (*Buddleia Davidii*), 10, 21
Butterfly weed (*Asclepias tuberosa*), 54

C

Caladium (*Caladium bicolor*), 107
Calendar, general, 26; January, 27; February, 27–28; March, 28; April, 28–29; May, 29; June, 30; July, 30–31; August, 31; September, 31; October, 32; November, 32; December, 32
Calendar, my garden: January, 70; February, 74; March, 78–79; April, 85; May, 89; June, 93; July, 98; August, 102; September, 106; October, 109; November, 111; December, 115
Calendula, pot-marigold (*Calendula officinalis*), 7, 64, 71, 72, 74, 76, 78, 87, 88, 97
California poppy (*Eschscholtzia californica*), 51, 61, 71, 72, 76
Callery pear (*Pyrus Calleryana*), 64, 113
Camellia japonica (*Camellia japonica*), 64; planting, 12, 112; fertilizing, 15–16, 99; pruning, 18, 19, 21, 22, 88; in design, 37, 39, 44, 45, 46; cultural requirements, 47, 61; propagation, 93–94, 107–8; early varieties: September Morn, 45; High Hat, 45; Morning Glow, 45; Arejisha, 45; Dikagura, 45; Mrs. K. Sawada, 45; midwinter varieties: Finlandia, 45; Blood of China, 45; Herme, 45; Sara Frost, 45; Flame, 45; Flame variegated, 45; Elegans, 45; Leucantha, 45
Camellia sasanqua (*Camellia sasanqua*), 64, 109; planting, 12, 112; fertilizing, 15–16, 99; pruning, 18, 19, 21, 22; in design, 37, 39, 44, 45, 46; cultural requirements, 47, 61; propagation, 93–94, 107–8
Campanula, bellflower (*Campanula*), 51, 64
Canada wild ginger (*Asarum canadense*), 54, 64
Canadian hemlock (*Tsuga canadensis*), 44, 47
Candytuft (perennial) (*Iberis sempervirens*), 11, 38, 50, 64, 87, 88, 99, 107, 110
Canna (*Canna generalis*), 12, 64, 81, 109, 112
Canterbury bell (*Campanula medium*), 51, 110
Cape jasmine, gardenia. *See* Gardenia
Cardinal flower (*Lobelia cardinalis*), 55
Carolina cherry laurel (*Prunus laurocerasus* var. *caroliniana*), 16, 39, 47, 60, 64
Carolina hemlock (*Tsuga caroliniana*), 44, 47
Carolina jessamine (*Gelsemium sempervirens*), 11, 36, 65, 99, 107
Carolina silverbell (*Halesia carolina*), 48, 54
Cassine holly, Dahoon holly (*Ilex cassine*), 40, 48
Castor bean (*Ricinus communis*), 7, 86
Catalpa (*Catalpa*), 48
Catesby's trillium (*Trillium nervosum*), 54, 64, 79
Cedar, red (*Juniperus virginiana*), 37, 47
Celosia, cockscomb (*Celosia argentea*), 61, 86, 91
Cherry (*Prunus* spp.), 20, 22, 48, 64, 67, 112
Chickweed (*Stellaria*), 68, 73, 112
Chinese elm (*Ulmus chinensis*), 47
Chinese holly (*Ilex cornuta*), 35, 39, 64, 109; in design, 37, 44, pruning, 88; propagation, 107–8. *See also* Burford holly
Christmas cherry, Jerusalem cherry (*Solanum pseudo-capsicum*), 8, 64, 76, 106, 114
Christmas fern (*Polystichum acrostichoides*), 54, 64, 76, 79
Christmas rose (*Helleborus niger*), 50
Chrysanthemum, mums (*Chrysanthemum* spp.), 50, 64, 87, 106, 109, 114; propagation of, 10, 81; spraying, 24; in design, 76; pruning, 92, 112; fertilizing, 92; staking, 97; Korean, 81; Masterpiece, 81; Baby Tears, 81; Cloud Nine, 82
Cineraria (*Senecio cruentus*), 66, 70
Clematis (*Clematis Jackmanii*), 20, 36, 65, 79, 88, 92, 107, 109; Ramona, 20; Henry, 20; Prince Phillip, 20; Crimson Star, 20; Nelly Moser, 20

[136] Index

Cleome, spider flower (*Cleome spinosa*), 64, 73, 81, 89, 91, 92, 99; in design, 52, 90, 97; pruning, 96; Pink Queen, 90; Helen Campbell, 90
Cleyera (*Cleyera japonica*), 44, 64
Climbing hydrangea (*Hydrangea petiolaris*), 65
Cockspur thorn, hawthorn (*Crataegus Crus-galli*), 54, 109
Colchicum, fall crocus (*Colchicum autumnale*), 64, 112
Coleus (*Coleus Blumei*), 10, 86, 87, 96, 106, 107
Columbine (*Aquilegia canadensis*), 12, 24, 50, 54, 68, 77, 110
Compost: definition of, 5; materials for, 5; how to make, 5; chemistry of, 6; benefits as mulch, 6, 7
Concord. *See* Grape
Confederate jasmine, star jasmine (*Trachelospermum jasminoides*), 10
Confederate violet (*Viola papilionacea*), 54
Conservation: list of protected plants in North Carolina and South Carolina, 55
Convexa holly (*Ilex crenata convexa*), 40. *See also* Japanese holly
Coral-bell (*Heuchera sanguinea*), 12, 50, 64, 68
Coral honeysuckle, trumpet honeysuckle (*Lonicera sempervirens*), 65
Coreopsis (*Coreopsis lanceolata*), 86
Cork-bark elm (*Ulmus alata*), 47
Corkscrew willow (*Salix matsudana* var. *tortuosa*), 41
Cornflower, bachelor's-button (*Centaurea cyanus*), 7, 61, 64, 71, 72, 73
Cosmos (*Cosmos bipinnatus*), 86
Cotoneaster (*Cotoneaster horizontalis*), 11, 21, 22, 37, 42
Crab apple (*Malus* spp.), 20, 22, 48, 64, 78, 92, 109
Crape myrtle (*Lagerstroemia indica*), 64, 97; propagation of, 11; pruning, 20, 21, 74; in design, 41, 45, 46, 60, 109; spraying, 92; Near East, 41, 97
Crinum, milk-and-wine lily (*Crinum*), 64, 98
Crocus (*Crocus biflorus*), 64, 68, 103
Croonenburg holly (*Ilex opaca* var. *Croonenburg*), 40. *See also* American holly
Cucumber magnolia (*Magnolia acuminata*), 47
Cuttings, 10, 11, 93–94, 97; house plants, 65; winter care of, 107–8

D
Daffodil (*Narcissus* spp.), 64, 76, 79, 112; fertilizing, 68; in design, 71, 73; winter damage, 78; removal of foliage, 88, 97; planting, 103–4, 108; February Gold, 38, 104; Golden Harvest, 38; Thalia, 48, 104; Ice Follies, 48; King Alfred, 104; Unsurpassable, 104; Dutch Master, 104; John Evelyn, 104; Actea, 104; Laurens Koster, 104; Geranium, 104
Dahlia (*Dahlia pinnata*), 10, 12, 81, 89, 92, 97, 98, 107
Daphne (*Daphne cneorum*), 10, 11, 64
Day lily (*Hemerocallis*), 12, 50, 61, 64, 69, 70, 81, 96, 112
Delphinium (perennial) (*Delphinium grandiflorum*), 49
Design: in base plantings, 34–35; in garden location, 35–36; in framing garden, 36–37; trees and shrubs in, 37; green gardens in, 38, 42, 43; shade and sun plants in, 39; hollies in, 39, 40; deciduous shrubs in, 41; shrub spacing in, 41; recommended Carolina shrubs for, 42–43; leaf size and texture in, 44, 109; flowering sequence in, 44–46; types of trees in, 46–47; number and placement of trees in, 46, 47; size of trees in, 48; plan for shady garden, 48; bedding plants in, 48; perennials in, 49–50, 51; biennials in, 51; annuals in, 52; wild flowers in, 52–54; native trees and shrubs in, 54–55; herbs in, 56–57; formal gardens in, 58; informal gardens in, 58, 59; color in, 59–60; for farm home, 60–61; in maintenance, 61–62; garden structures in, 62; combining food and ornamentals, 83–84. *See also* Conservation
Deutzia (*Deutzia gracilis*), 11, 21, 45, 46, 60, 64
Dianthus (*Dianthus*), 10, 11, 64, 87, 96, 97, 107, 109, 110; Persian Carpet, 97
Dock (*Rumex patientia*), 68, 73
Dogwood (*Cornus florida*), 64; pruning, 14, 22; in design, 41, 48, 54, 60, 61, 109; planting, 76, 112; propagation of, 79; watering, 108
Doronicum, leopard's-bane (*Doronicum caucasicum*), 49
Drummond phlox (*Phlox Drummondii*), 7, 61, 64, 71, 72, 74, 76, 78, 87, 97
Dutch hyacinth. *See* Hyacinth
Dutch iris (*Iris xiphium*), 64, 71, 97, 104, 112
Dutchman's-breeches (*Dicentra cucullaria*), 64
Dwarf orange (*Citrus taitensis*), 67, 73
Dwarf yaupon (*Ilex vomitoria compacta*), 40

E
Easter lily, Madonna lily (*Lilium candidum*), 81
Ebony spleenwort (*Asplenium platyneuron*), 54
Elaeagnus (*Elaeagnus*), 19, 45, 64
Elephant's-ear (*Colocasia antiquorum*), 81
Elm (*Ulmus* spp.), 47
English boxwood, dwarf boxwood (*Buxus sempervirens* var. *suffruticosa*). *See* Boxwood
English daisy (*Bellis perennis*), 51, 52, 64, 71, 72, 110
English hawthorn (*Crataegus oxyacantha*), 48
English laurel (*Prunus laurocerasus* var. *officinalis*), 39, 44, 60
Escallonia (*Escallonia*), 10
Espalier: definition of, 18; forms, 22; plants for, 22–23; techniques for, 22–23; in base plantings, 35
Euonymus (*Euonymus*), 11, 37, 64
Evening primrose (*Oenothera perennis*), 50, 64
Everblooming jasmine (*Jasminum floridum*), 43

F
Fairy lily, zephyr lily (*Zephyranthes candida*), 64, 93
Fertilizers: soil testing, 14; nature of, 14–15; basic elements of, 14–15; application calendar, 15; bulbs, 15, 68; trees and shrubs, 15; vegetables, 15, 88, 89, 97; quantities, 16; wood ashes, 16; dehydrated manures, 16; bone meal, 16; how to apply, 16, 17; for lawns, 17, 74, 103; iron chlorosis, 17, 88; for house plants, 73, 76
Fescue (*Festuca*), 17, 74, 103
Flowering almond (*Prunus glandulosa*), 11, 21, 45, 46, 64, 92
Flowering quince. *See* Japanese quince
Flowering tobacco (*Nicotiana alata*), 24, 60, 86, 91, 109
Flowers: cool-season seeds, 7; warm-season seeds, 8; cuttings of, 10; spraying of, 24; test plantings of, 71; use of cool-season annuals, 71, 72, 73; removal of faded flowers from, 76
Foam flower (*Tiarella cordifolia*), 54, 64
Forget-me-not (*Myosotis sylvatica*), 51, 52, 72, 108, 110
Forsythia (*Forsythia intermedia*), 11, 21, 37, 43, 45, 46, 60, 64, 69, 109
Foster's holly (*Ilex opaca* var. *Fosterii*), 40. *See also* American holly
Four o'clock (*Mirabilis jalapa*), 86, 91
Foxglove (*Digitalis purpurea*), 51, 110
Fragrant viburnum (*Viburnum Carlesii*), 21
French marigold (*Tagetes patula*), 64
Fringe tree, granddaddy-greybeard (*Chionanthus virginica*), 21, 48, 54
Fuchsia (*Fuchsia procumbens*), 10, 67, 86, 106, 107

G
Gaillardia (*Gaillardia aristata*), 31
Galax (*Galax aphylla*), 54
Gardenia, cape jasmine (*Gardenia jasminoides*), 45
Garden pink. *See* Dianthus
Garden record keeping, 25–26
Gazania (*Gazania*), 115
Geranium (*Pelargonium*), 64, 80, 82, 89, 113; propagation of, 10, 65, 66, 67, 93, 97; in design, 87, 99; spraying, 92; pruning, 96; as house plants, 106–7
Gerbera, Transvaal daisy (*Gerbera Jamesonii*), 10
Ginger lily (*Hedychium coronarium*), 64
Ginkgo (*Ginkgo biloba*), 48
Gladiolus (*Gladiolus*), 64, 81, 97, 107
Globe thistle (*Echinops exaltatus*), 64, 96
Gloriosa daisy (*Rudbeckia hirta*), 93
Glory-of-the-snow (*Chionodoxa Luciliae*), 64, 68, 103
Gloxinia (*Sinningia*), 114
Goldenchain tree (*Laburnum alpinum*), 11
Goldenrain tree (*Koelreuteria paniculata*), 48
Goldenrod (*Solidago odora*), 54
Gourd (*Cucurbita pepo*), 60, 86, 95
Grape (*Vitis* spp.), 60, 65, 69, 70, 82, 83, 92, 96, 101, 112; Concord, 101; Niagara, 101
Grape hyacinth (*Muscari botryoides*), 103
Great Solomon's seal (*Polygonatum commutatum*), 54
Green-in-gold, golden star (*Chrysogonum virginianum*), 64

H
Hackberry (*Celtis*), 47, 48
Hall's amaryllis (*Lycoris squamigera*), 64
Hanging baskets, 86, 87, 96; types of, 86; list of plants for, 86–87
Hardy begonia (*Begonia Evansiana*), 50, 64, 91, 92

Hawthorn (*Crataegus* spp.), 48, 54, 109
Heller holly (*Ilex crenata* var. *Helleri*), 35, 40, 42. See also Japanese holly
Hen-and-chicks (*Sempervivum tectorum*), 64
Henbit (*Lamium maculatum*), 68
Hepatica (round-lobed) (*Hepatica triloba*), 54, 64; (sharp-lobed) (*Hepatica acutiloba*), 54, 64
Herbs: types of, 56; harvesting, 56; most popular, 57
Hetz holly (*Ilex crenata* var. *Hetzi*), 35, 40. See also Japanese holly
Hibiscus, rose-mallow (*Hibiscus coccineus*), 10, 45, 46, 64, 92
Hickory, shagbark hickory (*Carya ovata*), 47
Holly (*Ilex* spp.), 10, 16, 39, 69, 93, 94, 99, 107, 109. See also American holly; Cassine holly; Chinese holly; Japanese holly; Possum-haw holly; Winterberry; Yaupon holly
Holly osmanthus (*Osmanthus aquifolium*), 37, 39, 44, 45, 46, 64
Hollyhock (*Althaea rosea*), 51, 92, 110
Honesty, money plant (*Lunaria annua*), 51, 64, 97, 112
Hoop-petticoat daffodil (*Narcissus bulbocodium*), 79
Hornbeam (*Carpinus*), 48
Hosta, plantain lily, funkia (*Hosta*), 76, 79, 81, 86, 96; Royal Standard, 81, 100
House plants: propagation of, 10; spraying, 24; winter care, 65–66, 106–7, 113–14; geranium and begonia cuttings, 65, 73; cineraria, 66–67; dwarf orange, 67; spathiphyllum, 67; fertilizing, 73, 76; pruning, 76. See also Window greenhouse
Hoya, wax-vine (*Hoya carnosa*), 10, 11
Hyacinth (*Hyacinthus*), 64, 71, 103, 104, 108
Hydrangea (florists' hydrangea) (*Hydrangea hortensia*), 21
Hypericum, St.-John's-wort (*Hypericum calycinum*), 21, 38, 45

I

Impatiens, patience plant (*Impatiens balsamina*), 10, 64, 81, 86, 89, 91, 92; propagation, 10, 87, 97, 106–7; in design, 52, 90; Tangerine, 90
Iris. See Bearded iris
Ironwood, American hornbeam (*Carpinus caroliniana*), 48, 64, 109
Italian arum (*Arum italicum*), 64, 112
Italian ryegrass (*Lolium multiflorum*), 103
Ivy (*Hedera helix*), 11, 35, 36, 62, 64, 86
Ivy-leaved geranium (*Pelargonium peltatum*), 86, 96

J

Jacob's ladder. See Polemonium
Japanese anemone, fall anemone (*Anemone hupehensis*), 50, 64
Japanese flowering cherry (*Prunus serrulata*), 20, 48, 64
Japanese holly (*Ilex crenata*), 39, 64; in design, 37–38, 44; characteristics of, 40; pruning, 88; spraying, 92; propagation of, 107–8. See also Convexa holly, Heller holly, Hetz holly
Japanese maple (*Acer palmatum*), 41, 64, 73, 92, 109
Japanese quince, flowering quince, cydonia, japonica (*Chaenomeles japonica*), 11, 20, 21, 22, 41, 45
Japanese snowball, snowball (*Viburnum tomentosum*), 11, 21, 46
Johnson grass (*Sorghum halepense*), 4, 83
Juniper (*Juniperus* spp.), 20, 35, 39, 62

K

Kerria, globeflower (*Kerria japonica*), 11, 21, 41, 64, 78
Kieffer pear (*Pyrus communis*), 112
Kochia, summer cypress (*Kochia scoparia*), 86

L

Lantana (*Lantana camara*), 10, 66, 67, 106
Larkspur (biennial) (*Delphinium cultorum*), 51, 61, 71, 72
Lawns, 102–3; fertilizing of, 17, 74, 103; Japanese beetles in, 92; watering of, 94
Leatherleaf viburnum (*Viburnum rhytidophyllum*), 43, 44
Lenten rose (*Helleborus orientalis*), 50
Leucothoe (*Leucothoe Catesbaei*), 42, 54
Ligustrum (*Ligustrum* spp.), 16, 18, 19, 37, 39, 44, 47, 64, 74, 88
Lilac (*Syringa vulgaris*), 11, 16, 21, 24, 45, 60
Linden (*Tilia*), 48
Liriope, lily-turf (*Liriope muscari*), 12, 50, 62, 76, 79, 81, 86, 110, 112
Live oak (*Quercus virginiana*), 47, 48
Lobelia (annual) (*Lobelia erinus*), 86
Loosestrife (*Lysimachia punctata*), 50, 64, 96
Loquat (*Eriobotrya japonica*), 22, 44
Lupine (*Lupinus polyphyllus*), 49, 53, 64, 87, 88, 110
Lycoris, red spider lily (*Lycoris radiata*), 64

M

Magnolia (evergreen) (*Magnolia grandiflora*), 11, 14, 22, 47, 48, 60, 64, 79, 112
Mahonia, Oregon hollygrape (*Mahonia Bealei*), 10, 20, 21, 39, 44, 46, 64, 73, 99
Maidenhair fern, American maidenhair fern (*Adiantum pedatum*), 44
Maiden pinks. See Dianthus
Maintenance: garden, 61–62; structures in, 62; weeding, 68, 73, 83, 97, 112; winter care, 68, 69, 78, 82; mulches, 69, 93; watering, 94–95, 110
Marigold (*Tagetes*), 8, 24, 52, 67, 68, 80, 86, 91, 92, 97
Michaelmas daisy. See Aster (perennial)
Milk-and-wine lily. See Crinum
Mock orange (*Philadelphus coronarius*), 11, 21, 45
Morning glory (*Ipomoea purpurea*), 86
Moss pink, thrift (*Phlox nivalis*), 54
Mottled wild ginger (*Asarum ariofolium*), 54, 64
Mountain andromeda, mountain pieris (*Pieris floribunda*), 42, 55
Mulch, 6, 7, 69, 93, 95, 96; definition of, 6; advantages and disadvantages of, 6, 7; replenishing, 110. See also Compost
Muscadine, scuppernong (*Vitis rotundifolia*), 101, 112; Magnolia, 101; Albemarle, 101; Carlos, 101; Chowan, 101; Roanoke, 101; Tarheel, 101; Scuppernong, 101; Hunt, 101; Nevermiss, 101. See also Grape

N

Nandina (*Nandina domestica*), 20, 21, 39, 64, 73, 109
Nasturtium (*Tropaeolum majus*), 52, 86
Niagara grape. See Grape

Nigella, love-in-a-mist (*Nigella damascena*), 86, 91
Norway maple (*Acer platanoides*), 47

O

Oak-leaf hydrangea (*Hydrangea quercifolia*), 21, 45
Oconee bell (*Shortia galacifolia*), 54
Oleander (*Nerium oleander*), 10, 11
Onion (*Allium*), 24, 71, 73, 84, 85, 104, 109, 113
Oriental poppy (*Papaver orientale*), 30, 50
Osmanthus, tea-olive (*Osmanthus Fortunei*), 37, 39, 44, 45, 46, 64, 88

P

Pachysandra (*Pachysandra terminalis*), 11, 30, 35, 38, 62, 64
Painted daisy (*Pyrethrum*), 31
Pansy (*Viola*), 51, 52, 64, 68, 80, 96, 113; planting, 72, 108, 110; fertilizing, 74, 76; winter damage, 78; summer replacement of, 87; propagation of, 104–5; Clear Crystals, 105
Parsley-haw, hawthorn (*Crataegus apiifolia*), 54
Peach (*Prunus* spp.), 18, 20, 67
Pear (*Pyrus* spp.), 20, 22, 65, 67
Pearlbush (*Exochorda racemosa*), 11, 21, 43, 45
Peegee hydrangea (*Hydrangea paniculata* var. *grandiflora*), 21, 45
Penstemon, beard-tongue (*Penstemon*), 10
Peony (*Paeonia lactiflora*), 12, 16, 50, 61, 64, 87, 88
Perennials: cuttings of, 10, 87, 97; layerage of, 11; division of, 11, 12; definition of, 49; popular varieties, 50; plan for border, 51; herbs, 56; self-seeding, 79, 91; watering, 94, 95; staking, 97; fertilizing of, 97
Periwinkle (annual) (*Vinca rosea*), 64, 81, 91, 92, 99; planting of, 8, 86, 97; in design, 52, 89, 90; propagation of, 90; pruning of, 96; Little Blanche, 90; Little Bright Eyes, 90; (perennial) (*Vinca major*), (*Vinca minor*), 11, 35, 62, 64, 86
Pesticides: plant enemies, 23; general uses, 23; home spraying calendar, 24; natural repellants, 24–25; sources of information, 25; for house plants, 73; boxwood leaf miners, 77; systemics, 77, 79; dormant sprays, 78; control of Japanese beetle, 91–92, 95
Petunia (*Petunia hybrida*), 7, 8, 10, 86, 91, 92, 96
Pfitzer juniper (*Juniperus chinensis*), 62
Photinia (*Photinia glabra*, *P. serrulata*), 37, 44, 47, 64, 76, 79, 88
Pieris, lily-of-the-valley shrub (*Pieris japonica*), 12, 15, 16, 21, 44, 46, 64, 93, 99
Pin oak (*Quercus palustris*), 47, 48
Pine (*Pinus* spp.), 20, 48, 60, 61
Pipsissewa (*Chimaphila maculata*), 54
Pittosporum (*Pittosporum tobira*), 44
Plants, my garden, 64–65
Plum (*Prunus* spp.), 20, 22, 48, 65, 67
Plumbago, leadwort (*Plumbago* spp.), 50, 64
Poet's laurel, Alexandrian laurel (*Danae racemosa*), 64
Poinsettia (*Euphorbia pulcherrima*), 29, 114
Polemonium, Jacob's ladder (*Polemonium caeruleum*), 54, 64
Pomegranate (*Punica granatum*), 45
Poppy anemone, spring anemone (*Anemone coronaria*), 64, 113

Portulaca, rose-moss (*Portulaca grandiflora*), 72, 86, 91
Possum-haw holly (*Ilex decidua*), 40, 54
Post oak (*Quercus stellata*), 47
Prickly pear (*Opuntia* spp.), 10, 86
Primrose, cowslip (*Primula vulgaris*), 12, 49, 64
Privet (*Ligustrum vulgare*), 37, 60. *See also* Ligustrum
Propagation: indoor seed planting, 7, 68, 75, 76; outdoor seed planting, 7; of cool-weather seeds, 7, 70, 71, 75; of warm-weather seeds, 8, 71, 75, 76, 88, 89; cultural requirements, 9; viability of seeds, 9; softwood cuttings, 10, 65, 73, 87, 97, 107; hardened green cuttings, 10, 11, 107-8; layerage, 11; by division, 11, 12, 69, 76, 79, 100
Pruning: year-around process, 17; reasons for, 17-19; espalier, 18, 22, 23; topiary, 18; guidelines for, 19; special plants, 19-21, 73, 74, 76; timetable, 21; house plants, 76. *See also* Shrubs
Pussywillow (*Salix discolor*), 44
Pyracantha, firethorn (*Pyracantha coccinea*), 11, 19, 21, 22, 37, 39, 109

R
Redbud (*Cercis canadensis*), 21, 41, 48, 54, 60, 64
Red cedar (*Juniperus virginiana*), 47
Red honeysuckle (*Lonicera sempervirens*), 65. *See also* Coral honeysuckle
Redhot poker, torchflower (*Kniphofia uvaria*), 44
Red maple (*Acer rubrum*), 47, 48, 92
Red-stemmed dogwood (*Cornus stolonifera*), 41, 64
Rhododendron (*Rhododendron* spp.), 45; planting of, 12; fertilizing of, 15-16; pruning, 21; in design, 39, 44, 54, 61, 99; Rosebay, 45. *See also* Azalea
River birch (*Betula nigra*), 41
Roman hyacinth (*Hyacinthus orientalis albulus*), 104
Rose (*Rosa* spp.), 45, 64, 89, 106, 109; propagation of, 10, 87, 97, 107-8; fertilization of, 15, 16, 79, 96; chlorosis of, 17; pruning of, 21, 74, 79, 96; spraying of, 24, 61, 78, 79, 84, 88, 92, 95, 96; in design, 36, 39; planting of, 76; watering, 95, 110; drainage, 98; Golden Showers, 76; The Fairy, 98, 99; Betty Prior, 98; New Dawn, 99; Mrs. Sam McGredy, 99
Rose-mallow. *See* Hibiscus
Russian olive (*Elaeagnus umbellata*), 41

S
Sage (*Salvia*), 31
Sandhill lupine (*Lupinus diffusus*), 53
Saucer magnolia, tulip tree (*Magnolia soulangeana*), 45, 78
Scabiosa, pincushion flower (*Scabiosa japonica*), 10
Scarlet sage (*Salvia splendens*), 52, 80, 86
Schipka laurel, schip laurel (*Prunus laurocerasus*, var. *schipkaensis*), 39, 64
Scilla, squill, Spanish bluebell (*Scilla hispanica*), 64, 68, 103
Scotch broom (*Cytisus scoparius*), 10, 21, 45
Sedum (*Sedum* spp.), 10, 50, 64
Seeds: indoor and outdoor, 70, 80; cool-season, 70, 71, 72, 75,

104-5; warm-season, 8, 75, 76, 88, 89; self-seeding, 72-73, 89, 91, 97, 99, 112. *See also* Propagation
Serviceberry, Juneberry, shadblow (*Amelanchier laevis*), 48
Shasta daisy (*Chrysanthemum maximum*), 50, 110
Shirley poppy (*Papaver rhoeas*), 51, 61, 71, 72, 76
Shore juniper (*Juniperus horizontalis conferta*), 20, 35, 39
Shrubs: propagation of, 10-11, 97; layerage, 11; soil preparation for, 12; transplanting, 12, 13, 76, 112; watering, 13, 94-95, 108; when to plant, 13, 76; container-grown, 13; specimen, 13; pruning, 13-14, 17, 18, 19, 21, 74, 96; weather-protection spray, 14; fertilizing, 15, 16, 74; spraying, 24; in base plantings, 34-35; garden framing, 37; in design, 37; in green gardens, 38; for sun and shade, 39; deciduous, 41; spacing, 41; how to select, 41, 46; evergreen, 42-43; flowering sequence, 44-45, 46; in woodland gardens, 54, 55; late-blooming azaleas, 78; winter care, 78
Siberian iris (*Iris sibirica*), 12
Silver maple (*Acer saccharinum*), 44, 47, 48
Skimmia (*Skimmia Reevesiana*), 42
Small-leaved linden (*Tilia cordata*), 47, 48
Small Solomon's seal (*Polygonatum biflorum*), 54
Smoke tree (*Cotinus*), 21
Snapdragon (*Antirrhinum majus*), 7, 8, 52, 64, 87, 96
Snowball, Japanese snowball (*Viburnum tomentosum*), 11, 21, 22, 45, 46, 64
Snowberry (*Symphoricarpos albus*), 11, 21
Snowdrop (*Galanthus nivalis*), 64, 68, 78, 79, 103
Snowflake (*Leucojum vernum*), 64, 68, 103
Snow-on-the-mountain, spurge (*Euphorbia marginata*), 86, 91
Snow trillium (*Trillium grandiflorum*), 54
Soil: nature of, 3; preparation of, 4, 103, 106, 108, 110, 111; organic matter in, 4; special problems of, 4; for trees and shrubs, 12; testing, 14; liming, 16; topsoil, 83. *See also* Compost
Sourwood (*Oxydendrum arborea*), 48, 54
Spanish bayonet (*Yucca aloifolia*), 54. *See also* Yucca
Spathiphyllum (*Spathiphyllum patinii*), 67
Spider lily, lycoris (*Lycoris radiata*), 112
Spiderwort (*Tradescantia* spp.), 50, 54, 64
Spirea (*Spiraea Vanhouttei*), 11, 21, 37, 45
Spring phlox, blue spring phlox (*Phlox divaricata*), 10, 50, 64, 76, 79, 88, 96, 110
Squill. *See* Scilla
Star magnolia (*Magnolia stellata*), 41, 45, 46, 64, 78, 109
Stock (*Matthiola incana*), 86
Stokesia, Stokes' aster (*Stokesia laevis*), 31
Strawberry geranium, strawberry begonia (*Saxifraga sarmentosa*), 64
Strawflower, everlasting (*Helichrysum bracteatum*), 86
Sugar maple (*Acer saccharum*), 47, 48
Summer cypress (*Kochia*), 86
Summer phlox, hardy phlox (*Phlox paniculata*), 10, 24, 50, 64, 96, 97
Summer spirea (*Spiraea bumalda* var. Anthony Waterer), 45
Sweet alyssum (*Lobularia maritima*), 7, 64, 71, 72, 73, 92
Sweet gum (*Liquidambar styraciflua*), 47, 48, 64

Sweet pea (annual) (*Lathyrus odoratus*), 72, 115
Sweet rocket (*Hesperis matronalis*), 51
Sweet shrub, sweet-betsy (*Calycanthus floridus*), 54
Sweet white violet (*Viola blanda*), 55
Sweet william (*Dianthus barbatus*), 51, 71, 108, 110
Sycamore (*Platanus occidentalis*), 47, 64, 92

T
Thermopsis (*Thermopsis caroliniana*), 50
Thornless honey locust (*Gleditsia triacanthos*), 47, 48
Thrift (*Phlox subulata*), 10, 50
Thunbergia, black-eyed Susan vine (*Thunbergia alata*), 86
Toad trillium (*Trillium sessile*), 54, 64
Tools: basic garden, 2; pruning, 2; motorized, 3
Topiary: definition of, 18
Trailing arbutus (*Epigaea repens*), 54
Trees: soil preparation for, 12; transplanting, 12, 13, 110, 112; staking, 13; watering, 13, 94-95, 108; when to plant, 13; container-grown, 13; specimen, 13; pruning, 13-14, 17, 18, 19; weather-protection spray, 14; fertilizing, 15, 16, 74; spraying program, 24, 78; in base planting, 35; as garden framing, 37; in design, 37, 46-48; types of, 47; size classification, 48; fruit trees, 67, 112; for small gardens, 67. *See also* Design, Pruning
Tree ivy (*Fatshedera lizei*), 64
Trout-lily (*Erythronium americanum*), 54
Trumpet vine, trumpet creeper (*Campsis radicans*), 37
Tulip (*Tulipa* spp.), 68, 71, 103, 108; Clusiana, 68; Fosteriana, 68; Kaufmanniana, 68
Tulip poplar (*Liriodendron tulipifera*), 47, 48, 64
Turk's-cap lily (*Lilium superbum*), 54, 64

V
Vegetables: cool-season, 7, 70, 71, 75, 102, 105; warm-season, 8, 75, 76, 88, 89; fertilizing, 15, 88, 89, 97; spraying, 24; cutworm protection, 82; crop continuity, 84-85; staking, 89, 97; watering, 94, 96; cabbage worms, 105
Venus's flytrap (*Dionaea muscipula*), 53
Verbena (*Verbena hybrida*), 10
Veronica, speedwell (*Veronica incana*), 31
Viburnum (*Viburnum* spp.), 21, 22, 41, 45, 46, 64
Vinca. *See* Periwinkle
Violet (*Viola* spp.), 10, 54, 64, 79
Virginia bluebell (*Mertensia virginica*), 50, 64, 79, 88, 91
Vitex, chaste tree (*Vitex agnus-castus*), 11, 21, 45

W
Wallflower (*Cheiranthus cheiri*), 51, 52, 72, 110
Wandering Jew (*Zebrina pendula*), 10, 66, 67, 80, 86, 106, 107
Wax-leaf ligustrum (*Ligustrum lucidum*), 37
Wax myrtle (*Myrica*), 43
Weigela (*Weigela florida*), 11, 22, 37, 45, 78, 112
White oak (*Quercus alba*), 47
White pine (*Pinus strobus*), 20, 48, 64. *See also* Pine
Wild flowers: distribution of, 52; sources, 53; for shade and sun,

Index [139]

53, 54; use of, 53–54; evergreen varieties, 54. *See also* Conservation
Wild geranium (*Geranium maculatum*), 54
Wild hyacinth, camass (*Camassia scilloides*), 54
Willow (*Salix* spp.), 11, 47
Willow oak (*Quercus phellos*), 47, 48, 64, 92
Window greenhouse, 65, 66, 80, 106–7, 113; location, 66; uses of, 66; warm-season plants in, 75
Winged euonymus (*Euonymus alatus*), 37, 41
Winter aconite (*Eranthis hyemalis*), 103
Winterberry (*Ilex verticillata*), 11, 40, 54
Winter honeysuckle, Sweet-Breath-of-Spring (*Lonicera fragrantissima*), 11, 21, 43–44
Winter jasmine (*Jasminum nudiflorum*), 11, 22, 44, 46
Wisteria (*Wisteria sinensis*), 30

Y
Yaupon (*Ilex vomitoria*), 40, 47, 48, 54, 76
Yellowwood (*Cladrastis lutea*), 48
Yucca, Spanish bayonet (*Yucca aloifolia*), 44, 54

Z
Zephyr lily, Zephyranthes (*Zephyranthes*), 64, 93
Zinnia (*Zinnia elegans*), 8, 52, 68, 80, 81, 86, 91
Zoysia, Manila grass (*Zoysia matrella*), 7, 17, 103